Abortion Bibliography

For 1971

Abortion Bibliography
For 1971

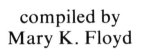

compiled by
Mary K. Floyd

Whitston Publishing Company
Incorporated
Troy, New York
1973

PREFACE

Abortion Bibliography for 1971 is the second annual list of books and articles surrounding the subject of abortion in the preceeding year. It appears serially each fall as a contribution toward documenting in one place as comprehensively as possible the literature of one of our central social issues. It is an attempt at a comprehensive world bibliography.

Searches in compiling this material have covered the following sources: *Bibliographic Index; Biological Abstracts; Books in Print; British Books in Print; British Humanities Index; Business Periodicals Index; Canadian Periodical Index; Cumulative Book Index; Current Index to Journals in Education; Current Literature of Venereal Disease; Education Index; Hospital Literature Index; Index to Catholic Periodicals and Literature; Index to Legal Periodicals; Index Medicus; Index to Nursing Literature; Index to Periodical Articles Related to Law; Index to Religious Periodical Literature; International Nursing Index; Library of Congress Catalog: Books: Subjects; Philosophers Index; Public Affairs Information Service; Readers Guide to Periodical Literature; Review for Religious; Social Sciences and Humanities Index.*

The bibliography is divided into two sections: a title section in alphabetical order; and a subject section. Thus, if the researcher does not wish to observe the subject heads of the compiler, he can use the title section exclusively. The 120 subject heads have been allowed to issue from the nature of the material indexed rather than being imposed from Library of Congress subject heads or other standard lists.

Countries are listed alphabetically under subjects: "Abortion: Africa," etc.; drugs are listed under the specific drug involved; and "Children," "College Students," and "Youth" are given seperate subject heads in this bibliography.

ABBREVIATIONS	TITLE
ABA	American Booksellers Association Bulletin (New York)
Acta Endocrinol	Acta Endocrinologica (Copenhagen)
Acta Genet Med Gemellol	Acta Geneticae Medicae et Gemellologie (Rome)
Acta Med Acad Sci Hung	Acta Medica Academiae Scietiarum Hungaricae (Budapest)
Acta Med Iugosl	Acta Medica Iugoslavica (Belgrade)
Acta Obstet Ginecol Hisp Lusit	Acta Obstetrica y Ginecologica Hispano-Lusitana (Barcelona)
Acta Obstet Gynecol Scand	Acta Obstetricia et Gynecologia Scandinavica (Lund)
Acta Pathol Microbiol Scand	Acta Pathologica et Microbiologica Scandinavica; Section A: Pathology (formerly Acta Pathologica et Microbiologica Scandinavica) Section B: Microbiology and Immunology (Copenhagen)
Acta Physiol Scand	Acta Physiologica Scandinavica (Stockholm)
Acta Univ Carol (Med)	Acta Universitatis Carolinae: Medica (Prague)
Adv Age	Advertising Age (Chicago)
Adv Surg	Advances in Surgery (Chicago)
Akush Ginekol	Akusherstvo i Ginekologiya (Moscow)
Akush Ginekol	Akusherstvo i Ginekologia (Sofiia)
Albany L Rev	Albany Law Review (Albany)
Am Druggist	American Druggist (New York)
Am Fam Physician	American Family Physician/GP (Brookside, Kansas)
Am J Juris or Amer J Juris	American Journal of Jurisprudence (Notre Dame, Indiana)
Am J Nurs or Amer J Nursing	American Journal of Nursing (New York)
Am J Obstet Gynecol	American Journal of Obstetrics and Gynecology (St. Louis)
Am J Orthopsych	American Journal of Orthopsychiatry (New York)

Am J Psychiatry	American Journal of Psychiatry (Hanover, New Hampshire)
Am J Public Health	American Journal of Public Health and the Nation's Health (New York)
Am J Vet Res	American Journal of Veterinary Research (Chicago)
Am State Assn J	American Statistical Association Journal (Washington)
Amer Med News	American Medical Association News (Chicago)
America	America (San Francisco)
Anesthesiology	Anesthesiology (Philadephia)
Ann Endocrinol	Annales d'Endocrinologie (Paris)
Ann Chir Gynaecol Fenn	Annales Chirurgiae et Gynaecologiae Fenniae (Helsinki)
Ann Intern Med	Annals of Internal Medicine (Philadelphia)
Ann NY Acad Sci	Annals of the New York Academy of Sciences (New York)
Ann Ostet Ginecol	Annali di Ostetricia e Ginecologia (Milan)
Ann Rev Med	Annual Review of Medicine (Palo Alto)
Ann Sanita Pubblica	Annali della Sanita Pubblica (Rome)
Antibiotiki	Antibiotiki (Moscow)
Arch Gynaekol	Archiv fur Gynaekologie (Munich)
Arch Ital Urol Nefrol	Archivio Italiano di Urologia e Nefrologia (Bologna)
Arch Mal Prof	Archives des Maladies Professionelles de Medecine du Travail et de Securite Sociale (Paris)
Arch Ostet Ginecol	Archivio di Ostetricia e Ginecologia (Naples)
Arch Pathol	Archives of Pathology (Chicago)
Arch Surg	Archives of Surgery (Chicago)
Arch Toxikol	Archiv fur Toxikologie; Fuehner-Wielands Sammlung von Vergiftungsfaellen (Berlin)
Arzt und Christ	Arzt und Christ (Vienna)
Atlan Adv	Atlantic Advocate (New Brunswick)
Aust Vet J	Australian Veterinary Journal (Sydney)
Australian Nurses J	Australian Nurses' Journal (Sydney)
Baylor L Rev	Baylor Law Review (Waco, Texas)
Bedside Nurs	Bedside Nurse (New York)
Beitr Gerichtl Med	Geitraege zur Gerichtlichen Medizin (Vienna)

Bibl Gynaecol	Bibliotheca Gynaecologica (Switzerland)
Biol Reprod	Biology of Reproduction (New York)
Birth Defects	Birth Defects (New York)
Boll Soc Ital Biol Sper	Bollettino della Societa Italiana di Biologia Sperimentale (Naples)
Bord Med	Bordeaux Medical (Bordeaux)
Br J Clin Pract	British Journal of Clinical Practice (Sussex)
Br J Prev Soc Med	British Journal of Preventive and Social Medicine (London)
Br J Psychiatry	British Journal of Psychiatry (London)
Br J Surg	British Journal of Surgery (Bristol)
Br Med J	British Medical Journal (London)
Br Vet J	British Veterinary Journal (London)
British J of Social Work	British Journal of Social Work
Broadcasting	Broadcasting (Washington)
Brux Med	Bruxelles-Medical (Brussels)
Buffalo L Rev	Buffalo Law Review (Buffalo)
Bull Acad Vet Fr	Bulletin de l'Academie Veterinaire de France (Paris)
Bull Fed Soc Gynecol Obstet Lang Fr	Bulletin de la Federation des Societes de Gynecologie et d'Obstetrique de Langue Francaise (Paris)
Bull Infirm Cath Canada	Bulletin des Infirmieres Catholiques du Canada (Quebec)
Bull Inst Natl Sante Rech Med	Bulletin de l'Institute National de la Sante et de la Recherche Medicale (Paris)
Bull NY Acad Med	The New York Academy of Medicine Bulletin (New York)
Bull Off Int Epizoot	Bulletin de l'Office International des Epizooties (Paris)
Bull Soc Sci Med Grand Duche Luxemb	Bulletin de la Societe des Sciences Medicales du Grand-Duche de Luxembourg
C Dgst	Catholic Digest (St. Paul)
C Mind	Catholic Mind (New York)
C R Acad Sci	Comptes Rendus Herdomadaires des Seances de l'Academie des Sciences; D: Sciences Naturelles (Paris)
C R Soc Biol	Comptes Rendus des Seances de la Societe de Biologie et de ses Foliales (Paris)

Calif Med	California Medicine (San Francisco)
Calif Nurse	California Nurses' Association: Bulletin (San Francisco)
Can Anesth Soc J	Canadian Anaesthetists' Society Journal (Toronto)
Can Doctor	Canadian Doctor (Gardenvale, Quebec)
Can Forum	Canadian Forum (Ontario)
Can Hosp	Canadian Hospital (Toronto)
Can Med Ass J	Canadian Medical Association Journal (Toronto)
Can Nurse	Canadian Nurse (Ottawa)
Can Psychiatr Assoc J	Canadian Psychiatric Association Journal (Ottawa)
Can Vet J	Canadian Veterinary Journal/Revue Veterinaire Canadienne (Ontario)
Canad J Public Health	Canadian Journal of Public Health (Toronto)
Cath Hosp	Catholic Hospital (Ottawa)
Cath World	Catholic World (New York)
Catholic Charities R	Catholic Charities Review (Washington)
Catholic Law	Catholic Lawyer (Brooklyn)
Cent Afr J Med	Central Africa Journal of Medicine (Salisbury)
Cesk Gynekol	Ceskoslovenska Gynekologie (Prague)
Cesk Zdrav	Ceskoslovenska Zdravotnictvi (Prague)
Chatelaine	Chatelaine (Toronto)
Chicago Stds	Chicago Studies (Mundelein, Illinois)
Chr Cent	Christian Century (Chicago)
Chr Today	Christianity Today (Washington)
Christ Nurse	Christian Nurse (Nagpur, India)
Christianity and Crisis	Christianity and Crisis (New York)
Christus	Christus (Mexico)
Clergy Monthly	Clergy Monthly
Clin Obstet Gynecol	Clinical Obstetrics and Gynecology (New York)
Clin Pediatr	Clinical Pediatrics (Philadelphia)
Collationes	Collationes
Columbia	Columbia (New Haven, Connecticut)
Commonweal	Commonweal (New York)
Criminal Law R	Criminal Law Review (London)
Cross Curr	Cross Currents (West Nyack, New York)
Daily Telegraph Mag	Daily Telegraph Magazine (London)
Del Med J	Delaware Medical Journal (Wilmington)

Demography	Demography (Washington)
Dist Nurs	District Nurse (London)
Doc Cath	Documentation Catholique (Paris)
Drake L Rev	Drake Law Review (Des Moines)
Dtsch Gesundheitsw	Deutsche Gesundheitswesen (Berlin)
Dtsch Med Wochenschr	Deutsch Medizinische Wochenschrift (Stuttgart)
Dtsch Tieraerztl Wochenschr	Deutsche Tieraerztliche Wochenschrift (Hannover, New York)
Duodecim	Duodecim (Helsinki)
East Afr Med J	East African Medical Journal (Nairobi)
Economist	Economist (London)
Educ Med Salud	Educacion Medica y Salud (Washington)
Endokrinologie	Endokrinologie (Leipzig)
Enfermeras	Enfermeras; Revista del Colegio Nacional de Enfermeras (Mexico)
Environmental Affairs	Environmental Affairs
Environmental Law	Environmental Law (Portland, Oregon)
Evol Psychiatr	Evolution Psychiatrique (Toulouse)
F Relations	Family Relations (Washington)
Fam Plann Perspect	Family Planning Perspectives (New York)
Family Coordinator	Family Coordinator (Minneapolis)
Family Health	Family Health Bulletin (Berkeley)
Fed Proc	Federation Proceedings: Federation of American Societies for Experimental Biology (Bethesda)
Fertil Steril	Fertility and Sterility (New York)
Folia Med	Folia Medica (Naples)
Friuli Med	Friuli Medico (Udine, Italy)
Furrow	Furrow
Geburtshilfe Frauenheilkd	Geburtshilfe und Frauenheilkunde (Stuttgart)
Ginecol Obstet Mex	Ginecologia y Obstetricia de Mexico
Ginekol Pol	Ginekologia Polaska (Warsaw)
God Zb Med Fak Skopje	Godisen Zbornik na Medicinslciot Fakultet vo Skopje
Good H	Good Housekeeping (New York)
Guardian	Guardian
Gynecol Obstet	Gynecologie et Obstetrique et Federation des Societies de Gynecologie et d'Obstetrique de Langue Francaise. Bulletin (Paris)

Gynecol Prat	Gynecologie Pratique (Paris)
HPR	Homiletic and Pastoral Review (New York)
HSMHA Health Rep	HSMHA Health Reports (Rockville, Maryland)
Harefuah	Harefuah (Tel Aviv)
Hastings L J	Hastings Law Journal (San Francisco)
Herder Korrespondenz	Herder-Korrespondenz (Briesgau, W. Germany)
Hosp Admin Can	Hospital Administration in Canada (Ontario)
Hosp Forum	Hospital Forum (New York)
Hosp Manage	Hospital Management (Chicago)
Hosp Physician	Hospital Physician (Oradell, New Jersey)
Hosp Progr	Hospital Progress (St. Louis)
Hospital	Hospital (Rio de Janiero)
Hospitals	Hospitals (Chicago)
Human Rights	Revue des Droits de l'Homme/Human Rights (Paris)
Humangenetik	Humangenetik (Berlin)
Humanist	Humanist
IA L Rev	Iowa Law Review (Iowa City, Iowa)
IPQ	IPQ/International Philosophical Quarterly (Bronx, New York)
Ill Med J	Illinois Medical Journal (Chicago)
Impact of Science on Society	Impact of Science on Society (Paris)
Indian J Med Res	Indian Journal of Medical Research (New Delhi)
Indian J Public Health	Indian Journal of Public Health (Calcutta)
Indian Journal of Adult Education	Indian Journal of Adult Education (New Delhi)
Indian Pediatr	Indian Pediatrics (Calcutta)
Indian Vet J	Indian Veterinary Journal (Madras)
Infirm Can	Infirmiere Canadienne (Ottawa)
Inquiry	Inquiry
Int J Fertil	International Journal of Fertility (Baltimore)
Int Surg	International Surgery Bulletin (Chicago)
Iowa L Rev	Iowa Law Review (Iowa City)
Ir Nurs News	Irish Nursing News (Dublin)

JAMA	Journal of the American Medical Association (Chicago)
J R Coll Gen Pract	Journal of the Royal College of General Practitioners (Dartmouth, England)
J Am Osteopath Assoc	Journal of the American Osteopathic Association (Chicago)
J Am Vet Med Assoc	Journal of the American Veterinary Medical Association (Chicago)
J Amer Med Ass	Journal of the American Medical Association (Chicago)
J Anim Sci	Journal of Animal Science (Albany)
J Biosoc Sci	Journal of Biosocial Science (London)
J Formosan Med Assoc	Journal of the Formosan Medical Association (Taipei)
J Indiana State Med Asso	Journal of the Indiana State Medical Association (Indianapolis)
J Iowa Med Soc	Journal of the Iowa Medical Society (Des Moines)
J Ir Med Assoc	Journal of the Irish Medical Association (Dublin)
J Kans Med Soc	Journal of the Kansas Medical Society (Topeka)
J Ky Med Ass	Journal of the Kentucky Medical Association (Louisville)
J La State Med Soc	Journal of the Louisiana State Medical Society (New Orleans)
J Med Assoc Ga	Journal of the Medical Association of Georgia (Atlanta)
J Med Assoc State Ala	Journal of the Medical Association of the State of Alabama (Montgomery)
J Med Assoc Thai	Journal of the Medical Association of Thailand (Bangkok)
J Med Genet	Journal of Medical Genetics (London)
J Med Lyon	Journal de Medecine de Lyon (Lyon)
J Med Soc NJ	Journal of the Medical Society of New Jersey (Trenton)
J Miss State Med Ass	Journal of the Mississippi State Medical Association (Jackson)
J Natl Med Ass	Journal of the National Medical Association (New York)
J Nerv Ment Dis	Journal of Nervous and Mental Disease (Baltimore)

J Nursing	Journal of Nursing (Taipei)
J Obstet Gynaecol Br Commonw	Journal of Obstetrics and Gynaecology of the British Commonwealth (London)
J Okla State Med Ass	Journal of the Oklahoma State Medical Association (Oklahoma City)
J Pastoral Care	Journal of Pastoral Care (New York)
J Philos	Journal of Philosophy (New York)
J Pract Nurs	Journal of Practical Nursing (New York)
J Psychiat Nurs	Journal of Psychiatric Nursing (Pitman, New Jersey)
J Rehabil	Journal of Rehabilitation (Washington)
J Reprod Fertil	Journal of Reproduction and Fertility (Oxford)
J Reprod Med	Journal of Reproductive Medicine (Chicago)
J Sci Med Lille	Journal des Sciences Medicales de Lille (Lille)
J Urban L	Journal of Urban Law (Detroit)
J Urol	Journal of Urology (Baltimore)
Jap J Midwife	Japanese Journal for Midwives (Tokyo)
Journal of Marriage and the Family	Journal of Marriage and the Family (Minneapolis)
Jurist	Jurist (Washington)
Katilolekti	Katilolekti (Helsinki)
Klin Monatsbl Augenheilkd	Klinische Monatsblaetter fuer Augenheilkunde und fuer Augenarztliche Fortbildung (Stuttgart)
Klin Wochenschr	Klinische Wochenschrift (Berlin)
Lab Anim Sci	Laboratory Animal Science (Argonne, Illinois)
Ladies Home Journal	Ladies Home Journal (New York)
Lakartidningen	Lakartidningen (Stockholm)
Lancet	Lancet (London)
Laval Med	Laval Medical (Quebec)
Life	Life (New York)
Liguorian	Liguorian (Liguori, Missouri)
Lijec Vjesn	Lijecnicki Vjesnik (Zagreb)
Lille Med	Lille Medical (Lille)
Linacre Quarterly	Linacre Quarterly (Milwaukee)
Lond Clin Med J	London Clinic Medical Journal (London)
Look	Look (New York)
Loyola U L Rev	Loyola University of Chicago Law

	Journal (Lincoln, Nebraska)
Lyon Med	Lyon Medical (Lyon)
McCalls	McCalls (New York)
MD State Med J	Maryland State Medical Journal (Baltimore)
Manch Med Gaz	Manchester Medical Gazette (Nottingham, England)
Marriage	Marriage (Meinrad, Indiana)
Matern Infanc	Maternidade e Infancia (Sao Paulo)
Med Ann DC	Medical Annals of the District of Columbia (Washington)
Med Econ	Medical Economics (Oradell, New Jersey)
Med Insight	Medical Insight (New York)
Med Interna	Medicina Interna/Internal Medicine (Bucharest)
Med J Aust	Medical Journal of Australia (Sydney)
Med J Malaya	Medical Journal of Malaya (Singapore)
Med Klin	Medizinische Klinik (Munich)
Med Leg Bull	Medico-Legal Bulletin (Richmond)
Med Leg Domm Corpor	Medecine Legale et Dommage Corporel (Paris)
Med Lett Drugs Ther	Medical Letter on Drugs and Therapeutics (New York)
Med Pregl	Medicinski Pregled (Novi Sad)
Med Times	Medical Times (Manorhaven, New York)
Med Welt	Medizinische Welt (Stuttgart)
Med World News	Medical World News (New York)
Medical Aspects of Human Sexuality	Medical Aspects of Human Sexuality (New York)
Ment Hyg	Mental Hygiene (New York)
Mental Health	Mental Health (London)
Mercer L Rev	Mercer Law Review (Macon, Georgia)
Mich Med	Michigan Medicine (East Lansing)
Midwife Health Visit	Midwife and Health Visitor (London)
Midwives Chron	Midwives Chronicle (London)
Milbank Mem Fund Q	Milbank Memorial Fund Quarterly (New York)
Minerva Ginecol	Minerva Ginecologica (Turin)
Minerva Med	Minerva Medica (Turin)
Minn Med	Minnesota Medicine (St. Paul)
Mod Hosp	Modern Hospital (Chicago)
Mod Treat	Modern Treatment (New York)

Munch Med Wochenschr	Muenchener Medizinische Wochenschrift (Munich)
N Engl J Med	New England Journal of Medicine (Boston)
NC L Rev or N C Law R	North Carolina Law Review (Chapel Hill, North Carolina)
NC Med J	North Carolina Medical Journal (Raleigh)
NRT	National Retired Teachers Association Journal (Long Beach)
NY L F	New York Law Forum (New York)
NY State J Med	New York State Journal of Medicine (New York)
NY Times Mag	New York Times Magazine (New York)
NZ Med J	New Zealand Medical Journal (Wellington)
Nagoya Med J	Nagoya Medical Journal (Nagoya)
Nat Cath Rep	National Catholic Reporter (Kansas City)
Nat R	National Review (New York)
Nation	Nation (New York)
Nature	Nature (London)
Neb L Rev	Nebraska Law Review (Lincoln)
Ned Tijdschr Geneeskd	Nederlands Tijdschrift voor Geneeskunde (Amsterdam)
Neue Ordnung	Neue Ordnung (Walberberg, W. Germany)
New Physician	New Physician (Flossmoor, Illinois)
New Society	New Society (London)
New Statesm	New Statesman (London)
Newsletter (Soc Hosp Attorneys)	Newsletter (Society of Hospital Attorneys (Chicago)
Newsweek	Newsweek (New York)
Nord Med	Nordisk Medicin (Stockholm)
Nord Psykiatr Tidsskr	Nordisk Psykiatrisk Tidsskrift (Middelfart)
Northwest Med	Northwest Medicine (Seattle)
Notre Dame Law	Notre Dame Lawyer (Notre Dame)
Nova	Nova
Nurs Forum	Nursing Forum (Hillsdale, New Jersey)
Nurs J India	Nursing Journal of India (New Delhi)
Nurs Mirror	Nursing Mirror and Midwives' Journal (London)
Nurs Outlook	Nursing Outlook (New York)

Nurs Times	Nursing Times (London)
Nursing	Nursing (Brussels)
OR	OR Nursing (Chicago)
Obstet Gynecol	Obstetrics and Gynecology (New York)
Ohio State Med	Ohio State Medical Journal (Columbus)
Okla L Rev	Oklahoma Law Review (Uorman)
Orv Hetil	Orvosi Hetilap (Budapest)
Pa Med	Pennsylvania Medicine (Lemoyne)
Pacific L J	Pacific Law Journal (Sacramento, California)
Parents	Parents Magazine (London)
Pathol Biol	Pathologie et Biologie (Paris)
Pathol Microbiol	Pathologia et Microbiologia (Basel)
Patient Care	Patient Care (Greenwich, Connecticut)
Pediatr Akush Ginekol	Pediatriia Akusherstov i Ginekologiia (Kiev)
Pediatrics	Pediatrics (Springfield, Illinois)
Pediatrie	Pediatrie (Bucharest)
Penn Med	Pennsylvania Medicine (Harrisburg)
Perspect Psychiat Care	Perspectives in Psychiatric Care (Hillsdale, New Jersey)
Physicians Manage	Physician's Management (Evanston, Illinois)
Pol Przegl Chir	Polski Przeglad Chirurgiczny (Warsaw)
Pol Tyg Lek	Polski Tygodnik Lekarski (Warsaw)
Political Quarterly	Political Quarterly (London)
Population Studies	Population Studies (London)
Postgrad Med	Postgraduate Medicine (Minneapolis)
Practitioner	Practitioner (London)
Prairie Rose	Prairie Rose (Bismarck, North Dakota)
Presse Med	Presse Medicale (Paris)
Priest	Priest (Huntington, Indiana)
Probl Gematol Pereliv Krove	Problemy Gematologii i Perelivaniia Krovi (Moscow)
Proc R Soc Med	Proceedings of the Royal Society of Medicine (London)
Psychiat News	Psychiatric News (Washington)
Public Health Rep	Public Health Reports (Washington)
Q Med Rev	Quarterly Medical Review (Bombay)
Quad Clin Ostet Ginecol	Quaderni di Clinica Ostetrica e Ginecologica (Parma)
R Soc Health J	Royal Society of Health Journal (London)

RI Med J	Rhode Island Medical Journal (Providence)
RN	RN; National Magazine for Nurses (Oradell, New Jersey)
Rad Med Fak Zagrebu	Radovi Medicinskog Fakultela u Zagrebu (Zagreb)
Radiology	Radiology (Syracuse)
Rass Int Clin Ter	Rassenga Internazionale di Clinica e Terapia (Naples)
Read Dig	Readers Digest (Pleasantville, New York)
Redbook	Redbook Magazine (New York)
Relations	Relations (Montreal)
Resident Staff Physician	Resident and Staff Physician (Port Washington, New York)
Rev Chil Obstet Ginecol	Revista Chilena de Obstetricia y Ginecologia
Rev Colomb Obstet Ginecol	Revista Colombiana de Obstetricia y Gynecologia (Bogota)
Rev Fr Endocrinal Clin	Revue Francaise d'Endocrinologie Clinique, Nutrition et Metabolisine (Paris)
Rev Fr Gynecol Obstet	Revue Francaise de Gynecologie et d'Obstetrique (Paris)
Rev Inst Med Trop Sao Paulo	Revista do Instituto de Medicina Tropical de Sao Paulo (Sao Paulo)
Rev Int Trach	Revue Internationale du Trachome (Marseille)
Rev Med Chil	Revista Medica de Chile (Santiago)
Rev Med Chir Soc Med Nat Iasi	Revista Medico-Chirurgicala a Societatie di Medici si Naturalisti din Iasi
Rev Med Liege	Revue Medicale de Liege (Liege)
Rev Med Suisse Romande	Revue Medicale de la Suisse Romande (Lausanne)
Rev Obstet Ginecol Venez	Revista de Obstetricia y Ginecologia de Venezuela (Caracas)
Rev Saude Publica	Revista de Saude Publica (Sao Paulo)
Revista Eclesiastica Brasileira	Revista Eclesiastica Brasileira (Petropolis, Brazil)
Revue Nouvelle	Revue Nouvelle (Brussels)
Riv Anat Patol Oncol	Rivista di Anatomia Patologica e di Oncologia (Padova)

Riv Ital Ginecol	Rivista Italiana di Ginecologia (Bologna)
Riv Ostet Ginecol	Rivista di Obstetricia e Ginecologia (Florence)
Rocky Mt Med J	Rocky Mountain Medical Journal (Denver)
Royal Inst of Great Britain Proc	Royal Institution of Great Britain. Proceedings (Essex)
S Afr Med J	South African Medical Journal (Capetown)
SD J Med	South Dakota Journal of Medicine (Sioux Falls)
Sairaanhoitaja	Sairaanhoitaja Sjukskoterskan (Helsinki)
Salud Publica Mex	Salud Publica de Mexico (Mexico City)
San Diego L Rev	San Diego Law Revue (San Diego)
Sanfujinka Jissai	Sanfujinka no Jissai (Tokyo)
Santa Clara Law	Santa Clara Lawyer (Santa Clara)
Sat R	Saturday Review (New York)
Sci Am	Scientific American (New York)
Sci N	Science News (Washington)
Science	Science (Washington)
Schweiz Arch Tierheilkd	Schweizer Archiv fuer Tierheilkunde (Zurich)
Scott Med J	Scottish Medical Journal (Glasgow)
Sem Hop Paris	Semaine des Hopitaux de Paris (Paris)
Sexual Behavior	Sexual Behavior (New York)
Shujutsu	Shujutsu (Tokyo)
Sign	Sign (Union City, New Jersey)
Singapore Med J	Singapore Medical Journal (Singapore)
Soc Biol	Social Biology (Chicago)
Soc Just	Social Justice Review (St. Louis)
Soc Sci Med	Social Science and Medicine (Oxford)
Social Action	Social Action (New Delhi)
South Med J	Southern Medical Journal (Birmingham)
Sov Zdravookhr	Sovetskoye Zdravookhraneniye (Moscow)
Spectator	Spectator (London)
St. Anth	St. Anthony Messenger (Cincinnati)
Stimm Zeit	Stimmen der Zeit (Freiburg)
Studies in Family Planning	Studies in Family Planning (New York)

Supplément	Le Supplément (Paris)
Surg Gynecol Obstet	Surgery, Gynecology and Obstetrics (Chicago)
Tablet	Tablet (London)
Tar Heel Nurse	Tar Heel Nurse (Raleigh, North Carloina)
Teratology	Teratology; Journal of Abnormal Development (Philadelphia)
Tex L Rev	Texas Tech Law Review (Austin)
Tex So Intra L Rev	Texas Southern Intramural Law Review (Houston)
Theologische Quartalschrift	Theologische Quartalschrift (Milwaukee)
Ther GGW	Therapie der Gegenwart (Berlin)
Ther Umsch	Therapeutische Umschaw (Berlin)
Therapeutique	Therapeutique (Paris)
Tidskr Sver Sjukskat	Tidskrift for Sveriges Sjukskoterskor (Stockholm)
Tidsskr Nor Laegeforen	Tidsskrift for den Norske Laegeforening (Oslo)
Tijdschr Diergeneeskd	Tijdschrift voor Diergeneckunde (Utrecht)
Tijdschr Ziekenverpl	Tijdschrift voor Ziekenverpleging (Leidschendam)
Time	Time (Chicago)
Todays Educ	Todays Education (Washington)
Today's Health	Today's Health (Chicago)
Toxicol Appl Pharmacol	Toxicology and Applied Pharmacology (New York)
Trans Pac Coast Obstet Gynecol Soc	Transactions of the Pacific Coast Obstetrical and Gynecological Society (Portland)
Trimuph	Trimuph (Washington)
US Cath	U.S. Catholic and Jubilee (Chicago)
US Med	U.S. Medicine (Washington)
Ugeskr Laeger	Ugeskrift for Laeger (Copenhagen)
Union Med Can	Union Medicale du Canada (Montreal)
Vet Rec	Veterinary Record (London)
Veterinariia	Veterinariia (Moscow)
Vogue	Vogue (New York)
Vopr Okhr Materin Det	Voprosy Okhrany Materinstva i Detstva (Moscow)
Wake Forest L Rev	Wake Forest Intramural Law Review (Winston-Salem, North Carolina)

Wall St J	Wall Street Journal (New York)
Wash L Rev	Washington Law Review (Seattle)
Washburn L J	Washburn Law Journal (Topeka, Kansas)
West Afr Med J	West African Medical Journal (Lagos, Nigeria)
West Indian Med J	West Indian Medical Journal (Kingston)
Wiad Lek	Wiadomosci Lekarskie (Warsaw)
Wien Klin Wochenschr	Wiener Klinische Wochenschrift (Vienna)
Wien Med Wochenschr	Wiener Medizinische Wochenschrift (Vienna)
Woman Physician	Woman Physician (New York)
World Health	World Health (Geneva)
Yale Review of Law and Social Action	Yale Review of Law and Social Action (New Haven)
Yonsei Med	Yonsei Medical Journal (Seoul)
Z Aerztl Fortbild	Zeitschrift fur Aerztliche Fortbildung (Jena)
Z Geburtshilfe Gynaekol	Zeitschrift fur Beburshilfe und Gynaekologie (Stuttgart)
Z Gesamte Hyg	Zeitschrift fur die Gesamte Hygiene und Ihre Grenzgebiete (Berlin)
Z Urol Nephrol	Zeitschrift fur Urologie und Nephrologie (Leipzig)
Zdravookhr Ross Fed	Zdravookhraneniye Rossiiskoi Federatzil (Moscow)
Zentralbl Gynaekol	Zentralblatt fuer Gynaekologie (Leipzig)
Zentralbl Veterinaermed	Zentralblatt fuer Veterinaermedizinl Journal of Veterinary Medicine (Berlin)

SUBJECT HEADINGS USED IN THIS BIBLIOGRAPHY

Abnormalities
Abortion: Africa
Abortion: Alaska
Abortion: Argentine
Abortion: Austria
Abortion: Australia
Abortion: Brazil
Abortion: Bulgaria
Abortion: Canada
Abortion: Chile
Abortion: China
Abortion: Colombia
Abortion: England
Abortion: Findland
Abortion: France
Abortion: Germany
Abortion: Great Britain
Abortion: Hungary
Abortion: India
Abortion: Italy
Abortion: Jamaica
Abortion: Japan
Abortion: Latin America
Abortion: Macedonia
Abortion: Malaysia
Abortion: Netherlands
Abortion: Nicaragua
Abortion: Pakistan
Abortion: Poland
Abortion: Romania
Abortion: Russia
Abortion: Scotland
Abortion: Singapore
Abortion: Sweden
Abortion: Switzerland
Abortion: Taiwan
Abortion: Yugoslavia
Ampicillin
Anesthesia

Antibodies
Artificial Abortion
Behavior
Benzylpenicillin
Birth Control
Candidiasis
Carbenicillin
Cephalosporins
Cervical Incompetence or
    Insufficiency
Children
Cesarean Section
Clinical Aspects
College Students
Complications
Contraception
Demography
Diagnosis
Dilatol
Duvadilan
Drug Therapy
Education and Abortion
Family Planning
Family Therapy
Fertility
Fetus
Genetics
Gynaecology
Habitual Abortion
Hemorrhage
History
Hormones
Hospitals and Abortion
Immigration and Emigration
Induced Abortion
Infection
Isoxysuprine
IUCD
Law Enforcement

TABLE OF CONTENTS

BOOKS

THE ABORTION ACT 1967; proceedings of a symposium held by the Medical protection society in collaboration with the Royal college of general practitioners, at the Royal college of obstetricians and gynaecologists, London, 7 February 1969. London: Pitman Medical Publishing Company, 1969.

Bates, Jerome E. and Edward S. Zawadzki. CRIMINAL ABORTION, a study in Medical Sociology. Springfield, Illinois: C. C. Thomas, 1964.

Brautigan, R. THE ABORTION: an historical romance. New York: Simon & Schuster, 1966.

David, Henry P. FAMILY PLANNING & ABORTION IN THE SOCIALIST COUNTRIES OF CENTRAL & EASTERN EUROPE. Bridgeport, Connecticut: Key Books Service, 1970.

Dickens, Bernard M. ABORTION & THE LAW. New York: Fernhill Ltd., 1966.

Dollen, Charles J. ABORTION IN CONTEXT: A Select Bibliography. Metuchen, New Jersey: Scarecrow Press, 1970.

Duffy, Edward A. THE EFFECT OF CHANGES IN THE STATE ABORTION LAWS. Washington: GPO, 1971.

Enden, Hugo van den. ABORTUS PRO/CONTRA. Een critische analyse. Met uitvoerige literatuuropgave. Baarn: Het Wereldvenster, 1971.

Family Planning Association. ABORTION IN BRITAIN: Conference Proceedings. London: Pitman Medical Publishing Company, 1971.

Faulkner, Lloyd C., editor. ABORTION DISEASES OF LIVESTOCK.

Springfield, Illinois: C. C. Thomas, 1968.

Feldman, David M. BIRTH CONTROL IN JEWISH LAW. New York: New York University Press, 1968.

Galbally, R. T. J., et al. THE RIGHT TO BE BORN. Melbourne: Australian Catholic Truth Society, 1970.

Granfield, David. ABORTION DECISION. Garden City: Doubleday & Company, 1969.

Greenwood, Douglas C. and Mary J. Roberts. HAVING A WONDERFUL ABORTION. Jericho, New York: Exposition Press, 1971.

Group For The Advancement Of Psychiatry. RIGHT TO ABORTION: A Psychiatric View. New York: Scribner's, 1970.

Hall, R. E. A DOCTOR'S GUIDE TO HAVING AN ABORTION. New York: New American Library, 1971.

Hart, Thomas M., editor. FIRST AMERICAN SYMPOSIUM ON OFFICE ABORTIONS: the proceedings. San Francisco: Society for Humane Abortion, 1970.

Hendin, David. EVERYTHING YOU NEED TO KNOW ABOUT ABORTION. New York: Pinnacle Books, 1971.

Simms, Madeleine and Keith Hindell. ABORTION LAW REFORMED. (Contemporary Issues Service). New York: Hummanities Press, 1971.

Hordern, Anthony. LEGAL ABORTION: the English experience. Elmsford, New York: Pergamon Press, 1971.

Jamain, Bernard. L'AVORTEMENT OU LA VIE. Paris: Spedim, 1971.

Kindregan, Charles. ABORTION, THE LAW & DEFECTIVE CHILDREN. New York: World Publishing Company, 1969.

Kindregan, Charles P. QUALITY OF LIFE: Reflections on the Moral Values of American Law. New York: Bruce Publishing Company, 1969.

Kummer, Jerone M., editor. ABORTION, LEGAL & ILLEGAL: A Dialogue Between Attorneys & Psychiatrists. 2nd edition. The Author, 1969.

Lader, Lawrence. ABORTION. Indianapolis: Bobbs-Merrill Company, 1966.

Lee, Nancy H. SEARCH FOR AN ABORTIONIST. Chicago: University of Chicago Press, 1969.

Ligtenberg, W. J. J. ABORTUS IN DE HUISARTSENPRAKTIJK. Leiden: Stenfert Kroese, 1967.

Newman, Sidney H. and Mildred B. Beck, editors. ABORTION OBTAINED & DENIED: Research Approaches. Bridgeport, Connecticut: Key Books Service, 1971.

Pelrine, Eleanor W. ABORTION IN CANADA. Chicago: New Press, 1971. New women series 1.

Purdue university. North central campus, Westville, Indiana. CUMULATED BIBLIOGRAPHY OF ARTICLES ON ABORTION AND BIRTH CONTROL IN PERIODICALS INDEXED IN READER'S GUIDE TO PERIODICAL LITERATURE AND IN SOCIAL SCIENCES AND HUMANITIES INDEX, March 1965-September 17, 1970. Lafayette, Indiana: The University, 1970.

Reitermann, Carl, editor. ABORTION & THE UNWANTED CHILD. New York: Springer Publishing Company, 1971.

Reproduction Research Information Service. CHROMOSOME STUDIES OF SPONTANEOUS HUMAN ABORTION: Bibliography 1961-1967. New York: International Publications Services, 1971.

Rosen, Harold, editor. ABORTION IN AMERICA. Boston: Beacon Press, 1971.

Saltman, Jules. ABORTIONS. New York: Grosset and Dunlap, 1971.

Schmidt, Mary S., complier. ABORTION: a selective bibliography. August, 1971. Harrisburg: State Library of Pennsylvania, Department of Education, 1971.

Schudder, Diane and Florence Kennedy. ABORTION RAP. New York: McGraw-Hill, 1971.

Schur, Edwin M. CRIMES WITHOUT VICTIMS-DEVIANT BEHAVIOR & PUBLIC POLICY: Abortion, Homosexuality, Drug Addiction. Englewood

Cliffs, New Jersey: Prentice-Hall, 1971.

Schwarz, Richard H. SEPTIC ABORTION. Philadelphia: J. B. Lippincott Company, 1968.

Shaw, Russell. ABORTION ON TRIAL. Eau Claire, Wisconsin: E. M. Hale and Company, 1971.

Siebel, von Wigand. SOZIOLOGIE DER ABTREIBUNG; empirische Forschung und theoretische Analyse. Stuttgart: F. Enke, 1971.

Siegrist, Harald O. DER ILLEGALE SCHWANGERSCHAFTS-ABRUCH, aus kriminologischer Sicht. Hamburg: Kriminalistik Verlag, 1971.

Sloane, Bruce R., editor. ABORTION: Changing Views & Practice. New York: Grune and Stratton, 1971.

Smith, David T., editor. ABORTION & THE LAW. Cleveland: The Press of Case Western Reserve University, 1967.

Sweden. Abortkommitté, 1965 ars. RÄTTEN TIL ABORT. Stockholm: Allmänna förlaget, 1971.

Tarnesby. ABORTION EXPLAINED. London: Sphere, 1971.

Volcher, Robert, et al. L'AVORTEMENT. Paris: Editions universitaires, 1971.

World Health Organization. ABORTION LAWS; a survey of current world legislation, Geneva. Geneva: WHO; London: HSMO, 1971.

Weinberg, Roy D. LAWS GOVERNING FAMILY PLANNING. Dobbs Ferry, New York: Oceana Publications, 1968.

Westoff, Leslie A. and Charles F. Westoff. FROM NOW TO ZERO; fertility, contraception and abortion in America. Boston: Little Brown, 1971.

Wieczorek, Veronika. CHROMOSOMENANOMALIEN ALS UR-ACHE VON FEHLGEBURTEN. Müchen: W. Goldmann, 1971.

Williams, Glanville. SANCTITY OF LIFE & THE CRIMINAL LAW. New York: Alfred A. Knopf, 1957.

PERIODICAL LITERATURE

TITLE INDEX

"Abnormal progesterone synthesis in placental tissue from a spontaneous abortion," by M. Wiener, et al. AM J OBSTET GYNECOL 111:942-946, December 1, 1971.

"Abortion," CAN MED ASSOC J 103:1314 passim, December 5, 1970.

"Abortion," J NATL MED ASSOC 63:481-485, November, 1971.

"Abortion," J OKLA STATE MED ASSOC 64:295-296, July, 1971.

"Abortion," LANCET 2:646-647, September 18, 1971.

"Abortion," SAIRAANHOITAJA 47:135-139, February 25, 1971.

"Abortion," by S. Galvin. PRAIRIE ROSE 40:7, January-March, 1971.

"Abortion," by A. M. Kennedy. CAN MED ASSOC J 104:70, January 9, 1971.

"Abortion," by L. Myers. JAMA 217:215, July 12, 1971.

"Abortion," by P. Riga. PRIEST 27:24-31, January, 1971; Reply by P. Driscoll 27:73-76, May, 1971.

"Abortion. Is it a therapeutic procedure in psychiatry?" by C. V. Ford, et al. JAMA 218:1173-1178, November 22, 1971.

"The Abortion Act after three years," by M. Simms. POLITICAL QUARTERLY 42:269-286, July-September, 1971.

"The Abortion Act, 1969--a review of the first year's experience," by S. B. Kwa, et al. SINGAPORE MED J 12:250-255, October, 1971.

"The Abortion Act 1967. (b). The social aspects," by N. M. Cogan. R SOC HEALTH J 90:295-298, November-December, 1970.

"The Abortion Act 1967. (c). Implications for the family," by J. Kemp. R SOC HEALTH J 90:299-301 passim, November-December, 1970.

"The Abortion Act: a reply," by M. Simms. CRIMINAL LAW R 86-88, February, 1971.

"The Abortion Act: what has changed?" by J. M. Finnis. CRIMINAL LAW R p3-12, January, 1971.

"Abortion ads rapped by NAB president," BROADCASTING 80:26, February 1, 1971.

"'Abortion airlift' in the military?" MED WORLD NEWS 12:4-5, June 11, 1971.

"Abortion: allegations, actions, and ad interim," by D. S. Wert. PENN MED 74:59-62, May, 1971.

"Abortion and the argument from innocence," by M. Kohl. INQUIRY 14: 147-151, Summer, 1971.

"Abortion and contraception in family planning. A commentary," by C. F. Coffelt. J REHABIL 7:13-15, July, 1971.

"Abortion and the courts," by B. Roberts, et al. ENVIRONMENTAL LAW 1:225-237, Spring, 1971.

"Abortion and electrocution. An exceptional industrial accident," by H. Esteve. ARCH MAL PROF 32:559-562, September, 1971.

"Abortion and euthanasia: a reply," by R. D. Lamm, et al. ROCKY MT MED J 68:40-42, February, 1971.

"Abortion and experiences with 500 Lippes' intrauterine devices," by M. Ribarić. LIJEC VJESN 92:443-450, 1970.

"Abortion and immigration," by D. C. Wallace. MED J AUST 1:659-660, March 20, 1971.

"Abortion and immigration," by V. H. Wallace. MED J AUST 1:404-405, February 13, 1971.

"Abortion and the law," CHRIST NURSE 238:9, December, 1971.

"Abortion and the law," TABLET 225:218-219, March 6, 1971.

"Abortion and the law," by B. A. Brody. J PHILOS 68:357-369, June 17, 1971.

"Abortion and the law," by O. Dijkstra. CLERGY MONTHLY pp409-422; 478-485, 1971.

"Abortion and the law," by O. Dijkstra. SOCIAL ACTION (India) pp324-340, 1971.

"Abortion and the law. (interviews)," by R. Lucas, et al. AMER MED NEWS 14:10 , April 19, 1971.

"Abortion and maternal Rh immunization," by W. Q. Ascari. CLIN OBSTET GYNECOL 14:625-634, June, 1971.

"Abortion and morality," by P. R. Ehrlich, et al. SAT R 54:58, September 4, 1971.

"Abortion and normative ethics," by S. Hauerwas. CROSS CURR 21:399-414, Fall, 1971.

"Abortion and obstetrical shock," by J. C. Lagorce, et al. BULL FED SOC GYNECOL OBSTET LANG FR 23:245-246, April-May, 1971.

"Abortion and the obstetrician," by I. Donald. LANCET 1:1233, June 12, 1971.

"Abortion and one nurse's conscience," NURS TIMES 67:680-681, June 3, 1971.

"Abortion and pluralist society," by C. F. Magistro. NAT R 23:476-478 +, May 4, 1971.

"Abortion and the psychiatrist," by W. Burke. HPR 71:199-207, December, 1970.

"Abortion and public opinion: the 1960-1970 decade," by J. Blake. SCIENCE 171:540-549, February 12, 1971.

"Abortion and public policy: what are the issues?" by E. C. Moore.

NY L F 17:411, 1971.

"Abortion and the reverence for life," by P. W. Rahmeier. CHR CENT 88:556-560, May 5, 1971; Reply by R. H. Hamill 88:957-958, August 11, 1971.

"Abortion and sterility of neuro-endocrine origin," by J. Belaisch. ANN ENDOCRINOL 31:975-977, September-October, 1970.

"Abortion and sterilization: an insight into obstetrician-gynecologists' attitudes and practices," by A. T. Fort. SOC BIOL 18:192-194, June, 1971.

"Abortion and suicidal behaviors: observations on the concept of 'endangering the mental health of the mother', " by H. L. Resnik, et al. MENT HYG 55:10-20, January, 1971.

"Abortion and the unemancipated minor," by M. Lipman. CALIF NURSE 67:8, September, 1971.

"Abortion as a public health problem," KATILOLEHTI 76:234-237, May, 1971.

"Abortion associated with mycotic infection in a cow in Hyderabad," by Z. Ahmed, et al. INDIAN VET J 48:446-449, May, 1971.

"Abortion battle," NEWSWEEK 77:110, May 3, 1971.

"Abortion: the burden of proof has been reversed," by L. Myers. J AMER MED ASS 217:215, July 12, 1971.

"Abortion: Canada Medical Association prepares Members of Parliament for anticipated Commons debate with reminder of current policy," CAN MED ASS J 105:522-523, September 4, 1971.

"Abortion: the Catholic presentation," AMERICA 124:62, January 23, 1971.

"Abortion caused by chromosomal abnormalities and estrogen insufficiency of the corpus luteum," by J. Cohen. PRESSE MED 78:1744, September 26, 1970.

"Abortion caused by chromosome aberration, with special reference to habitual abortion," by K. Watanabe. SANFUJINKA JISSAI 20:826-832, August, 1971.

"Abortion: a changing scene," by J. Cottam. LANCET 2:1193-1194, November 27, 1971.

"Abortion clinics studied in British Columbia to take pressure off hospitals," HOSP ADMIN CAN 13:17, January, 1971.

"Abortion committee 1965: woman's right to abortion as considerate and early as possible," by G. Bergström, et al. LAKARTIDNINGEN 68: 4137-4150, September 8, 1971.

"Abortion complicated by Clostridium perfringens infection," by J. A. Pritchard, et al. AM J OBSTET GYNECOL 111:484-492, October 15, 1971.

"Abortion--constitutional law--a law prohibiting all abortions except those performed 'for the purpose of saving the life of the mother,' which does not augment a compelling state interest, unconstitutionally infringes on the mother's ninth amendment right to choose whether to bear children," TEX L REV 49:537, March, 1971.

"The abortion controversy," by E. B. Smith. J NATL MED ASSOC 62: 379, September, 1970.

"Abortion: the counterattack," MED WORLD NEWS 12:4-5, April 30, 1971.

"Abortion: the crunch; How to protest abortion," by W. F. Buckley, Jr. NAT R 23:444-445, April 20, 1971.

"Abortion, death, and the sanctity of life," by H. L. Smith. SOC SCI MED 5:211-218, June, 1971.

"The abortion decision," by D. W. Millard. BRITISH J OF SOCIAL WORK 1:131-148, Summer, 1971.

"Abortion due to C. pyogenes?" by T. J. Smith. VET REC 87:519-520, October 24, 1970.

"Abortion due to Pseudomonas aeruginosa. Protection of the pregnant guinea pig by vaccination," by R. Durieux, et al. GYNECOL OBSTET 69:301-308, August-October, 1970.

"Abortion: an environmental convenience or a constitutional right?" by M. J. Sikora, Jr. ENVIRONMENTAL AFFAIRS 1:469-527, November, 1971.

"Abortion following ultra-short-wave hyperthermia. Animal experiment studies," by F. Dietzel, et al. ARCH GYNAEKOL 209:237-255, 1970.

"Abortion games," by D. Baird. LANCET 2:1145, November 20, 1971.

"Abortion games," by I. M. Ingram. LANCET 2:1197, November 27, 1971.

"Abortion games: an inquiry into the working of the act," by I. M. Ingram. LANCET 2:969-970, October 30, 1971.

"Abortion: high court showdown," MED WORLD NEWS 12:5-6, April 9, 1971.

"Abortion: how it's working," NEWSWEEK 78:50-52, July 19, 1971.

"Abortion in Hawaii: the first 124 days," by R. G. Smith, et al. AM J PUBLIC HEALTH 61:530-542, March, 1971.

"Abortion in Japan; cond from Family Life, December, 1970," by P. Popenoe. C DGST 35:27-29, September, 1971.

"Abortion in the Maori in historical perspective," by L. K. Gluckman. NZ MED J 74:323-325, November, 1971.

"Abortion in mice induced by ellagic acid," by N. Moe. ACTA PATHOL MICROBIOL SCAND (A) 79:487-490, 1971.

"Abortion in neural tube defect fraternities," by A. D. McDonald. BR J PREV SOC MED 25:220-221, November, 1971.

"Abortion in New York City. Preliminary experience with a permissive abortion statute," by J. J. Rovinsky. OBSTET GYNECOL 38:333-342, September, 1971.

"Abortion in New York City: the first nine months," by J. Pakter, et al. FAM PLANN PERSPECT 3:5-12, July, 1971.

"Abortion in New York State since July 1970," by H. S. Ingraham, et al. MOD TREAT 8:7-26, February, 1971.

"Abortion in the north-east of Scotland," by I. MacGillivray. J BIOSOC SCI 3:89-92, January, 1971.

"Abortion in perspective," by D. Ball. NEW SOCIETY 244, August 5, 1971.

"Abortion in perspective," by R. J. Endres. AM J OBSTET GYNECOL 111:436-439, October 1, 1971.

"Abortion in SR Macedonia," by A. Lazarov, et al. GOD ZB MED FAK SKOPJE 16:413-428, 1970.

"Abortion in U.S.A.," by H. C. McLaren. LANCET 2:713, September 25, 1971.

"Abortion in an upstate community hospital," by R. R. Murray. CLIN OBSTET GYNECOL 14:141-148, March, 1971.

"Abortion in women with latent toxoplasma infections," by P. Janssen, et al. KLIN WOCHENSCHR 48:25-30, January 1, 1970.

"Abortion investigation: one year leave of absence for bearing a child," TIDSKR SVER SJUKSKOT 38:12, September 22, 1971.

"Abortion: is it a therapeutic procedure in psychiatry?" by C. V. Ford, et al. J AMER MED ASS 218:1173-1178, November 22, 1971.

"Abortion is not the answer," by A. I. Weisman. JAMA 217:1553-1554, September 13, 1971.

"Abortion issue," by D. Kucharsky. CHR TODAY 15:36, April 23, 1971.

"Abortion kills unborn baby," by P. O'Boyle. SOC JUST 63:372-373 +, February, 1971.

"Abortion law in the supreme court," by W. J. Curran. N ENGL J MED 285:30-31, July 1, 1971.

"Abortion law reform," by F. Rosner. JAMA 216:147, April 15, 1971.

"Abortion law reform and repeal: legislative and judicial developments," by R. Roemer. AM J PUBLIC HEALTH 61:500-509, March, 1971.

"Abortion-law reform is inevitable, even in Texas," by J. C. Evans. CHR CENT 88:548-549, May 5, 1971; Discussion 88:1051-1052, September 8, 1971.

"Abortion law still binding," NAT CATH REP 7:16, February 19, 1971.

"Abortion laws," SOC JUST 63:374-376, February, 1971.

"Abortion laws: a constitutional right to abortion," NC L REV 49:487, April, 1971.

"Abortion laws (in various states): a constitutional right to abortion," by R. L. Welborn. N C LAW R 49:487-502, April, 1971.

"The abortion laws: A severe case of resistance to change," by R. A. Schwartz. OHIO STATE MED J 67:33-38, January, 1971.

"Abortion: laws which legislate morality should be eliminated," by J. A. Merrill. J OKLA STATE MED ASS 64:295-296, July, 1971.

"Abortion: the legal ramifications in Illinois," by F. M. Pfiefer. ILL MED J 139:273, March, 1971.

"Abortion legislation and right to life," by H. Medeiros. SOC JUST 64: 84-86, June, 1971; also in OR 149,5:7, February 4, 1971.

"Abortion legislation in North Carolina," by A. Mandetta. TAR HEEL NURSE 33:8-11, March, 1971.

"Abortion legislation: the Romanian experience," by H. P. David, et al. STUDIES IN FAMILY PLANNING 2:205-210, October, 1971.

"Abortion: litigative and legislative processes," by R. Lucas, et al. HUMAN RIGHTS 1:23-53, July, 1971.

"Abortion: medical aspects in a municipal hospital," by D. P. Swartz, et al. BULL NY ACAD MED 47:845-852, August, 1971.

"Abortion mortality statistics," by R. L. Burt. OBSTET GYNECOL 38: 950-951, December, 1971.

"Abortion: new restraints on private clinics," LANCET 2:1074, November 13, 1971.

"Abortion--1970," by E. M. Gold. AM J PUBLIC HEALTH 61:487-488, March, 1971.

"Abortion--1970," by F. R. Lock. J LA STATE MED SOC 123:309-316, September, 1971.

"Abortion; old figures, new facts," ECONOMIST 236:19, August 15, 1970.

"'Abortion-on-demand' a boon to moonlighting doctors," by M. J. Connor. MED TIMES 99:155 passim, October, 1971.

"Abortion on request: is it really 'liberal'?" by W. E. Kimble. TEX SO INTRA L REV 1:173, 1971.

"Abortion or contraception?" BR MED J 3:261-262, July 31, 1971.

"Abortion or contraception?" by W. Wood, et al. BR MED J 3:476-477, August, 1971.

"Abortion or no abortion--what decides?" by C. McCance, et al. J BIOSOC SCI 3:116-120, January, 1971.

"Abortion: parameters for decision," by R. Gerber. IPQ 11:561-584, December, 1971.

"Abortion: physician and hospital attitudes," by R. E. Hall. AM J PUBLIC HEALTH 61:517-519, March, 1971.

"Abortion: pro and con," by T. I. Steinman. N ENGL J MED 284:728-729, April 1, 1971.

"The abortion problem from the medical viewpoint," by H. Husslein. WIEN MED WOCHENSCHR 121Suppl 2:3-7, November 20, 1971.

"Abortion problems," by C. B. Goodhart. ROYAL INST OF GREAT BRI-TAIN PROC 43:378-393, December, 1970.

"Abortion: a profitable business," by S. Beauman. DAILY TELEGRAPH MAG 20+, November 26, 1971.

"The abortion program in Japan," by T. Wagatsuma. J REHABIL 7:16-19, July, 1971.

"Abortion: public health concerns and needed psychosocial research," by H. P. David. AM J PUBLIC HEALTH 61:510-516, March, 1971.

"Abortion: a question of right or wrong?" by R. W. Fox. ABA J 57:667, July, 1971.

"Abortion: questions to ask," ECONOMIST 239:24+, May 1, 1971.

"Abortion rap," by D. Schulder, et al. NATION 213:342-343, October 11, 1971.

"Abortion: the rearguard in birth control," by J. M. Kummer. J REPROD MED 5:167-174, October, 1970.

"Abortion referral services: New York State," by L. S. Goldsmith. PHYSICIANS MANAGE 11:36, September, 1971.

"Abortion referral services--profiteers under fire," by T. W. Welch. NEW PHYSICIAN 20:571-575, September, 1971.

"Abortion reform," by R. D. Lamm, et al. YALE REVIEW OF LAW AND SOCIAL ACTION 1:5-63, Spring, 1971.

"Abortion reform and the courts; Florida and Michigan Supreme court decisions," AMERICA 125:52, August 7, 1971.

"Abortion repeal in Hawaii: an unexpected crisis in patient care," by J. F. McDermott, Jr., et al. AM J ORTHOPSYCHIATRY 41:620-626, July, 1971.

"Abortion requests at District of Columbia General Hospital," HSMHA HEALTH REP 86:698, August, 1971.

"Abortion revolution: inconsistent change," J MISS STATE MED ASS 12:129-130, March, 1971.

"Abortion: rhetoric and reality," CHR CENT 88:871, July 21, 1971; Discussion 88:1052-1053, September 8, 1971.

"Abortion--The S. A. scene," by J. H. Hagger. AUSTRALAS NURSES J 5:17, October, 1971.

"Abortion screening and counseling: a brief guideline for physicians," by J. C. Butler, et al. POSTGRAD MED 50:208-212, October, 1971.

"Abortion sequel--Rh problems," NORTHWEST MED 70:29, January, 1971.

"The abortion situation," CAN MED ASSOC J 104:941, May 22, 1971 +.

"Abortion situation in Switzerland and the need for sociomedical measures," by H. Stamm. GEBURTSHILFE FRAUENHEILKD 31:241-250, March, 1971.

"Abortion standards, New York City Board of Health," by M. C. McLaughlin. CLIN OBSTET GYNECOL 14:25-35, March, 1971; also in MOD TREAT 8:27-37, February, 1971.

"Abortion statements in Canada: Catholic clarity, Protestant ambivalence," by G. Lane. CHR CENT 88:1303-1304, November 3, 1971.

"Abortion story," by D. Gould NEW STATESM 82:465, October 8, 1971.

"Abortion: a survey of current legislation," WHO CHRON 25:328-333, July, 1971.

"Abortion tangle in New York," by A. Bosco. MARRIAGE 53:28-32 +, July, 1971.

"Abortion techniques and services: a review and critique," by D. Harting, et al. AM J PUBLIC HEALTH 61:2085-2105, October, 1971.

"Abortion: a theological judgment," by J. Dedek. CHICAGO STDS 10: 313-333, Fall, 1971.

"Abortion throughout antiquity and in the books of Hippocrates," by J. P. Pundel. BULL SOC SCI MED GRAND DUCHE LUXEMB 108:19-30, March, 1971.

"Abortion throughout the world," by J. De Moerloose. NURS TIMES 67: 678-680, June, 1971.

"Abortion throughout the world," by A. Monti. MINERVA GINECOL 23: 764-765, September 30, 1971.

"Abortion: two opposing legal philosophies," by R. J. Gerber. AM J JURIS 15:1, 1970.

"Abortion under paracervical block," by A. J. Penfield. NY STATE J MED 71:1185-1189, June 1, 1971.

"Abortion U.S.A. --1971," by A. F. Guttmacher. RESIDENT STAFF PHYSICIAN 17:114+, September, 1971.

"Abortion: what you should know," by P. M. Sarrel, et al. VOGUE 158: 93-94, August 1, 1971.

"Abortion: where have we been? Where are we going," by T. Crist.

NC MED J 32:347-351, August, 1971.

"Abortion; why not?" ECONOMIST 239:29, June 26, 1971.

"Abortion with cerebral air embolism after 4 years," by H. Wojahn. BEITR GERICHTL MED 27:97-100, 1970.

"Abortion--with complications," by D. Brett, et al. NURS TIMES 67:1209-1210, September 30, 1971.

"An abortion with an unusual course (cervical pregnancy)," by J. Richon, et al. BULL FED SOC GYNECOL OBSTET LANG FR 22:243-246, April-May, 1970.

"Abortion: woman's right and legal problem," by H. Moody. CHRISTIANITY & CRISIS 31:27-32, March 8, 1971.

"Abortion: 'a woman's right to decide'," by P. Worthington. DAILY TELEGRAPH 11, September 1, 1971.

"Abortions and the law," by C. C. Copenhaver. MED LEG BULL 219: 1-7, July, 1971.

"Abortions and unrecognized trophoblastic disease," by A. H. DeCherney, et al. N ENGL J MED 285:407-408, August 12, 1971.

"Abortions as the cause of ectopic pregnancy," by K. Kurčiev, et al. GOD ZB MED FAK SKOPJE 16:405-411, 1970.

"Abortions at the University Gynecological Clinic in Erlangen during 1950-1968," by W. Rummel, et al. MED KLIN 65:1123-1125, June 5, 1970.

"Abortions by resident physicians in a municipal hospital center," by J. J. Kopelman, et al. AM J OBSTET GYNECOL 111:666-671, November 1, 1971.

"Abortions for poor and nonwhite women: a denial of equal protection?" by A. Charles, et al. HASTINGS L J 23:147, November, 1971.

"Abortions of cows after invasion by Theileria annulata (Dschunkowsky and Luhs, 1904)," by J. Waltschowski, et al. ZENTRALBL VETERINAERMED (B) 17:895-903, September, 1970.

"Abortions performed in New York State from July 1-October 31, 1970: a preliminary report," HOSP FORUM 39:10-14, March, 1971.

"Abortion's psychological price," by K. J. Sharp. CHR TODAY 15:4-6, June 4, 1971.

"Abortions under the N.H.S.," by H. G. Arthure. BR MED J 4:617, December 5, 1970.

"Abortions under the N.H.S.," by M. Simms. BR MED J 1:52, January 2, 1971.

"Abortive confusion," ECONOMIST 239:61, May 15, 1971.

"Abortive effects and comparative metabolism of chlorcyclizine in various mammalian species," by A. J. Steffek, et al. TERATOLOGY 1:399-406, November, 1968.

"About abortion," JAMA 215:286, January 11, 1971.

"Abruptio placenta with renal failure," by S. Johnson. MIDWIVES CHRON 85:344-345, October, 1971.

"Abruptio placentae," by B. McDonnell. MIDWIFE HEALTH VISIT 7: 177:181, May, 1971.

"Abschaffung des 218 StGB?" by E. W. Böckenförde. STIMM ZEIT 188: 147-167, September, 1971.

"Accidental haemorrhage. The present position," by A. P. Barry. J IR MED ASSOC 64:494-497, September 23, 1971.

"Accidental intravenous injection in extra-amniotic sodium chloride abortion," by B. Gustavii. LAKARTIDNINGEN 68:2723-2728, June 2, 1971.

"Ace renal insufficiency in obstetrics," by C. Ponticelli, et al. ARCH ITAL UROL NEFROL 42:142-159, 1969.

"The act 4 years after (operation of the Abortion Act, 1967; Great Britain)," by D. Steel. MENTAL HEALTH p6-9, Summer, 1971.

"Action of prostaglandin in the pregnant woman," by S. Karim. ANN NY ACAD SCI 180:483-498, April 30, 1971.

"Active management in modern treatment of gestosis," by A. Cretti. GINEKOL POL 42:437-440, April, 1971.

"Acute intestinal obstruction caused by lithopaedion," by S. A. Zaheer. BR J SURG 58:401-402, May, 1971.

"Acute renal failure after septic abortion," by G. Staude, et al. Z UROL NEPHROL 64:23-28, January, 1971.

"Acute renal insufficiency with diffuse intravascular coagulation in 2 fatal cases of septic abortion," by L. E. Ribeiro, et al. ACTA OBSTET GINECOL HISP LUSIT 19:215-224, April, 1971.

"Acute suppurated thyroiditis in children. Apropos of a case," by P. Beauvais, et al. PEDIATRIE 26:633-641, September, 1971.

"Adolescent attitudes toward abortion: effects on contraceptive practice," by I. W. Gabrielson, et al. AMER J PUBLIC HEALTH 61:730-738, April, 1971.

"Age distribution of 715 mothers having had an early spontaneous abortion," by P. Lazar, et al. C R ACAD SCI (D) 272:2852-2855, June 2, 1971.

"Aggressive management of incomplete or inevitable abortion. Report of 1002 septic and aseptic patients," by J. L. Breen, et al. J MED SOC NJ 67:711-715, November, 1970.

"Aggressive treatment of septic abortion," by L. G. Keith, et al. AM FAM PHYSICIAN 3:98-103, June, 1971.

"Alerte au traducianisme," by A. Ple. SUPPLEMENT 96:59-71, February, 1971.

"Allergic abortions," by A. Burthiault. GYNECOL PRAT 20:123-128, 1969.

"The alternative abortion," by B. N. Branch, et al. MED AM DC 40: 691-696, November, 1971.

"Alternative to abortion," by L. N. Bell. CHR TODAY 15:17-19, June 18, 1971.

"Ambivalence on abortion," TIME 97:40, May 3, 1971.

"The American Catholic: contraception and abortion," by J. Fitzgerald.
LINACRE 38:264-267, November, 1971.

"American Psychiatric Association joins others in high court abortion
case," PSYCHIAT NEWS 6:1+, September 15, 1971.

"Amniocentesis and abortion: methods and risks," by F. Fuchs. BIRTH
DEFECTS 7:18-19, April, 1971.

"Amniocentesis: medical and social implications," by R. Adams. REV
MED SUISSE ROMANDE 91:389-400, June, 1971.

"Amnioscopy in patients with bad obstetric history and high risk pregnancies," by K. H. Ng. MED J MALAYA 26:59-61, September, 1971.

"Amniotic fluid volume. A measurement of the amniotic fluid present in
72 pregnancies during the first half of pregnancy," by D. L. Smith.
AM J OBSTET GYNECOL 110:166-172, May 15, 1971.

"Anaesthetic practice and pregnancy," by D. D. Moir. LANCET 1:1027,
May 15, 1971.

"Analysis of complications after legal interruption of pregnancy in
Poland," by E. Chroscielewski. MED LEG DOMM CORPOR 3:16-17,
January-March, 1970.

"Analysis of the contraceptive program and control of abortion in Chile
(1964-1969)," by B. Viel, et al. REV MED CHIL 99:486-494, July,
1971.

"Analysis of 480 births after bleeding during pregnancy," by H. Wallner,
et al. MUNCH MED WOCHENSCHR 113:690-695, April 30, 1971.

"Analysis of human chorionic gonadotropin: comparison between the
biologic test in frogs and the immunologic pregnancy test," by G.
Cobellis, et al. RIV ANAT PATOL ONCOL 33:857-863, 1968.

"Analysis of internal indications for termination of pregnancy," by V.
Fialová, et al. CESK GYNEKOL 36:344-346, July, 1971.

"Analysis of 2,746 abortions treated at their Managua General Hospital,"
by C. Guido, et al. INT SURG 56:125-127, August, 1971.

"Anesthesia in abortions," by B. E. Marbury. CLIN OBSTET GYNECOL

14:81-84, March, 1971.

"Anesthesia, pregnancy, and miscarriage: a study of operating room nurses and anesthetists," by E. N. Cohen, et al. ANESTHESIOLOGY 35:343-347, October, 1971.

"Anesthetic-induced abortion?" by D. H. Carr. ANESTHESIOLOGY 35: 335, October, 1971.

"Anomaly of the maternal karyotype in 2 cases of habitual abortion and fetal abnormalities," by M. Vitse, et al. BULL FED SOC GYNECOL OBSTET LANG FR 20:466-469, November-December, 1968.

"Anti-abortion campaign," TIME 97:70+, March 29, 1971.

"Antinuclear factor in 2 patients with recurrent abortions," by C. Abrahams, et al. LANCET 1:498-499, February 26, 1972.

"Application of genetics in gynecology and obstetrics," by A. L. Castelazo. ENFERMERAS 18:4-11, January-February, 1971.

"Application of the randomized response technique in obtaining quantitative data," by B. G. Greenberg, et al. AM STAT ASSN J 66:243-250, 1971.

"Are abortions really necessary?" by R. J. Pion. ANN INTERN MED 75:961-962, December, 1971.

"The art of abortion. 1. Curettage of the pregnant uterus," by B. W. Newton. POSTGRAD MED 50:131-136, August, 1971.

"The art of abortion. 2. Induction of labor and other methods," by B. W. Newton. POSTGRAD MED 50:213-220, September, 1971.

"Artificial abortion," by S. Tojo, et al. SHUJUTSU 25:58-65, January, 1971.

"Artificial abortion and immunization with antigens A or B in women with blood group O," by M. Jakubowska, et al. POL TYG LEK 25:1263-1264, August 17, 1970.

"Artificial abortion in women with heart defects," by Z. Piechowiak, et al. GINEKOL POL 42:371-375, 1971.

"Aspectos biológicos, éticos e jurídicos do abôrto," by J. Snoek.

REVISTA ECLESIÁSTICA BRASILEIRA pp878-890, 1971.

"Aspiration abortion without cervical dilation," by S. Goldsmith, et al. AM J OBSTET GYNECOL 110:580-582, June 15, 1971.

"Assessing the demographic effect of a family planning programme," by W. Brass. PROC R SOC MED 63:1105-1107, November, 1970.

"Assumption of attitudes toward abortion during physician education," by S. R. Wolf, et al. OBSTET GYNECOL 37:141-147, January, 1971.

"Attempt at abortion with potassium permanganate tablets," by A. Le Coz, et al. BULL FED SOC GYNECOL OBSTET LANG FR 20:190-191, April-May, 1968.

"Attempts to isolate H-1 virus from spontaneous human abortions: a negative report," by S. J. Newman, et al. TERATOLOGY 3:279-281, August, 1970.

"Attendance at family planning centers," by O. Texier. EVOL PSYCH-IATR 34:595-637, July-September, 1969.

"Attenders at a contraceptive clinic for single women," by M. Wadsworth, et al. J BIOSOC SCI 3:133-143, April, 1971.

"Attitudes and practices of North Carolina obstetricians: the impact of the North Carolina Abortion Act of 1967," by W. B. Walker, et al. SOUTH MED J 64:441-445, April, 1971.

"Attitudes toward Michigan's abortion law and experience of Michigan physicians with requests for abortion," by B. Serena, et al. MICH MED 70:309-316, April, 1971.

"Avoidable factors in maternal deaths," by H. Arthure. MIDWIFE HEALTH VISIT 7:381+, October, 1971.

"Awareness and acceptance of different family planning in a rural popu-lation," by H. S. Gandhi, et al. INDIAN J PUBLIC HEALTH 13:130-143, July, 1969.

"Baterial abortion and shock," by H. Franke. ZENTRALBL GYNAEKOL 92:385-391, March 28, 1970.

"Bacterial infection of the placenta in cases of spontaneous abortion.

Correlation with the histological lesions," by M. Veron, et al. PATHOL BIOL 19:129-138, February, 1971.

"Behavior of maternal antiplacental IgA, IgM a nd IgG immunoglobulins in recurrent abortion," by U. Montemagno, et al. MINERVA GINECOL 21: 1083-1086, August 31, 1969.

"The biggest killer," DIST NURS 14:186, December, 1971.

"Biological properties of Escherichia coli isolated from pathological material," by M. S. Venugopal, et al. PATHOL MICROBIOL 37:420-424, 1971.

"The biologist's dilemma," by C. B. Goodhart. NATURE (London) 229: 213, January 15, 1971.

"Birth control," by R. S. Kirk, et al. SCIENCE 170:1256 passim, December 18, 1970.

"Birth control," by M. Verhaeghe. LILLE MED 14:924-938, October, 1969.

"Birth control. Future of the different contraceptive and abortion methods," by R. Vokaer. GYNECOL OBSTET 70:15-44, January-February, 1971.

"Birth control. Problem of the gynecologist from the medical, moral and religious point of view," by S. Fossati. MINERVA GINECOL 22:664-668, July 15, 1970.

"Birth control and induced abortion," by E. A. Bendek. REV COLOMB OBSTET GINECOL 21:579-586, November-December, 1970.

"Birth control in Singapore and the IUCD," MED J AUST 1:566, March 13, 1971.

"Birth control survey in a lower social group in Melbourne," by C. Wood, et al. MED J AUST 1:691-696, March 27, 1971.

"Birth control--the views of women," by J. A. Hurst. MED J AUST 2:835-838, October 31, 1970.

"Birth planning and eugenics," by J. Benoist. UNION MED CAN 97:613-616, May, 1968.

"Birthright," by V. Dillon. SIGN 50:27-29, July, 1971.

"Birthright: alternative to abortion," by J. B. Breslin. AMERICA 125: 116-119, September 4, 1971; Discussion 125:217, 273, October 2, 16, 1971.

"Birthright: a better answer," by I. Critelli, et al. ST ANTH 79:12-18, November, 1971.

"Birthright's goal: stop 100,000 abortions," NAT CATH REP 7:6, September 10, 1971.

"Black hospital in Kansas ordered to halt abortions: Douglass Hospital, Kansas City," HOSPITALS 45:21, August 16, 1971.

"Blood alkaline phosphatase activity before and after interruption of pregnancy," by H. Skalba, et al. WIAD LEK 24:1503-1506, August 15, 1971.

"Bougie-induced abortion at mid-pregnancy and placental function: histological and histochemical study of the placenta," by Y. Manabe, et al. ENDOKRINOLOGIE 57:389-394, 1971.

"The British candidate for termination of pregnancy: a quantified survey of psychiatric referrals," by R. G. Priest. BR J PSYCHIATRY 118: 579-580, May, 1971.

"Calcified extra-uterine foetus co-existing with normal intra-uterine pregnancy," by F. M. Bulwa. EAST AFR MED J 48:109-115, March, 1971.

"California's 1967 therapeutic abortion act: abridging a fundamental right to abortion," PACIFIC L J 2:186, January, 1971.

"California's Therapeutic Abortion Act upheld and struck down," NEWSLETTER: (SOC HOSP ATTORNEYS) 4:1-2, August, 1971.

"Canadian Nurses' Association board rescinds all statements on abortion," CAN NURSE 67:5, November, 1971.

"Cardinal Cooke condemns State's abortion law," OR 53 (144) 11, December 31, 1970.

"Cardinal Terence Cooke launches new service; birthright for mothers,"

OR 17 (161) 4, April 29, 1971.

"Cardinals condemn abortion; pastoral letters," by P. O'Boyle, et al. OR 4 (148) 4, January 28, 1971.

"Case of amniotic fluid embolism and secondary afibrinogenemia in artificial abortion," by V. M. Shikhatova. AKUSH GINEKOL 45:68, March, 1969.

"Case of habitual abortion in a patient with primary hyperparathyroidism (current obstetrical clinico-diagnostico-therapeutic and statistical aspects)," by C. Zanoner. FRIULI MED 24:227-240, May-June, 1969.

"A case of latent (subacute) hypofibrinogenemia due to retained dead fetus," by B. Georgiev, et al. AKUSH GINEKOL (Sofiia) 10:165, 1971.

"Case of severe lesion of the urinary bladder in the course of induced abortion," by W. Maternik, et al. POL PRZEGL CHIR 43:1035-1038, June, 1971.

"A Catholic abortion," TRIUMPH 6:7-12, April, 1971.

"Catholics and liberalized abortion laws," by N. J. Rigali. CATH WORLD 213:283-285, September, 1971; Discussion 214:101-102, December, 1971.

"Catholics against the Vatican," by C. Goodhart. SPECTATOR 274, August 21, 1971.

"Cause and effect; decline in birthrate with new abortion law," SCI AM 225:242, October, 1971.

"A cause of reproductive failures," by M. Massobrio, et al. MINERVA GINECOL 23:507-535, June, 1971.

"Causes and sequelae of abortion," by K. I. Zhuravleva, et al. ZDRA-VOOKHR ROSS FED 15:22-25, February, 1971.

"Cephalosporins in the treatment of septic abortion," by R. F. Soto, et al. REV OBSTET GINECOL VENEZ 30:509-515, 1970.

"Cerclage in the Gynecologic Department in Kragujevac and Arandelo-vac," by M. Duric, et al. MED PREGL 23:255-257, 1970.

"Cervical cerclage in the treatment of incompetent cervix. A retrospective analysis of the indications and results of 164 operations," by M. Seppälä, et al. ACTA OBSTET GYNECOL SCAND 49:343-346, 1970.

"Cervical insufficiency in pregnancy," by R. Wawryk, et al. WIAD LEK 24:1513-1519, August 15, 1971.

"Cervico-isthmic gapings and abortions of the 1st trimester," by H. Serment, et al. BULL FED SOC GYNECOL OBSTET LANG FR 23: 197-201, April-May, 1971.

"Cervico-segmentary insufficiency in pregnancy," MINERVA GINECOL 21:802-809, July 15, 1969.

"Change in attitudes about illegal abortion," by G. Dotzauer. BEITR GERICHTL MED 27:45-60, 1970.

"Changes in the thrombelastograph following blood loss during late spontaneous abortion," by L. V. Terskaia. AKUSH GINEKOL 45:70-72, September, 1969.

"Changes in uterine volume during hypertonic saline induced abortions," by A. Kivikoski, et al. ACTA OBSTET GYNECOL SCAND 9:Suppl:45, 1971.

"Changes of panorama in the abortion mortality," by O. Pribilla, et al. BEITR GERICHTL MED 27:76-85, 1970.

"Changing attitudes and practices concerning abortion: a sociomedical revolution," by A. F. Guttmacher. MARYLAND STATE MED J 20: 59-63, December, 1971.

"Changing trends in mortality and morbidity from abortion in Singapore (1964 to 1970)," by M. C. Cheng, et al. SINGAPORE MED J 12:256-258, October, 1971.

"Chaplains condemn abortion," C MIND 69:4, February, 1971.

"Children of cardiac patients," by J. Palmade. BORD MED 4:1939-1940 passim, June, 1971.

"Chorionic villi and syncytial sprouts in spontaneous and induced abortions," by T. Fujikura, et al. AM J OBSTET GYNECOL 110:547-555, June 15, 1971.

"Christian values in the legislative process in Britain in the sixties," by F. Dowrick. AMER J JURIS 16:156-183, 1971.

"Chromosomal abortion," by M. Massobrio, et al. MINERVA GINECOL 23:443-472, May 31, 1971.

"Chromosomal studies in relation to abortion," by P. Adler, et al. J AM OSTEOPATH ASSOC 70:1319-1323, August, 1971.

"Chromosome aberrations in oogenesis and embryogenesis of mammals and man," by G. Röhrborn. ARCH TOXIKOL 28:115-119, 1971.

"Chromosome abnormalities in early spontaneous abortions," by D. T. Arakaki, et al. J MED GENET 7:118-124, June, 1970.

"Chromosome findings in women with habitual abortions and fetal mal-formations," by E. Golob, et al. WIEN KLIN WOCHENSCHR 83:668-670, September 24, 1971.

"Chromosome pathology in spontaneous abortions," by C. Zara. ARCH OSTET GINECOL 75:215-225, May-June, 1970.

"Chromosome studies in selected spontaneous abortions. 3. Early pregnancy loss," by D. H. Carr. OBSTET GYNECOL 37:570-574, May, 1971.

"Chromosome studies in selected spontaneous abortions. Polyploidy in man," by D. H. Carr. J MED GENET 8:164-174, June, 1971.

"Chromosomic abortions. The value of new data and the interest of further research," by R. Debre. INDIAN J PEDIATR 38:114-118, March, 1971.

"Chronic typhoid abscess of body wall," by T. A. Stoker, et al. PROC R SOC MED 64:1000-1001, September, 1971.

"Cigarette smoking and abortion. Consecutive prospective study of 4,312 pregnancies," by B. Palmgren, et al. LAKARTIDNINGEN 68: 2611-2616, May 26, 1971.

"Civil liability for abortion," by A. R. Holder. J AMER MED ASS 215: 355-356, January 11, 1971.

"Civil rights in the United States and abortion," by D. Wuerl. OR 2 (146) 9-10, January 14, 1971.

"Claim abortion can eliminate stress," NAT CATH REP 8:5, December 17, 1971.

"A clearing house for abortion appointments," by E. F. Daily. FAM PLANN PERSPECT 3:12-14, July, 1971.

"A clergyman's view," by J. G. Chatham. J MISS STATE MED ASSOC 12:116-117, March, 1971.

"Clinical and statistical considerations of recurrent abortion," by G. Pritsivelis, et al. MINERVA GINECOL 21:1067-1069, August 31, 1969.

"Clinical aspects of human reproduction," by P. O. Hubinont. BRUX MED 49:71-75, February, 1969.

"Clinical aspects of poisonings with chemical abortifacients," by M. Canale. MINERVA GINECOL 21:1183-1185, September 30, 1969.

"Clinical attitude towards bleeding in early pregnancy," by P. Järvinen. DUODECIM 87:389-391, 1971.

"Clinical condition of women with pathological development of ovum and fetus," by P. Dráč, et al. CESK GYNEKOL 36:49-50, February, 1971.

"Clinical direction," BR MED J 4:382, November 13, 1971.

"Clinical experience in midwifery. Threatened abortion," by K. Zenki. JAP J MIDWIFE 25:47-49, January, 1971.

"Clinical experience with basal temperature rhythm," by J. P. Durkan. FERTIL STERIL 21:322-324, April, 1970.

"Clinical experiences with pregnancy interruption with a vacuum extractor," by C. Flämig, et al. ZENTRALBL GYNAEKOL 91:1567-1570, November 29, 1969.

"Clinico-statistical considerations on a second series of cases of premature detachment of the normally inserted placenta (5-year period 1964-1968)," by A. Muziarelli, et al. MINERVA GINECOL 23:657-670, September 15, 1971.

"Clostridium welchii septicotoxemia. A review and report of 3 cases," by L. P. Smith, et al. AM J OBSTET GYNECOL 110:135-149, May 1, 1971.

"Coagulation failure after vaginal termination of pregnancy," by S. V. Sood. BR MED J 4:724, December 18, 1971.

"Coeliac disease presenting as recurrent abortion," by R. A. Joske, et al. J OBSTET GYNAECOL BR COMMONW 78:754-758, August, 1971.

"Coincidence of a submucous uterine myoma with pregnancy," by I. Philadelphy, et al. ZENTRALBL GYNAEKOL 92:1317-1319, October 3, 1970.

"Colpocytodiagnosis of threatened abortion," by O. I. Lopatchenko. VOPR OKHR MATERIN DET 15:27-30, December, 1970.

"Combination of a surgical and drug treatment in isthmo-cervical insufficiency during pregnancy," by H. Hertel, et al. GEBURTSHILFE FRAUENHEILKD 29:9-15, January, 1969.

"Combined use of the aspiration method and abortion forceps in induced abortion between the 13th and 18th week of pregnancy," by A. Atanasov, et al. AKUSH GINEKOL (Sofiia) 9:223-228, 1970.

"The complete family planning service at King's College Hospital," by P. Newton. NURS TIMES 66:1399-1400, October 29, 1970.

"Complications of abortion," by J. Stallworthy. NURS MIRROR 132:21-25, January 8, 1971.

"Complications of amnioinfusion with hypertonic saline for midtrimester abortion," by R. C. Goodlin. AM J OBSTET GYNECOL 110:885-886, July 15, 1971.

"The concept of necessity in the laws and deontology," by C. Palenzona. MINERVA GINECOL 23:917-920, November 15, 1971.

"Concept of relationship between law and deontology," by C. Palenzona. MINERVA MED Suppl 40:19+, May, 1971.

"Concerning the journal's abortion issue," by V. J. Freda. AM J PUBLIC HEALTH 61:1284-1285, July, 1971.

"Consequences of the legalization of induced abortion in Eastern Europe," by A. Klinger. THER UMSCH 27:681-692, October, 1970.

"Consequences of a liberalization of the abortion laws," by Gunnar, et al.

LAKARTIDNINGEN 68:2714-2715, June 2, 1971.

"Considerations on 200 cases of vaginal burns by potassium permanganate," by J. A. Guerrero, et al. GINECOL OBSTET MEX 29:275-279, March, 1971.

"Constitutional law-abortion-statutory limitation on reasons for abortion is violation of fundamental right to privacy," MERCER L REV 22: 461, Winter, 1971.

"Constitutional law-abortions: abortion as a ninth amendment r ight," WASH L REV 46:565, May, 1971.

"Constitutional law-due process and abortion," NEB L REV 51:340, Winter, 1971.

"Constitutional law-mother's right to abort is greater than unquickened child's right to live," J URBAN L 48:969, June, 1971.

"Content of chorionic gonadotropins in urine of women with threatened abortion," by A. T. Berko. PEDIATR AKUSH GINEKOL 1:37-40, January-February, 1971.

"Content of microelements in blood and placental tissue in normal pregnancy and abortion," by P. I. Fogel. PEDIATR AKUSH GINEKOL 2: 33-37, 1971.

"Content of silicon, aluminum, titanium in blood in normal pregnancy and threatened abortion," by L. I. Priakhina. PEDIATR AKUSH GINEKOL 1:35-37, January-February, 1971.

"Content of vitamin E in blood and estriol excretion in women with threatened abortion," by L. Ia. Davidov, et al. PEDIATR AKUSH GINEKOL 1:33-35, January-February, 1971.

"Contraception," by H. Winn. CLIN OBSTET GYNECOL 13:701-712, September, 1970.

"Contraception and abortifacients," by E. Diamond. LINACRE 38:122-126, May, 1971.

"Contraception and abortion among Aleuts and Eskimos in Alaska: a demographic study," by H. D. Alpern. J REPROD MED 7:239-244, November, 1971.

"Contraception by intra-uterine device," by M. Lancet, et al. HAREFUAH 78:223-226, March 1, 1970.

"Contraceptive practices among college women," by T. Crist. MEDICAL ASPECTS OF HUMAN SEXUALITY 5,11:168-176, November, 1971.

"Contractibility of the human uterus and the hormonal situation. Studies on therapy with progesterone in pregnancy," by P. Mentasti, et al. MINERVA GINECOL 21:685-687, May 31, 1969.

"Contrasts in world abortion laws," by P. Brookes. DAILY TELEGRAPH p12, May 18, 1971.

"Contribution to the diagnosis of infections swine abortion," by F. Kemenes, et al. ZENTRALBL VETERINAERMED (B) 18:170-176, March, 1971.

"The control of fertility," by J. McEwan. PRACTITIONER 206:406-407, March, 1971.

"Coordination of outpatient services for patients seeking elective abortion," by C. H. Siener, et al. CLIN OBSTET GYNECOL 14:48-59, March, 1971.

"Counseling women who are considering abortion," by J. M. Kummer. J PASTORAL CARE 25:233-240, December, 1971.

"Counsellor: threatening risks for practically indefensible solutions," by I. Cedermark. LAKARTIDNINGEN 68:5859-5862, December 8, 1971.

"Course of delivery following cerclage for cervical incompetence," by R. Artal, et al. HAREFUAH 81:65-68, July 15, 1971.

"Course of pregnancy following cerclage for cervical incompetence," by R. Artal, et al. HAREFUAH 81:63-65, July 15, 1971.

"Court denies abortion for mental patient," PSYCHIAT NEWS 6:9, December 15, 1971.

"Court strikes antiabortion law in Illinois," by J. DeMuth. NAT CATH REP 7:16, February 12, 1971.

"Criminal abortion. A clinical case and medicolegal aspects," by F. De Gennaro. MINERVA GINECOL 21:1002-1005, August 15, 1969.

"Criminal law: a call for statutory abortion law reform in Oklahoma," OKLA L REV 24:243, May, 1971.

"Criminal law-the Iowa abortion statute is not unconstitutionally vague and does not deny equal protection," DRAKE L REV 20:666, June, 1971.

"Criminal liability for abortion," by A. R. Holder. J AMER MED ASS 215:175-176, January 4, 1971.

"Critical study of single-time and double-time methods of artificial pregnancy interruptions," by W. Weise, et al. ZENTRALBL GYNAEKOL 92:841-848, June 27, 1970.

"Cultivation of lymphocytes from cord blood, obtained postmortem and from live infants, for chromosome analysis," by Z. Papp, et al. ORV HETIL 112:2287-2288, September 19, 1971.

"Current status of the qualitative and quantitative problem of the limitation of births," by L. Bussi. MINERVA MED 62:1592-1593, April 14, 1971.

"Cytogenetic aspects of habitual abortion. 1. Chromosome analysis of couples with history of habitual abortion," by K. Koike. NAGOYA MED J 16:59-72, November, 1970.

"Cytogenetic investigation of spontaneous abortions," by A. M. Kuliev. HUMANGENETIK 12:275-283, 1971.

"Cytogenetics and malformation in abortions," by D. H. Carr. FED PROC 30:102-103, January-February, 1971.

"Cytohormonal studies of vaginal smears performed during the treatment of imminent abortions," by B. Wierstakow, et al. GINEKOL POL 41: 977-984, September, 1970.

"D.C. abortion law is upheld," NAT CATH REP 7:3-4, April 30, 1971.

"De bisschoppelijke verklaring in verband met abortus: Een vraaggesprek met Mgr. Heuschen," COLLATIONES 220-228, 1971.

"Death from sickle-cell crises after abortion," BR MED J 3:125, July 10, 1971.

"Debate at the Abortion Meeting," by H. Bengtsson. LAKARTIDNINGEN 68:5863-5871, December 8, 1971.

"Debate: should abortion be available on request?" by B. Nathanson. SEXUAL BEHAVIOR 1,7:64-81, October, 1971.

"Decidual-cell necrosis after injection of hypertonic saline for therapeutic abortion," by B. Gustavii, et al. LANCET 2:826, October 9, 1971.

"Declaration du Secretariat de l'episcopat Francais sur l'avortement; July 2, 1970," DOC CATH 67:729, August 2-16, 1970.

"The Declaration of Oslo," S AFR MED J 44:1281, November 14, 1970.

"Defects and limitations of cervical cerclage," by J. Richon, et al. BULL FED SOC GYNECOL OBSTET LANG FR 23:82-86, January-March, 1971.

"A defense of abortion," by J. J. Thomson. PHIL PUB AFFAIRS 1:47-66, Fall, 1971.

"Definition and etiology of threatened abortion," by A. Mestrallet. LYON MED 18:Suppl:17-19, 1971.

"Delayed abortion due to coalescence defect in the decidual," by G. Bruniquel. BULL FED SOC GYNECOL OBSTET LANG FR 21:469-473, September-October, 1969.

"Demand abortions in public hospitals: medicolegal opinion," by H. B. Alsobrook, Jr. J LOUISIANA STATE MED SOC 123:29-30, January, 1971.

"The demand for abortion in an urban Malaysian population," by O. S. Ooi. MED J MALAYA 25:175-181, March, 1971.

"Demographic adaptations to urban conditions," by G. M. Korostelev, et al. SOV ZDRAVOOKHR 29:35-36, 1970.

"The demographic effects of birth control and legal abortion," by H. Sjövall. LAKARTIDNINGEN 67:5261-5272, November 4, 1970.

"A demographic study on the relationships of nuptiality, child mortality, and attitude toward fertility to actual fertility in Hsueh-Chia township in Twiwan. I. Relationship of marriage cohort and marriage age to actual fertility," by H. Y. Wu. J FORMOSAN MED ASSOC 69:243-255, May 28, 1970.

"Demonstration of one of the early symptoms of abortion caused by bio-variectomy in the pregnant female rat," by M. Clabaut, et al. C R SOC BIOL 164:1958-1962, 1970.

"Dermatological aspects of pregnancy interruption," by G. W. Korting. MED WELT 43:1685-1691, October 22, 1971.

"Determination of C-reactive protein in metrorrhagic blood with special reference to the diagnosis of threatened abortion," by C. Zanoner. FRIULI MED 24:413-421, July-August, 1969.

"Die deutschen Bischöfe über die Verantwortung für das menschliche Leben," HERDER KORRESPONDENZ 544-555, 1971.

"Development and retention durations of 716 zygotes, products of pre-cocious spontaneous abortions," by J. Boué, et al. C R ACAD SCI (D) 272:2992-2995, June 7, 1971.

"Diagnosis and management of internal abortion. Clinico-statistical study on 204 cases," by G. Zucconi, et al. RIV OSTET GINECOL 24: 323-333, November, 1969.

"Diagnostic value of combined dynamic tests in corpus luteum deficien-cy," by P. Kićović. MED PREGL 22:577-580, 1969.

"Dial for abortion," TIME 97:64, March 15, 1971.

"Difficulties encountered apropos of toxic abortions. Apropos of a case," by C. Vitani, et al. MED LEG DOMM CORPOR 2:153-154, April-June, 1969.

"Discussion session three," by C. S. Anglin. CANAD J PUBLIC HEALTH 62:56-57, September, 1971.

"Disseminated intravascular coagulation complicating hysterotomy in elderly gravidas," by R. E.Sabbagha, et al. OBSTET GYNECOL 38: 844-847, December, 1971.

"Divorce et avortement; interview," by A. Renard. DOC CATH 67:1088-1089, December 6, 1970.

"Doctor claims hundreds of fetuses die needlessly," NAT CATH REP 7:3, March 15, 1971.

"Doctor Hodgson's choice," by E. Kiester. FAMILY HEALTH 3:14-17, June, 1971.

"Doctor, I want an abortion," PATIENT CARE 5:28-33, April 15, 1971.

"Doctors and the population problem," by J. Briggs. LANCET 1:805, April 17, 1971.

"Don't blame the doctors," by J. R. Wilson. SPECTATOR 51, July 10, 1971.

"Double septicemia due to Streptococcus and Candida," by R. Le Lourd, et al. BORD MED 4:3197-3208, November, 1971.

"Dr. Daly says law prohibiting abortion should be repealed," NAT CATH REP 7:8, April 2, 1971.

"Drug-induced arrest of a pathological labor," by J. Huter. BULL FED SOC GYNECOL OBSTET LANG FR 20:Suppl:432-434, 1968.

"Drug store: abortion information center?" AM DRUGGIST 162:12-14, August 24, 1970.

"The duration of the positive pregnosticon-planotest reaction following evacuation of the uterine cavity," by E. Reinold. Z GEBURTSHILFE GYNAEKOL 174:75-79, 1971.

"The dynamics of the Danilin reaction in the artificial interruption of pregnancy," by R. A. Podgurskaia, et al. AKUSH GINEKOL 47:71-73, February, 1971.

"Early abortion in the human," by M. Bygdeman, et al. ANN NY ACAD SCI 180:473-482, April 30, 1971.

"Early complications from artificial abortion," by J. Jurukovski, et al. GOD ZB MED FAK SKOPJE 16:503-507, 1970.

"Early gynecological complications as the result of legal abortion," by E. Lunow, et al. ZENTRALBL GYNAEKOL 93:49-58, January 9, 1971.

"Easy abortion; who's to blame?" by L. Piguet. US CATH 36;39-40,

February, 1971.

"Education about abortion," by E. S. Gendel, et al. AM J PUBLIC
HEALTH 61:520-529, March, 1971.

"Effect of criminal and induced abortion on the morbidity and mortality
of women," by I. Kiene. Z GESAMTE HYG 16:274-276, April, 1970.

"The effect of induced abortion on fetomaternal transfusion," by I. Cseh,
et al. ORV HETIL 112:2763-2764, November 14, 1971.

"Effect of therapy in threatened abortion," by F. S. Baranovskaia, et al.
PEDIATR AKUSH GINEKOL 1:41-44, January-February, 1971.

"Effect of vitamin E on the placenta and fetus," by L. V. Knysh.
AKUSH GINEKOL 44:30-34, September, 1968.

"Effects of the abortion law, 1967, on a gnyaecological unit," by E. E.
Rawlings, et al. LANCET 2:1249-1251, December 4, 1971.

"The effects of legalized abortion in England," by J. V. O'Sullivan.
HOSP PROGR 52:75-78, June, 1971.

"The effects of prostaglandins E 2 and F 2 alpha administered by different routes on uterine activity and the cardiovascular system in pregnant and non-pregnant women," by S. M. Karim, et al. J OBSTET
GYNAECOL BR COMMONW 78:172-179, February, 1971.

"The efficacy and acceptability of intravenously administered prostaglandin F as an abortifacient," by A. I. Csapo, et al. AM J OBSTET
GYNECOL 111:1059-1063, December 15, 1971.

"Efficacy and tolerance of intravenous prostaglandins F 2 and E 2,"
by C. H. Hendricks, et al. AM J OBSTET GYNECOL 111:564-579,
October 15, 1971.

"Efficacy of combined bacterins for experimental immunization of sheep
against ovine vibriosis and chlamydial abortion of ewes," by W. A.
Meinershagen, et al. AM J VET RES 32:51-57, January, 1971.

"18-year-old may consent to abortion: Washington (D.C.) Hospital
Center," NEWSLETTER (SOC HOSP ATTORNEYS) 4:5, March, 1971.

"83% in ob-gyn poll take liberal abortion view," AMER MED NEWS 14:3,

May 17, 1971.

"Eine pastoralmedizinische Anmerkung zum Problem der Humanonto-genese," by M. Vodopivec. THEOLOGISCHE QUARTALSCHRIFT 222-227, 1971.

"Elective abortions available under New York Medicaid," NEWSLETTER (SOC HOSP ATTORNEYS) 4:1, July, 1971.

"Electrocardiographic abnormalities in the course of induced abortions," by J. Horeau, et al. SEM HOP PARIS 47:2034-2039, July 10, 1971.

"Electrolyte changes and serious complications after hypertonic saline instillation," by R. L. Berkowitz. CLIN OBSTET GYNECOL 14:166-178, March, 1971; also in MOD TREAT 8:114-126, February, 1971.

"Electrolyte dynamics in hypertonic saline-induced abortions," by F. D. Frigoletto, et al. OBSTET GYNECOL 38:647-652, November, 1971.

"Electrolytes, enzymes and hormones in women with spontaneous and habitual abortions," by B. Kiutukchiev, et al. AKUSH GINEKOL (Sofiia) 10:89-98, 1971.

"Embryonic development in patients with recurrent abortions," by B. J. Poland. FERTIL STERIL 22:325-331, May, 1971.

"Emergency room vacuum curettage for incomplete abortion," by B.R. Marshall. J REPROD MED 6:177-178, April, 1971.

"The emotional scars of abortion," by H. S. Arnstein. LADIES HOME J 88:121+, May, 1971.

"En marge du rapport Bird: la femme devant l'avortement," by M. Marcotte. F RELATIONS 358:81-85, March, 1971.

"Endometritis and abortion by association of Lippes' loop and pregnancy with intraplacental insertion of the apparatus," by A. Notter, et al. BULL FED SOC GYNECOL OBSTET LANG FR 21:460, September-October, 1969.

"Endotoxin shock in septic abortions," by E. Hirvonen. ANN CHIR GYNAECOL FENN 60:196-201, 1971.

"Enzootic abortion of ewes," by W. O. Neitz. BULL OFF INT EPIZOOT

70:367-372, May, 1968.

"Enzootic 'viral' (Rakeia) abortion in goats," by J. Lecoanet, et al.
BULL ACAD VET FR 44:61-64, January, 1971.

"Enzymatic activity of the blood and obstetrical physiopathology. I.
Serum glutamic-oxalacetic (SGOT) and glutamic-pyruvic (SGPT) transaminases in normal pregnancy and in some pathological obstetrical
conditions," by A. Valsecchi, et al. MINERVA GINECOL 22:943-
949, October 15, 1970.

"An epidemiological analysis of abortion in Georgia," by R. W. Rochat,
et al. AM J PUBLIC HEALTH 61:543-552, March, 1971.

"Epizootics of toxoplasmosis causing ovine abortion," by W. A. Watson,
et al. VET REC 88:120-124, January 30, 1971.

"Erklärung der skandinavischen Bischöfe uber die Abtreibung," HERDER
KORRESPONDENZ 478-485, 1971.

"Erythropoetic activity of placental and abortion blood serum and the
preparations obtained from them," by V. I. Gudim, et al. PROBL
GEMATOL PERELIV KROVI 16:27-32, June, 1971.

"La escalada del aborto," CHRISTUS 36:29, February, 1971.

"Estimates of induced abortion in urban North Carolina," by J. R.
Abernathy, et al. DEMOGRAPHY 7:19-29, February, 1970.

"Ethical issues in community and research medicine," by A. J. Dyck.
N ENGL J MED 284:725-726, April 1, 1971.

"The ethics of a cottage industry in an age of community and research
medicine," by P. Ramsey. N ENGL J MED 284:700-706, April 1, 1971.

"Etiologic incidence of rickettsial and coxsackie infection in pregnancy
interruptions: serologic study," by J. Y. Gillet, et al. BULL FED SOC
GYNECOL OBSTET LANG FR 21:213-216, April-May, 1969.

"Etiology of repeated spontaneous abortions," by M. Gaudefroy, et al.
J SCI MED LILLE 89:309-311, August-September, 1971.

"Eugenic prophylaxis in the light of international legislation," by R.
D'Andrea. ANN SANITA PUBBLICA 32:25-49, January-February, 1971.

37

"Evaluation of fertility control of periodic abstinence," by W. M. Moore. PRACTITIONER 205:38-43, July, 1970.

"Evaluation of periodic continence as a family planning method. Acceptance among low socioeconomical levels in Cali, Colombia," by V. R. Guerrero, et al. REV COLOMB OBSTET GINECOL 22:13-18, January-February, 1971.

"Evaluation of periodic continence as a method of family planning," by R. Guerrero, et al. REV COLOMB OBSTET GINECOL 21:545-552, November-December, 1970.

"Examination and evaluation of 141 cases with uterine perforation," by S. Sugiyama, et al. SANFUJINKA JISSAI 20:545-551, May, 1971.

"Experience and complications with the use of hypertonic intra-amniotic saline solution," by H. Berk, et al. SURG GYNECOL OBSTET 133: 955-958, December, 1971.

"Experience in education of couples about birth control in under developed countries (Reunion and Maurice islands)," by R. Traissac. BULL FED SOC GYNECOL OBSTET LANG FR 22:187-190, April-May, 1970.

"Experience in the use of the NAPP-1 apparatus for fluothane anesthesia in minor gynecologic surgery," by V. A. Glotova, et al. NOV MED PRIBOROSTR 2:41-45, 1970.

"Experience with the Kovács method of extra-amniotic glucose injection," by I. Kocsis, et al. ORV HETIL 112:1585-1587, July 4, 1971.

"Experiences in the genetic counseling office," by M. Avčin. WIEN MED WOCHENSCHR 120:356-359, May 16, 1970.

"Experiences with cerclage," by G. Ruzicska, et al. ORV HETIL 112: 1628-1631, July 11, 1971.

"Experimental action of a strain of trachoma agent on the gestation in rats," by P. Giroud. REV INT TRACH 46:113-116, 1969-1970.

"Experimental findings on the effects of administration of fluorouracil in pregnancy. II. Treatment of mice and rabbits with FU," by V. Lauro, et al. MINERVA GINECOL 22:281-285, March 15, 1970.

"An exploratory study of troops and their families practising contraception," by R. N. Varma, et al. INDIAN J MED RES 59:321-329, February, 1971.

"Extend the indications of medical abortion," by H. Zaidman. GYNECOL OBSTET 70:243-244, March-April, 1971.

"Extra-amniotic instillation of Rivanol and catheterization of the uterus in late legal abortion," by C. A. Ingemanson. LAKARTIDNINGEN 68: 2729-2731, June 2, 1971.

"Extraovular transcervical injection of rivanol for interruption of pregnancy," by S. A. Nabriski, et al. AM J OBSTET GYNECOL 110:54-56, May 1, 1971.

"Failure in interruption of pregnancy and its management," SANFUJIN-KA JISSAI 20:610, May, 1971.

"The family enters the hospital," by G. M. Abroms, et al. AM J PSY-CHIATRY 127:1363-1370, April, 1971.

"Family group therapy for children with self-induced seizures," by S. S. Libo, et al. AM J ORTHOPSYCHIATRY 41:506-509, April, 1971.

"Family planning," by H. Husslein. WIEN KLIN WOCHENSCHR 82:553-554, July 31, 1970.

"Family planning and conjugal roles in New York City poverty areas," by S. Polgar, et al. SOC SCI MED 4:135-139, July, 1970.

"Family planning and demography," by J. Henripin. UNION MED CAN 97:608-612, May, 1968.

"Family planning and maternal and child health," by J. M. Yang. YON-SEI MED J 11:67-76, 1970.

"Family planning and present law situation in Austria," by H. Husslein. WIEN KLIN WOCHENSCHR 83:141-144, March 5, 1971.

"Family planning and the reduction of fertility and illegitimacy: a preliminary report on a rural southern program," by J. D. Beasley, et al. SOC BIOL 16:167-178, September, 1969.

"Family Planning Association. Conference on Health Services and Public and Health Act 1968. J R COLL GEN PRACT 17:117-119, February, 1969.

"Family planning. Clinical practice and problems," by H. J. Staemmler, et al. DTSCH MED WOCHENSCHR 96:959-964, May 28, 1971.

"Family planning comes of age," by L. M. Hellman. AM J OBSTET GYNECOL 109:214-224, January 15, 1971.

"Family planning. Critical review of the Resolution of Family Planning," by B. Stambolović. LIJEC VJESN 92:493-500, 1970.

"Family planning--a health priority," J MED ASSOC STATE ALA 40: 414-415, December, 1970.

"Family planning--how, when and where," by U. Borell. NORD MED 86: 840-842, July 15, 1971.

"Family planning in China," by S. Ornstedt. LAKARTIDNINGEN 68: 2582-2583, May 26, 1971.

"Family planning in Cordoba (Argentine Republic)," by M. A. Agliozzo, et al. GINECOL OBSTET MEX 28:105-110, July, 1970.

"Family planning in the developing world," by W. G. Povey. OBSTET GYNECOL 36:948-952, December, 1970.

"Family planning in the Negro ghettos of Chicago," by D. J. Bogue. MILBANK MEM FUND Q 48:283-307, April, 1970.

"Family planning in a rural area using intrauterine devices," by R. C. Ramirez. REV CHIL OBSTET GINECOL 35:11-13, 1970.

"Family planning physicians answer abortion critics," AMER MED NEWS 14:1+, April 19, 1971.

"Family planning policies and practice in population control," by A. Wiseman. R SOC HEALTH J 91:134-138, May-June, 1971.

"Family planning with special reference to the intrauterine contraception using intrauterine pessary of the Dana-Super type," by C. Zwahr. ZENTRALBL GYNAEKOL 93:645-650, May 8, 1971.

"The family-size umbrella," by M. Woolacott. GUARDIAN 11, January 11, 1971.

"Family therapy in the treatment of anorexia nervos," by A. Barcai.

AM J PSYCHIATRY 128:286-290, September, 1971.

"Faut-il légaliser l'avortement?" by R. Troisfontaines. NRT 93:489-512, May, 1971.

"Fertility after insertion of an IUCD in Taiwan's family-planning program," by R. Freedman, et al. SOC BIOL 18:46-54, March, 1971.

"Fertility in balanced heterozygotes for a familial centric fusion translocation, t(DgDg)," by J. A. Wilson. J MED GENET 8:175-178, June, 1971.

"Fetal death in the cow, with observations from a practice," by W. Zindel. SCHWEIZ ARCH TIERHEILKD 112:130-138, March, 1970.

"Fetal indications for therapeutic abortion," by A. C.Barnes. ANNU REV MED 22:133-144, 1971.

"Fetal losses in a high prevalence area of chronic Chagas' disease," by J. R. Teruel, et al. REV INST MED TROP SAO PAULO 12:239-244, July-August, 1970.

"A fetal salvage program: the use of plasma diamine oxidase as a fetal monitor," by A. B. Weingold, et al. INT J FERTIL 16:24-35, January-March, 1971.

"Feticide: mens rea with partial immunity?" WASHBURN L J 10:403, Spring, 1971.

"Fetus as a legal entity-facing reality," SAN DIEGO L REV 8:126, 1971.

"Fever of unknown etiology," by D. B. Louria. DEL MED J 43:343-348, November, 1971.

"A field trial of the fluorescence antibody test for toxoplasmosis in the diagnosis of ovine abortion," by J. F. Archer, et al. VET REC 88: 206-208, February 20, 1971.

"The fifth horseman. A specter of therapeutic abortion," by R. L. Burt. OBSTET GYNECOL 37:616-617, April, 1971.

"1st experiments concerning the vaccination of horses against rhinopneumonia (viral abortion of mares) with a live vaccine from cell cultures)," by A. Mayr, et al. BULL OFF INT EPIZOOT 70:133-140,

May, 1968.

"500 outpatient abortions performed under local anesthesia," by I. K. Strausz, et al. OBSTET GYNECOL 38:199-205, August, 1971.

"The fluorescent antibody technic for the diagnosis of equine herpes virus abortion in comparison with conventional diagnostic methods," by U. Luttmann, et al. DTSCH TIERAERZTL WOCHENSCHR 78:623-627, December 1, 1971.

"The foetus began to cry---abortion," NURS J INDIA 62:325+, October, 1971.

"Folic acid and habitual abortion," by G. Brigato, et al. MINERVA GINECOL 22:471-474, May 15, 1970.

"Follow-up after abortion," by L. A. Pike. BR MED J 2:767, June 26, 1971.

"For direct words on abortion," by P. Ramsey. N ENGL J MED 285: 1541-1542, December 30, 1971.

"Four years' experience with the Lippes Loop as a method of family planning," by L. L. Williams, et al. WEST INDIAN MED J 20:12-16, March, 1971.

"France: free abortions, now!" NEWSWEEK 77:54+, April 19, 1971.

"France: we've had one," ECONOMIST 239:34, April 10, 1971.

"Free abortions, now! proposed reforms," NEWSWEEK 77:54+, April 19, 1971.

"French women admit having abortions," CAN HOSP 48:1+, May 15, 1971.

"From womb into tomb," by R. Engel. LIGUORIAN 59:22-24, December, 1971.

"The function of glucocorticoids of the adrenal cortex in pregnancy and in abortion," by M. I. Zhiliaev. PEDIATR AKUSH GINEKOL 4:33-35, July-August, 1968.

"Functional studies in women with habitual abortion and premature labor," by B. Kiutukchiev, et al. AKUSH GINEKOL (Sofiia) 9:461-469, 1970.

"Further comment on People v. Belous," CATHOLIC LAW 16:92, Winter, 1970.

"Further field studies on the fluorescent antibody test in the diagnosis of ovine abortion due to toxoplasmosis," by J. F. Archer, et al. VET REC 88:178-180, February 13, 1971.

"Gaping uterine isthmus (85 cases)," by H. Serment, et al. REV FR GYNECOL OBSTET 64:509-514, October, 1969.

"A general-practitioner survey of the Abortion Act 1967," by J. R. Eames, et al. PRACTITIONER 207:227-230, August, 1971.

"Genetic aspects of spontaneous abortions," by J. Cousin. J SCI MED LILLE 89:313-315, August-September, 1971.

"Genetic consequences of contraception in Santiago," by R. Cruz-Coke. REV MED CHIL 99:190-194, February, 1971.

"Genetics in therapeutic abortion," by A.C. Christakos. SOUTH MED J 64:Suppl:105-108, February, 1971.

"Genome unbalance and reproductive wastage in man and mammals," by C. E. Ford. NORD MED 86:1545, December 16, 1971.

"Geographic distribution of legal abortion in Bulgaria," by G. Stoimenov, et al. AKUSH GINEKOL (Sofiia) 10:112-116, 1971.

"Geographic distribution of need for family planning and subsidized services in the United States," by R. C. Lerner. AM J PUBLIC HEALTH 60:1944-1955, October, 1970.

"Group therapy following abortion," by N. R. Bernstein, et al. J NERV MENT DIS 152:303-314, May, 1971.

"A guide for the Catholic nurse on abortion," IR NURS NEWS 5, Spring, 1971.

"Guide for women," by A. J. Margolis, et al. REDBOOK 136:26, January, 1971.

"Guide to abortion laws in the United States," by L. Lader. REDBOOK 137:51-58, June, 1971.

"Guidelines for therapeutic abortion in Oregon: adopted September 26, 1971 by the Oregon Medical Association House of Delegates," NORTHWEST MED 70:854, December, 1971.

"Gynaecologist and patient alone should be allowed to determine legal abortions," by E. Sjövall. LAKARTIDNINGEN 68:4150-4151, September 8, 1971.

"Gynecological indications of a new progestational agent with prolonged action," by M. Goisis, et al. MINERVA GINECOL 22:339-367, March 31, 1970.

"Gynecologist: abortion--a decision between the woman and her physician," by N. G. Holmberg. LAKARTIDNINGEN 68:5845-5848, December 8, 1971.

"Gynecology and obstetrics," by D. N. Danforth. SURG GYNECOL OBSTET 132:221-225, February, 1971.

"Habitual abortion," by N. Vaglio. MINERVA GINECOL 21:1059-1061, August 31, 1969.

"Has abortion become all too easy?" by L. Edmunds. DAILY TELEGRAPH 11, August 20, 1971.

"Health legislation. Abortion: a survey of current legislation," WHO CHRON 25:328-333, July, 1971.

"Hematoma of the broad ligament of the uterus caused by uterine perforation," by H. Murooka, et al. SANFUJINKA JISSAI 20:534-539, May, 1971.

"Hemorrhage. A persistent source of obstetrical emergency," by G. C. Lewis, Jr. J KY MED ASSOC 69:105-109, February, 1971.

"Heparin for septic abortion and the prevention of endotoxic shock," by R. R. Margulis, et al. OBSTET GYNECOL 37:474-483, March, 1971.

"High court abortion debate relaxed, decorous," AMER MED NEWS 14:9, December 20, 1971.

"High court hears abortion cases," by J. McLellan. NAT CATH REP 8:4, December 24, 1971.

"Histochemical studies on the chorion in pregnant women treated with gestanon (preliminary report)," by Ts. Despotova, et al. AKUSH GINEKOL (Sofiia) 8:461-465, 1969.

"Hormonal and placental changes after intra-amniotic injection of hypertonic saline," by R. L. Berkowitz, et al. CLIN OBSTET GYNECOL 14:179-191, March, 1971.

"Hormonal contraception. Clinical experience, gained up to now and present-day problems," by J. Teter. POL TYG LEK 25:1641-1643, November 2, 1970.

"Hormonal studies and clinical observations in patients with threatening abortion or premature birth, respectively treated with depot-17-alpha-hydroxyprogesterone-caproate," by F. Tóth, et al. Z GEBURTSHILFE GYNAEKOL 175:168-175, October, 1971.

"Hormone produces abortion in 9," AM DRUGGIST 162:73, July 13, 1970.

"Hospital streamlines abortion policy: Atlantic City, N.J.," MOD HOSP 117:46, August, 1971.

"How do nurses feel about euthanasia and abortion?" by N. K. Brown, et al. AM J NURS 71:1413-1416, July, 1971.

"How safe is abortion?" by H. Price. LANCET 2:1419, December 25, 1971.

"Human chromosome abnormalities. 2. Occurrence in spontaneous abortion and antenatal detection by amniocentesis," by L. J. Butler. MIDWIFE HEALTH VISIT 7:105-108, March, 1971.

"Human infection by Vibrio fetus," by I. A.Cooper, et al. MED J AUST 1:1263-1267, June 12, 1971.

"Human life and abortion," by P. Harrington. CATHOLIC LAWYER 17:11-44, Winter, 1971.

"The human person: experimental laboratory or privileged sanctuary?" by C. Carroll. HOSP PROGR 52:35-41, June, 1971.

"The humanity of the unborn child," by E. Diamond. CATHOLIC LAWYER 17:174-180, Spring, 1971.

"Hungary clamps down on abortions," J AMER MED ASS 215:2122, March 29, 1971.

"Hydatidiform mole with a co-existent fetus diagnosed in advance by ultrasound," by P. Jouppila, et al. ANN CHIR GYNAECOL FENN 60:89-91, 1971.

"Hypertonic solutions to induce abortion," by I. L. Craft, et al. BR MED J 2:49, April 3, 1971.

"Hysteroscopy (preliminary report)," by R. Q. Guerrero, et al. GINECOL OBSTET MEX 27:683-691, June, 1970.

"Iatrogenic paracervical implantation of fetal tissue during therapeutic abortion. A case report," by L. R. Ayers, et al. OBSTET GYNECOL 37:755-760, May, 1971.

"Identification of meconium by the determination of acid phosphatase and spectrophotometric analysis," by E. Eliakis, et al. MED LEG DOMM CORPOR 4:163-168, April-June, 1971.

"Illinois Catholic Conference on Abortion," SOC JUST 63:414, March, 1971.

"Illinois court holds abortion 'on demand' legal," HOSPITALS 45:29, February 16, 1971; Supreme Court temporarily stays ruling. 17, March 1, 1971.

"Immediate and remote complications of repeated induced abortion," by B. Kh. Aronov. PEDIATR AKUSH GINEKOL 4:53-55, July-August, 1970.

"Immediate postpartum IUD insertion," by L. Banharnsupawat, et al. OBSTET GYNECOL 38:276-285, August, 1971.

" Imminent abortion, a statistical investigation of symptomatology and results of treatment," by N. B. Mossing, et al. UGESKR LAEGER 133: 1206-1209, June 25, 1971.

"Immunological rejection as a cause of abortion," by M. G. Kerr. J RE-PROD FERTIL 3:Suppl:49-55, April, 1968.

"Immunoserologic properties of antigens from Vibrio fetus of ovine origin," by L. L. Myers, et al. AM J VET RES 31:1773-1777, October, 1970.

46

"The impact of desired family size upon family planning practices in rural East Pakistan," by P. W. Mosena. JOURNAL OF MARRIAGE AND THE FAMILY 33,3:567-570, August, 1971.

"The impact of a liberalized abortion law on the medical schools," by M. L. Stone, et al. AM J OBSTET GYNECOL 111:728-735, November 1, 1971.

"The impact of liberalized abortion laws on family planning," by E. W. Overstreet. J REHABIL 7:20-21, July, 1971.

"Impact on hospital practice of liberalizing abortions and female sterilizations," by A. D. Claman, et al. CAN MED ASSOC J 105:35-41, July 10, 1971.

"Importance of colposcopic examinations after delivery and intrauterine interventions," by J. Simon. ZENTRALBL GYNAEKOL 93:1220-1226, August 28, 1971.

"Importance of the uterine anatomic factor in the etiology of recurrent abortion," by C. Orlandi, et al. MINERVA GINECOL 21:1061-1064, August 31, 1969.

"In defense of human life," by P. O'Boyle. COLUMBIA 50:5, December, 1970.

"In defense of unborn human life," SOC JUST 64:54-55, May, 1971.

"In defense of unborn human life; pastoral letter," OR 18 (162) 5, May 6, 1971.

"In a permissive society: defense of life," by G. Nicolini. OR 29 (173) 3-4, July 22, 1971.

"In vitro lymphoblastic transformation of blood lymphocytes applied to the study of repeated spontaneous abortions," by D. Alcalay, et al. GYNECOL OBSTET 70:59-61, January-February, 1971.

"In what measure should abortion be penalized," by P. DeBoeck. NURSING 43:15-21, July-August, 1971.

"Inadequacy of a one-method family-planning program," by R. G. Potter. SOC BIOL 18:1-9, March, 1971.

"Inaugural address: 7th National Conference of the Indian Academy of Pediatrics," by S. K. Shah. INDIAN PEDIATR 7:1-3, January, 1970.

"The incidence of illegal abortion (Great Britain)," by W. H. James. POPULATION STUDIES 25:327-339, July, 1971.

"Incidence of uterine perforations in criminal abortions," by E. Rosenzweig, et al. RAD MED FAK ZAGREBU 18:221-224, 1970.

"Increase in plasma progesterone caused by undernutrition during early pregnancy in the ewe," by I. A. Cumming, et al. J REPROD FERTIL 24:146-147, January, 1971.

"Indications for therapeutic abortion in Aberdeen, 1956-1967," by K. J. Dennis. J BIOSOC SCI 3:101-105, January, 1971.

"Individuation und Personalisation: Die anthropologische Relevanz embryonalbiologischer Entwicklungsphasen," by A. van Melsen. THEOLOGISCHE QUARTALSCHRIFT 228-237, 1971.

"Induced abortion," MED LETT DRUGS THER 12:98-100, November 27, 1970.

"Induced abortion," by A. W. Mante. TIJDSCHR ZIEKENVERPL 24:248-253, March 16, 1971.

"Induced abortion," by A. Sikkel. NED TIJDSCHR GENEESKD 115: 1119-1120, June 26, 1971.

"Induced abortion and its medico-legal aspects," by D. Q. Garcia REV OBSTET GINECOL VENEZ 30:517-523, 1970.

"Induced abortion and its trends in Yugoslavia," by B. M. Berich. AKUSH GINEKOL 46:67-68, November, 1970.

"Induced abortion--contraception," by O. Koller. TIDSSKR NOR LAEGEFOREN 91:629-632, March 30, 1971.

"Induced abortion for psychiatric indication," by S. Meyerowitz, et al. AM J PSYCHIATRY 127:1153-1160, March, 1971.

"Induced abortion in New York City. A report of six separate studies," by R. E. Hall. AM J OBSTET GYNECOL 110:601-611, July 1, 1971.

48

"Induction of abortion by the intravenous administration of prostaglandin F 2. A critical evaluation," by N. Wiqvist, et al. ACTA OBSTET GYNECOL SCAND 50:381-389, 1971.

"The induction of abortion by prostaglandin F 2," by K. Kinoshita, et al. AM J OBSTET GYNECOL 111:855-857, November, 1971.

"Induction of abortion by prostaglandins E (PGE1 and PGE2)," by M. P. Embery. J REPROD MED 6:256-259, June, 1971.

"Induction of abortion in the rabbit by hydrocortisonacetate," by G. Wagner. ACTA ENDOCRINOL 155:Suppl:89, 1971.

"Induction of lactogenesis and abortion by prostaglandin F2-alpha in pregnant rats," by R. P. Deis. NATURE (London) 229:568, February 19, 1971.

"Induction of midtrimester abortion by intra-amniotic administration of prostaglandin F 2. A preliminary report," by M. Bygdeman, et al. ACTA PHYSIOL SCAND 82:415-416, July, 1971.

"Induction of mid-trimester therapeutic abortion by intra-amniotic urea and intravenous oxytocin," by I. Craft, et al. LANCET 2:1058-1060, November 13, 1971.

"Induction of therapeutic abortion by intra-amniotic injection of urea," by J. O. Greenhalf, et al. BR MED J 1:28-29, January 2, 1971.

"Induction of therapeutic abortion with urea," by J. O. Greenhalf. BR MED J 2:107, April 10, 1971.

"Induction of therapeutic abortion with urea," by M. Pugh, et al. BR MED J 1:345, February 6, 1971.

"Infected abortion and disseminated intravascular coagulation (DIC). Heparin prevention and early diagnosis of the DIC," by W. Kuhn, et al. MED WELT 22:1199-1200, July 24, 1971.

"Influenza and rhino-pneumonia in horses in France," by A. Brion. BULL OFF INT EPIZOOT 70:149-169, May, 1968.

"Inhibition of prostaglandin release and the control of threatened abortion," by A. Tothill, et al. LANCET 2:381, August 14, 1971.

"The injurious effects of smoking on gestation," by L. Vértes. ZEN-TRALBL GYNAEKOL 92:1395-1398, October 17, 1970.

"Insufficiency of the cervix uteri," by B. Budínská. ACTA UNIV CAROL (MED) 16:377-427, 1970.

"Integration of the family planning in the health care of the German Democratic Republic," by K. H. Mehlan. Z AERZTL FORTBILD 64: 429-432, May 1, 1970.

"International cooperation in family planning," by M. Strachan. NURS OUTLOOK 19:103, February, 1971.

"International discussion on abortion," SAIRAANHOITAJA 47:484-486, June 10, 1971.

"Interruption of pregnancy by the abdominal route," by M. Blažek, et al. CESK GYNEKOL 36:342-343, July, 1971.

"Interruption of pregnancy by various steroids," by H. Selye, et al. FERTIL STERIL 22:735-740, November, 1971.

"Interruption of pregnancy from the legal viewpoint," by W. Becker. THER GGW 110:1362-1376, September, 1971.

"Intra-abdominal chicken-bone abscess," by R. N. Berk, et al. RADIO-LOGY 101:311-333, November, 1971.

"Intra-abdominal sepsis," by W. A. Altemeier, et al. ADV SURG 5:281-333, 1971.

"Intra-amnial introduction of hypertonic solutions--a method for inter-ruption of pregnancy," by I. Atanasov, et al. AKUSH GINEKOL (Sofiia) 10:155-158, 1971.

"Intrauterine injection of hypertonic solutions," by L. P. Bengtsson. LAKARTIDNINGEN 68:2721-2722, June 2, 1971.

"Intrauterine injection of 20 per cent saline for inducing abortion," by M. C. Cheng, et al. SINGAPORE MED J 12:259-263, October, 1971.

"An invitational symposium," J REPROD MED 6:274-301, June, 1971.

"Iodine salivary clearance in a group of hyperthyroid women with a history of recurrent or habitual abortion," by A. Viglione, et al. MINERVA GINECOL 21:1077-1079, August 31, 1969.

"Is abortion on demand good medicine?" by E. G. Kilroy. OHIO STATE MED J 67:39-46, January, 1971.

"Is reaction to the population problem misplaced?" by R. L. Day PEDIATRICS 47:952-955, May, 1971.

"Isolation of a herpesvirus from the canine genital tract: association with infertility, abortion and stillbirths," by G. Poste, et al. VET REC 88:229-233, February 27, 1971.

"Isolation of V. fetus from aborted sows," by V. F. Shatalov. VETER-INARIIA 3:49-50, March, 1971.

"It's a new game," TRIUMPH 6:46, March, 1971.

"The Jamaican male and family planning," by B. I. Morgan, et al. WEST INDIAN MED J 20:5-11, March, 1971.

"Japan's 22 year experience with a liberal abortion law," by Y. Hayasaka, et al. LINACRE 38:33-44, February, 1971.

"Juridical and legal-political problems of birth regulation," by G. Kaiser. MED KLIN 63:1526-1530, September, 1968.

"Ketamine for dilatation and curettage," by S. Galloon. CAN ANAESTH SOC J 18:600-613, November, 1971.

"Killing the problem even if it is human," by B. Daly. MARRIAGE 53: 72, February, 1971.

"The Kings County Abortion story," by L. A. Walton. CLIN OBSTET GYNECOL 14:149-152, March, 1971; also in MOD TREAT 8:97-100, February, 1971.

"Late abortion and difficulties of evacuation of the uterus," by H. Serment, et al. BULL FED SOC GYNECOL OBSTET LANG FR 21: 174-176, April-May, 1969.

"L'avortement et la responsabilité du chrétien; declaration des évêques catholiques des pays nordiques, Goeteborg, juillet 1971," DOC CATH 68:1076-1084, December 5, 1971.

"Law and the unborn child; the legal and logical inconsistencies," NOTRE DAME LAW 46:349, Winter, 1971.

"Law on abortion as it may appear to the layman," by C. P. Harrison. CAN DOCTOR 37:82-83, June, 1971.

"Law professor named special guardian of unborn children in New York City," HOSPITALS 45:27, December 16, 1971.

"Learning abortion care," by A. Goldmann. NURS OUTLOOK 19:350-352, May, 1971.

"Legal abortion and mental health," by C. Thonet. REV CHIL OBSTET GINECOL 35:209-213, 1970.

"Legal abortion in Sweden: thirty years' experience," by J. O. Ottosson. J BIOSOC SCI 3:173-192, April, 1971.

"Legal abortion in the U.S.A. A preliminary assessment," by M. Potts, et al. LANCET 2:651-653, September 18, 1971.

"Legal abortion mess; Women's medical group, New York," by A. Barry. MCCALLS 98:30+, January, 1971.

"Legal abortion: who, why and where," TIME 98:67-70, September 27, 1971.

"Legal abortions: Early medical complications. An interim report of the joint program for the study of abortion," by C. Tietze, et al. FAMILY PLANN PERSPECT 3:6-14, October, 1971.

"Legal abortions in Canada," by L. E. Rozovsky. CAN HOSP 48:39-41, February, 1971.

"Legal abortions in Finland," by P. A. Jarvinen. ANN CHIR GYNAECOL FENN 60:65-66, 1971.

"Legal abortions--a social problem," by E. Sjövall. LAKARTIDNINGEN 68:5279-5285, November 10, 1971.

"Legal abortions, socioeconomic status, and measured intelligence in the United States," by J. E. Cohen. SOC BIOL 18:55-63, March, 1971.

"Legal and illegal situation in Switzerland," by H. Stamm. BIBL

GYNAECOL 55:1-43, 1970.

"Legal authority of health departments to regulate abortion practice," by W. J. Curran. AMER J PUBLIC HEALTH 61:621-626, March, 1971.

"Legal interruption of pregnancy," GYNECOL OBSTET 70:127-132, January-February, 1971.

"Legal possibilities of pregnancy interruption for eugenic or fetal indications," by D. Krauss. MUNCH MED WOCHENSCHR 113:1505-1512, November 5, 1971.

"Legal reforms on pregnancy interruption," by A. Eser. MED WEIT 17: 721-729, April 24, 1971.

"Legal regulation of abortion in England (Abortion Act 1967)," by K. Händel. BEITR GERICHTL MED 27:72-75, 1970.

"Legal theory of value assessment and medical aspects of the need to protect the beginning of life," by J. Gerchow, et al. BEITR GERICHTL MED 27:67-71, 1970.

"Legal view of abortion," by C. A. Gravenor, Jr. CAN DOCTOR 37:44+, March, 1971.

"Legalized abortion: the conscience clause and coercion," by D. Cavanagh. HOSP PROGR 52:86-90, August, 1971.

"Legalized abortion is not 'progress'," by A. Nowlan. ATLAN ADV 61:64-65, March, 1971.

"The legalizing of contraceptives and abortions," by E. Szabady. IMPACT OF SCIENCE ON SOCIETY 21:265-270, July-September, 1971.

"Let us be born, by R. Joyce, et al. A Review," by P. Marx. CATH WORLD 212:218, January, 1971.

"Let's look at abortion (discussion of the issues from the points of view of a physician, a pastor, an ethicist and a young woman who underwent the experience," SOCIAL ACTION 37:3-39, March, 1971.

"Letter from doctor will do for abortion: Vancouver General Hospital," CAN HOSP 48:18, April, 1971.

"Letter on abortion morality," by M. Hurley. SOC JUST 64:241-242, November, 1971.

"Letters to editor," CATH WORLD 212:173-174, January, 1971.

"Letters to John and Mary Ann, preamble to an exodus," by L. Gilbert. TRIUMPH 6:24-26, October, 1971.

"Lettre pastorale de l'épiscopat Hollandais sur l'avortement direct," DOC CATH 68:486-489, May 16, 1971.

"Leukocytic and thrombocytic isoimmunization in pregnancy," by M. Minev. AKUSH GINEKOL 10:213-218, 1971.

"Level of histamine in peripheral blood in patients with bacterial shock," by A. D. Makatsariia, et al. AKUSH GINEKOL 46:40-43, October, 1970.

"Liberal abortion policy upheld in California by the California Medical Association," AMER MED NEWS 14:6, March 29, 1971.

"A liberal law does not include 'abortion on request'," by R. Gillon. LAKARTIDNINGEN 68:3560-3563, August 4, 1971.

"Liberalizing abortion laws; teacher opinion poll. National education association, research division," TODAYS ED 60:5, May, 1971.

"Life and living it," by Y. Cross, et al. NURS MIRROR 133:49-51, October 15, 1971.

"Life or death, maturity or decline," by M. S. Roach. INFIRM CAN 13:17, July, 1971.

"Life our greatest asset? Moralistic and theologic discussion of pregnancy interruption," by A. Ziegler. WIEN MED WOCHENSCHR 121: Suppl 2:9-13, November 20, 1971.

"Lineup on abortion: experts see Supreme Court closely divided," AMER MED NEWS 14:12-13, December 6, 1971.

"Literacy and family planning in India," by V. J. Marsick. INDIAN JOURNAL OF ADULT EDUCATION 32,7:8-10, 21, July, 1971.

"Live abortion to be investigated," NAT CATH REP 7:7, May 7, 1971.

"Locums for God," by C. Storr. NEW STATESMAN 78, July 16, 1971.

"Logistic problems of legal abortion," by E. W. Overstreet. AM J PUBLIC HEALTH 61:496-499, March, 1971.

"The logistics of abortion services in the absence of restrictive criminal legislation in the United States," by C. W. Tyler, Jr., et al. AM J PUBLIC HEALTH 61:489-495, March, 1971.

"Long-term results of treatment with a delayed-action progestational hormone in threatened abortion," by P. Scillieri. MINERVA GINECOL 22:413-416, April 15, 1970.

"Luteinizing hormone titration in the anterior pituitary of women who died during pregnancy and the post-abortion period," by M. De la Lastra. REV MED CHIL 98:782-785, November, 1970.

"MDs, legislature act to curb New York abortion agencies," AMER MED NEWS 14:3, June 7, 1971.

"Mad scramble for abortion money," by H. Eisenberg. MED ECON 48: 35+, January 4, 1971.

"Main causes of repetitive abortion revealed by hysterography," by P. Dellenbach, et al. J RADIOL ELECTROL MED NUCL 52:522-523, August-September, 1971.

"Malthus on population quality," by E. Cocks. SOC BIOL 18:84-87, March, 1971.

"Management of incomplete abortion as an outpatient procedure," by A. Allen, et al. CENT AFR J MED 17:91-96, May, 1971.

"Management of incomplete abortion with vacuum curettage," by D. L. Hill. MINN MED 54:225-228, March, 1971.

"Marriage and child care in those classified as mentally retarded," by J. B. Fotheringham. CAN MED ASSOC J 104:813-816, May 8, 1971.

"Marshall's ruling ripped," NAT CATH REP 7:14, February 26, 1971.

"Maryland ruling permits abortion referral ads," ADV AGE 43:21, January 3, 1972.

"Massachusetts RN's do not have to help with abortions," HOSP MANAGE 112:17, August, 1971.

"Maternal herpes-simplex infection causing abortion. Histopathologic study of the placenta," by A. G. Garcia. HOSPITAL 78:1267-1274, November-December, 1970.

"Maternal serologic analysis and histoimmunologic localization of IgG, IgM and IgA immunoglobulins in ovular tissue during the 1st trimester," by U. Montemagno, et al. ARCH OSTET GINECOL 74:58-71, January-February, 1969.

"Mechanism of selection and decision-making in therapeutic abortion," by C. Farmer. J BIOSOC SCI 3:121-127, January, 1971.

"Medical abortion in South Australia. The first 12 months under new lesiglation," by A. F. Connon. MED J AUST 2:608-614, September 18, 1971.

"A medical case for abortion liberalization," by M. L. Taymor. ARCH SURG 102:235, March, 1971.

"Medical-legal considerations of abortion in New York State under the new abortion law," by L. Holtzman. CLIN OBSTET GYNECOL 14:36-47, March, 1971; also in MOD TREAT 8:39-49, February, 1971.

"Medical obligations imposed by abortion," by F. J. Ingelfinger. N ENGL J MED 284:727, April 1, 1971.

"Medical pressures to tighten the Abortion Act," by N. Hagger. TIMES p14, June 17, 1971.

"Medical record of women with habitual abortion," by I. Penev. AKUSH GINEKOL (Sofiia) 9:470-478, 1970.

"Medical records aren't fishing grounds: court," MOD HOSP 116:68-70, March, 1971.

"Medical responsibility," by K. Chaturachinda. J MED ASSOC THAI 54:149-152, March, 1971.

"Medicolegal opinion. Re: on demand abortions in public hospitals," by H. B. Alsobrook, Jr. J LA STATE MED SOC 123:29-30, January, 1971.

"Medicolegal problems caused by the use of oxytocics," by R. C. Clingolani. MINERVA MEDICOLEG 90:5-10, January-June, 1970.

"Der medizinische Umgang mit dem praenatalen Leben," by W. Mende. THEOLOGISCHE QUARTALSCHRIFT 214-221, 1971.

"Meeting the needs of the single parent family," FAMILY COORDINATOR 20,4:327-336, October, 1971.

"Meeting the problems of today's families through extension programs," FAMILY COORDINATOR 20,4:337-340, October, 1971.

"Memorandum on The Medical Termination of Pregnancy Bill 1971; presented to Shrimati Indira Gandhi, Prime Minister of India, by Archbishop Angelo Fernandes," OR 39 (183) 4, September 30, 1971.

"Meningitis with Escherichia coli (O119B14)," by I. Voiculescu, et al. MED INTERNA 23:1007-1011, August, 1971.

"Menstrual disturbances after interruption," by D. Andreev. FOLIA MED 12:263-269, 1970.

"Methods of abortion," by W. T. Fullerton. J BIOSOC SCI 3:128-131, January, 1971.

"3. Methotrexate and concentration of chorionic gonadotropin," by L. Lajos, et al. ORV HETIL 112:2077-2080 passim, August 29, 1971.

"Methoxyflurane in therapeutic abortion," by M. H. Lawrence. BR J CLIN PRACT 25:414-416, September, 1971.

"Mid-trimester abortion by extra-ovular catheter stimulation of the uterus," by W. H. Godsick. J REPROD MED 7:281, December, 1971.

"Midtrimester abortion: clinical experience with amniocentesis and hypertonic instillation in 400 patients," by J. M. Mackenzie, et al. CLIN OBSTET GYNECOL 14:107-123, March, 1971; also in MOD TREAT 8:72-88, February, 1971.

"Mid-trimester abortions, fetal weight and ethics," by R. C. Goodlin. CALIF MED 114:85-86, March, 1971.

"Military hospitals struggle to keep balanced approach on abortions," US MED 7:4+, November 1, 1971.

"Miscarriages, premature birth and perinatal death of infants in employed and unemployed women," by N. Aresin, et al. ZENTRALBL GYNAE-KOL 93:441-444, April 3, 1971.

"Missouri Catholic bishops' statement on abortion," OR 29 (173) 11, July 22, 1971.

"Model abortion program set up in Wickersham Hospital, New York City," HOSP MANAGE 111:7, May, 1971.

"Modern therapy of endotoxic shock in septic abortion," by B. Krznar, et al. ACTA MED IUGOSL 25:23-36, 1971.

"Moonlighting medics: liberal abortion law proves to be a bonanza for New York (N.Y.) doctors," by M. J. Connor. WALL ST J 177:1+, June 1, 1971.

"The morality of abortion," by M. O'Brien. FURROW 21:762-769, December, 1970.

"Morbidity and mortality in the offspring of 300 consanguineous couples in Florence," by U. Bigozzi, et al. ACTA GENET MED GEMELLOL 19:515-528, October, 1970.

"Morbidity and mortality of abortions," by H. Arthure. LANCET 2:310-311, August 7, 1971.

"More on rights," LANCET 1:791-792, April 17, 1971.

"Morphological abnormalities of the uterus and abortion," by R. Iizuka, et al. SANFUJINKA JISSAI 20:833-841, August, 1971.

"Morphological changes in the kidneys in acute renal insufficiency following an abortion," by N. F. Kan'shina, et al. ARKH PATOL 32:59-64, 1970.

"Morphology of abortive ovum," by P. Dráč, et al. CESK GYNEKOL 36: 48-49, February, 1971.

"Morphology of the kidneys in acute post-abortion renal insufficiency," by N. F. Kan'shina, et al. AKUSH GINEKOL 45:36-39, March, 1969.

"Mortality and morbidity of abortion," by P. Huntingford. LANCET 1:1012-1013, May 15, 1971.

"Mortality and morbidity of legal abortion," by A. Czeizel, et al. LANCET 2:209-210, July 24, 1971.

"Mortality of abortion," by M. D. Buckley-Sharp. LANCET 2:490-491, August 28, 1971.

"Mortality of abortion," by M. R. Henzl. LANCET 2:368, August 14, 1971.

"Mortality of abortion," by P. Kestleman. LANCET 2:607, September 11, 1971.

"Motivations, acceptance and refusal of contraceptive methods," by F. Jamet. BULL INST NATL SANTE RECH MED 23:1333-1346, November-December, 1968.

"Multiple enzyme deficiencies in placental tissue from two blighted-ovum abortions," by J. B. Edlow, et al. AM J OBSTET GYNECOL 111:365-368, October 1, 1971.

"My experience in uterine perforation," SANFUJINKA JISSAI 20:611-612, May, 1971.

"My experience in uterine perforation--self examination," SANFUJINKA JISSAI 20:612-613, May, 1971.

"My method in prevention of uterine perforation," by F. Kikuchi. SAN-FUJINKA JISSAI 20:604-606, May, 1971.

"My method in prevention of uterine perforation," by G. Ozawa. SAN-FUJINKA JISSAI 20:607-608, May, 1971.

"My method in prevention of uterine perforation," by T. Shinoara. SAN-FUJINKA JISSAI 20:609, May, 1971.

"My method in prevention of uterine perforation," by Y. Tamano. SAN-FUJINKA JISSAI 20:608-609, May, 1971.

"My method in prevention of uterine perforation," by H. Yoshida. SAN-FUJINKA JISSAI 20:606-607, May, 1971.

"Mycotic abortion in man: a case report," by R. A. Franciosi, et al. J REPROD MED 4:25-28, February, 1970.

"National Council on family relations: position paper on abortion,"
FAMILY COORDINATOR 20,4:401-402, October, 1971.

"Neurovegetative reactivity in women during interruption of unwanted
pregnancy in the 2nd trimester by intra-amniotic instillation of saline
solution," by B. Kiutukchiev, et al. AKUSH GINEKOL 8:482-485, 1969.

"The new abortion law and problems caused by it," by I. Kettunen,
KATILOLEHTI 76:505-510, November, 1971.

"The new abortion laws and practical-vocational nursing education,"
J PRACT NURS 1:27 passim, January, 1971.

"New abortion laws: how are they working?" by T. Irwin. TODAYS
HEALTH 48:20-23+, March, 1970.

"New liberal abortion laws, issues and problems," by H. Freilich. HOSP
MANAGE 111:1+, May, 1971.

"New national program of family planning in the United States," by S. C.
Scheyer. SALUD PUBLICA MEX 12:657-661, September-October, 1970.

"New York abortion reform and conflicting municipal regulations: a
question of home rule," BUFFALO L REV 20:524, Winter, 1971.

"New York abortion reform law: considerations, application and legal
consequences--more than we bargained for?" ALBANY L REV 35:
644, 1971.

"New York City abortions nearly equal births," AMER MED NEWS 14:9,
July 12, 1971.

"New York obstetricians' abortion stand," MED WORLD NEWS 12:12G,
April 2, 1971.

"New York State Department of Health; report on abortions," by H.
Ingraham. SOC JUST 63:377-384, February, 1971.

"New York's obstetricians surveyed on abortion," by R. C. Lerner, et al.
FAM PLANN PERSPECT 3:56, January, 1971.

"New wave of abortion," by J. Kettle. CAN DOCTOR 37:61-62, July,
1971.

"Nidation inhibition and abortion following rape," by E. Böhm, et al. MED KLIN 66:989-996, July 2, 1971.

"96% of women abort when given hormone," AM DRUGGIST 162:47, October 19, 1970.

"Nixon takes stand against abortion," NAT CATH REP 7:5, April 16, 1971.

"No new abortion laws, checks show," NAT CATH REP 7:5, September 10, 1971.

"Noise induced lesions with special reference to abortions in cattle," by E. Aehnelt. DTSCH TIERAERZTL WOCHENSCHR 77:543-547 contd, October 15, 1970.

"Noise induced lesions with special reference to abortions in cattle," by R. Kramer. DTSCH TIERAERZTL WOCHENSCHR 77:568-571 concl, November 1, 1970.

"Note doctrinale sur l'avortement," DOC CATH 68:285-290, March 21, 1971.

"Now-generation churchmen and the unborn," by H. B. Kuhn. CHR TODAY 15:38, January 29, 1971.

"The nurse and the abortion patient," by H. Virjo. SAIRAANHOITAJA 47:478-480, June 10, 1971.

"The nurse and placenta praevia and abruptio. Her function in protecting both mother and child," by G. Rosenheim, et al. BEDSIDE NURSE 3:31-32, December, 1970.

"Nurses and abortion," TIME 97:60, May 31, 1971.

"Nurses' feelings a problem under new abortion law," AMER J NURS 71:350+, February, 1971.

"Nurses opinion on induced abortions," by C. P. Sporken. TIJDSCHR ZIEKENVERPL 24:242-247, March 16, 1971.

"The nurse's role in family planning," by A. Rooke. NURS TIMES 67: 727-730, June, 1971.

"Nursing care in an abortion unit," by B. Yaloff, et al. CLIN OBSTET GYNECOL 14:67-80, March, 1971.

"Nursing care study: abortion--with complications," by D. Brett, et al. NURS TIMES 67:1209-1210, September 30, 1971.

"Nursing interviews helpful at abortion clinic: New York," AMER J NURSING 71:352-353, February, 1971.

"Observations on the anti-gestation effect of Aimax (methallibure) in recently bred gilts," by J. U. Akpokodje, et al. CAN VET J 12:110-114, May, 1971.

"Obstetrical complications of uterine malformations," by G. Poizat. REV MED LIEGE 25:763-764, December 1, 1970.

"Occurrence of incompatibility in the ABO and Rh systems following abortion," by A. Jasiewicz. ZENTRALBL GYNAEKOL 93:295-297, February 27, 1971.

"Occurrence of recurrent abortion among patients in our hospital in the last 3 years," by R. Palagi, et al. MINERVA GINECOL 21:1064-1066, August 31, 1969.

"Official statistics of legal abortions in England," by K. Händel. MED KLIN 65:524-526, March 13, 1971.

"On being reviewed," by M. Simms. HUMANIST 86:336-337, November, 1971.

"On a case of dicoumarin necrosis," by B. Danilov, et al. REV MED CHIR SOC MED NAT IASI 75:479-483, April-June, 1971.

"On combined estro-progestogenic and antireactional treatment in threatened abortion," by M. Goisis, et al. MINERVA GINECOL 23:547-552, June, 1971.

"On legal abortion," by I. K. Furier. MED J AUST 1:489-496, February 27, 1971.

"On the presence of anti-fetal antibodies in women after spontaneous abortion," by G. Gabbrielli, et al. BOLL SOC ITAL BIOL SPER 45:601-602, May 15, 1969.

"On the use of isoxysuprine in threatened abortion," by A. Julitta, et al. MINERVA GINECOL 21:867-868, July 15, 1969.

"100 clinical cases of pregnancy complications treated with a 19-nor-progesterone, registered as 31.458 Ba and followed until term," by M. Lanvin, et al. BULL FED SOC GYNECOL OBSTET LANG FR 20:110-117, April-May, 1968.

"100 college students form group to oppose abortion," NAT CATH REP 8:5, December 10, 1971.

"1,000 mourn innocents slain by abortion," NAT CATH REP 7:12, January 15, 1971.

"1,452 cases," by S. Lee, et al. AM J OBSTET GYNECOL 108:1294-1297, December 15, 1970.

"An open letter on the abortion problem," SOC JUST 64:86-93, June, 1971.

"Ontario Human Rights Commission finds no bias in abortion demotion," CAN NURSE 67:17-18, September, 1971.

"Opinions on abortion from medical practitioners," by R. A. Gregson, et al. NZ MED J 73:267-273, May, 1971.

"Opposition to eased abortions seen mounting," HOSP PROGRESS 52: 24-25, February, 1971.

"The organization and function of therapeutic abortion committees," by E. Wilson. CAN HOSP 48:38-40, December, 1971.

"Our experience in the diagnosis and therapy of recurrent abortion," by I. Coghi, et al. MINERVA GINECOL 21:1070-1073, August 31, 1969.

"Our experience with the Krause method in the Clinica y Maternidad Conchita," by L. de A. Benavides. GINECOL OBSTET MEX 26:641-647, November, 1969.

"An outbreak of bovine abortions associated with leptospirosis," by S. G. Knott, et al. AUST VET J 46:385-386, August, 1970.

"An outbreak of mare abortion in Japan due to infection with equine rhinopneumonitis virus," by T. Shimizu, et al. BULL OFF INT EPIZOOT 70:251-256, May, 1968.

"Outpatient abortion," by P. Diggory. LANCET 2:767-768, October 2, 1971.

"Outpatient abortion: New York style," by B. L. Shaw. RN 34:44-49, October, 1971.

"Outpatient abortions," LANCET 2:656, September 18, 1971.

"Outpatient intra-amniotic injection of hypertonic saline," by T. D. Kerenyl. CLIN OBSTET GYNECOL 14:124-140, March, 1971.

"Outpatient saline abortion," by H. Schulman, et al. OBSTET GYNECOL 37:521-526, April, 1971.

"Outpatient termination of pregnancy," by S. C. Lewis, et al. BR MED J 4:606-610, December 4, 1971.

"Ovine abortion due to experimental toxoplasmosis," by W. A. Watson, et al. VET REC 88:42-45, January 9, 1971.

"The oxytocic effect of acridine dyes and their use in terminating mid-trimester pregnancies," by B. V. Lewis, et al. J OBSTET GYNAECOL BR COMMONW 78:838-842, September, 1971.

"The oxytocic effect of acridine dyes and their use in the termination of mid-trimester pregnancies," by V. Lewis, et al. J REPROD FERTIL 25:456-457, June, 1971.

"Oxtocin administration in abortions induced with hypertonic saline," by J. D. Schulman, et al. LANCET 2:606-607, September 11, 1971.

"PGE compounds for induction of labour and abortion," by M. Embrey. ANN NY ACAD SCI 180:518-523, April 30, 1971.

"Papal falibility," CHR CENT 87:1309, November 4, 1970; Discussion 88:21, January 6, 1971.

"Paracevical block anaesthesia for evacuation of the uterus," by V. E. Aimakhu. WEST AFR MED J 20:277-279, August, 1971.

"Parent and child: minor's right to consent to an abortion," SANTA CLARA LAW 11:469, Spring, 1971.

"Parental consent for abortion is appealed to Supreme Court," AMER MED

NEWS 14:8, August 2, 1971.

"Parental consent not necessary to minor's therapeutic abortion: California," NEWSLETTER (SOC HOSP ATTORNEYS) 4:1, July, 1971.

"The Parliament requested overhaul in sterilization law," LAKARTID-NINGEN 67:5732, December 2, 1970.

"Participation of low-income urban women in a public health birth control program," by Z. L. Janus, et al. PUBLIC HEALTH REP 85: 859-867, October, 1970.

"Parting shots: well-kept-secret weapon in the sexual revolution," by W. A. McWhirter. LIFE 71:69, July 9, 1971.

"Pathogenesis of abortion in acute nitrite toxicosis in guinea pigs," by D. P. Sinha, et al. TOXICOL APPL PHARMACOL 18:340-347, February, 1971.

"Pathologic findings after hypertonic saline instillation in midtrimester abortion," by A. Blaustein, et al. CLIN OBSTET GYNECOL 14:192-203, March, 1971; also in MOD TREAT 8:127-138, February, 1971.

"Pathological structures of the placenta examined under the electron microscope. 1st observations of villi of aborted human ova," by R. Herbst, et al. GYNECOL OBSTET 70:369-376, August-October, 1971.

"Peculiarities of ampicillin use in acute renal failure," by M. I. Kuzin, et al. ANTIBIOTIKI 16:553-558, June, 1971.

"Pelvic short wave diathermy given inadvertently in early pregnancy," by A. H. Imrie. J OBSTET GYNAECOL BR COMMONW 78:91-92, January, 1971.

"Perinatal risk associated with maternal genital herpes simplex virus infection," by A. J. Nahmias, et al. AM J OBSTET GYNECOL 110: 825-837, July 15, 1971.

"Perirenal masses simulating renal tumors," by J. W. Fenlon, et al. J UROL 106:448-450, October, 1971.

"Personality factors and referral for therapeutic abortion," by P. C. Olley. J BIOSOC SCI 3:106-115, January, 1971.

"Perspectives of abortion," by T. Glenister. TABLET 225:300+, March 27, 1971; 326-327, April 3, 1971; 350-351, April 10, 1971.

"Petrified fetus (lithopedion) in a 74-year-old woman," by N. N. Tiraspolskaia, et al. PEDIATR AKUSH GINEKOL 4:61, July-August, 1970.

"The pharmacodynamic action of caffeine. Deductions in clinical obstetrics," by A. Crainicianu. MINERVA GINECOL 23:984-989, December 15, 1971.

"Phoenix of abortional freedom; is a penumbral or ninth-amendment right about to arise from the nineteenth-century legislative ashes of a fourteenth-century common-law liberty?" by C. C. Means, Jr. NY L F 17:335, 1971.

"Physician attitudes on abortion and the Kansas abortion law," by R. Bettis. J KANS MED SOC 72:344-349, August, 1971.

"Physicians and methods of birth planning," by P. J. Donaldson. RI MED J 53:419-423 passim, August, 1970.

"Physician's association abortion meeting. Conclusions of the presiding committee," by U. Borell, et al. LAKARTIDNINGEN 68:5842-5844, December 8, 1971.

"Physician's viewpoint," by K. Newmann. AM DRUGGIST 164:8, December 13, 1971.

"Pilot study of single women requesting a legal abortion," by J. F. Pearson. J BIOSOC SCI 3:417-448, October, 1971.

"Plain meaning of abortion," by G. L. Hallett. AMERICA 124:632-633, June 19, 1971.

"Planned parenthood 40 years in Alabama," by O.T. Bolding, et al. J MED ASSOC STATE ALA 40:451 passim, January, 1971.

"Plasma levels of progesterone in early pregnancy after removal of the foetoplacental unit, and following removal of corpus luteum," by P. E. Lebech. ACTA ENDOCRINOL 155:Suppl:134, 1971.

"Plasma progesterone during abortion induced by intra-amniotic hypertonic saline," by T. H. Holmdahl, et al. ACTA OBSTET GYNECOL SCAND 9:Suppl:48, 1971.

"Plasma progesterone in pregnancy interrupted by the intrauterine injection of hypertonic saline," by T. H. Holmdahl, et al. ACTA ENDOCRINOL 66:82-88, January, 1971.

"The politics of abortion," by C. Goodhart. SPECTATOR 484, April 10, 1971.

"The politics of abortion," by R. Taylor. TABLET 225:568-569, June 12, 1971.

"Politics of death," by R. Kirk. NAT R 23:315, March 23, 1971.

"Politics of social change: abortion reform. The role of health professionals in the legislative process," by M. A. Pond. AMER J PUBLIC HEALTH 61:904-909, May, 1971.

"Population, contraception and abortion," J R COLL GEN PRACT 21: 377-378, July, 1971.

"A population policy for Britain," LANCET 1:534, March 13, 1971.

"Porcine mycotic abortion caused by Aspergillus fumigatus," by R. W. Mason. AUST VET J 47:18-19, January, 1971.

"Possibility of conservative treatment in uterine perforation from the standpoint of morphology," by K. Kobayashi, et al. SANFUJINKA JISSAI 20:529-533, May, 1971.

"Possibility of prognosis of threatened abortion," by G. P. Mandruzzato, et al. MINERVA GINECOL 22:476-477, May 15, 1970.

"Post abortum bacteremic shock and coagulopathies of consumption," by M. Dumont, et al. GYNECOL OBSTET 70:109-123, January-February, 1971.

"Postabortal and postpartum tetanus, " by B. K. Adadevoh, et al. J OBSTET GYNAECOL BR COMMONW 77:1019-1023, November, 1970.

"Postabortion septicemia caused by Clostridium welchii. Report of 4 cases," by J. Cantillo, et al. REV COLOMB OBSTET GINECOL 22: 247-255, July-August, 1971.

"Postpartal counseling on family planning in the hospital," by D. Langnickel. ARCH GYNAEKOL 211:363-364, June 4, 1971.

"Practitioner in social medicine: why has the fetus been forgotton?" by B. Lindegard. LAKARTIDNINGEN 68:5854-5858, December 8, 1971.

"Pregnancy continuing to term despite a surgical evacuation procedure in the early weeks," by R. Gaskell. MANCH MED GAZ 50:14-16, 1971.

"Pregnancy in the 4th month; spontaneous abortion. Acute hemorrhagic pancreatitis. (Presentation of a clinical case)," by P. Dulea, et al. MED INTERNA 23:1513-1516, December, 1971.

"Pregnancy interruption and its influence on the hormonal activity of the thyroid," by W. Hartwig, et al. REV FR ENDOCRINOL CLIN 12:27-32, January-February, 1971.

"Pregnancy interruption during toxoplasmosis," by P. Hengst. DTSCH GESUNDHEITSW 26:1611-1614, August 19, 1971.

"Pregnancy interruption from the infant health viewpoint," by G. Krebs. ARCH GYNAEKOL 211:361, June 4, 1971.

"Pregnancy preservation with hormones," by G. A. Hauser. THER UMSCH 28:438-443, 1971.

"Prenatal diagnosis and the prevention of birth defects," by R. H. Heller. MD STATE MED J 20:59-62, May, 1971.

"Prenatal mortality and genetic wastage in man," by M. G. Kerr. J BIOSOC SCI 3:223-237, April, 1971.

"Preoperative instruction for the patient undergoing elective abortion," by D. F. Kallop. CLIN OBSTET GYNECOL 14:60-66, March, 1971.

"Preparing students for abortion care," by D. Malo-Juvera. NURS OUT-LOOK 19:347-349, May, 1971.

"Pre-pregnancy care--a logical extension of prenatal care," by R. F. Friesen. CAN MED ASSOC J 103:495-497, September 12, 1970.

"Present indications of prostaglandins," by P. Thibault. PRESSE MED 79:400, February 20, 1971.

"The present seriousness of criminal abortion," by M. Monrozies. GYNECOL OBSTET 70:79-94, January-February, 1971.

"President Nixon issues statement," by R. Nixon. OR 18 (162) 5, May 6, 1971.

"President on abortion: executive order to military hospitals," NEWS-WEEK 77:129 , April 19, 1971.

"Presidential address: 7th National Conference of the Indian Academy of Pediatrics," by J. N. Pohowalla. INDIAN PEDIATR 7:4-7, January, 1970.

"Presidential morality, abortion and federal-state law," by W. J. Curran. AMER J PUBLIC HEALTH 61:1042-1043, May, 1971.

"Prevention of abortion and premature delivery," by K. Watanabe. SANFUJINKA JISSAI 20:428-433, April, 1971.

"Prevention of abortion in hospital personnel," by M. Isokoski, et al. SAIRAANHOITAJA 47:486-488, June 10, 1971.

"Prevention of uterine injury during induced abortion," by S. Sugiyama. SANFUJINKA JISSAI 20:494-495, April, 1971.

"Prevention of uterine perforation," by M. Kusumoto. SANFUJINKA JISSAI 20:540-544, May, 1971.

"The price of a child," by M. Chartier, et al. BULL FED SOC GYNECOL OBSTET LANG FR 22:506-510, November-December, 1970.

"Priest asks study of fetuses' rights," NAT CATH REP 7:3, April 23, 1971.

"Problems diminish as New York City's hospitals perform 165,000 legal abortions in the first year," MOD HOSP 117:46, August, 1971.

"Problems of listeriosis in gynecology and obstetrics," by M. Pommier, et al. SEM HOP PARIS 47:2489-2491, November 8, 1971.

"Problems of termination of pregnancy in European socialistic countries," by J. Koubek. CESK ZDRAV 19:413-419, October, 1971.

"Procedure to follow in the case of a nonpregnant women consulting because of several previous spontaneous abortions," by M. Gaudefroy. J SCI MED LILLE 89:323-324, August-September, 1971.

"Procedure to follow in the case of a woman having had repeated spontaneous abortions and beginning another pregnancy," by L. Corette. J SCI MED LILLE 89:325-332, August-September, 1971.

"Procedures for abortions at The New York Lying-In Hospital," by R. E. Kaye. CLIN OBSTET GYNECOL 14:153-165, March, 1971; also in MOD TREAT 8:101-113, February, 1971.

"Progesterone depot in threatened abortion," by A. P. Camilleri, et al. OBSTET GYNECOL 38:893-895, December, 1971.

"The prognosis of threateden abortion," by A. Johannsen. ACTA OBSTET GYNECOL SCAND 49:89-93, 1970.

"Prognosis of threatened abortion," by J. M. Thoulon. LYON MED 18: Suppl:21-5, 1971.

"Prognosis of threatened abortion. A comparative study with the use of vaginal cytology and urinary gonadotropin immunoassay," by A. F. Youssef, et al. AM J OBSTET GYNECOL 109:8-11, January, 1971.

"Prognostic importance of determining excretion of chorionic gonado-tropin in the diagnosis of spontaneous abortion," by A. T. Berko. AKUSH GINEKOL 47:37-41, June, 1971.

"Prognostic value of vaginal exfoliative cytodiagnosis in habitual abor-tion," by I. Penev. AKUSH GINEKOL (Sofiia) 8:335-344, 1969.

"Progress against abortion," by N. St. John-Stevas. TABLET 225:1022, October 23, 1971.

"Prolonged amenorrhea after abortion during intensive treatment with progestagens," by J. P. Pundel. GYNECOL PRAT 22:77-85, 1971.

"Prostaglandins," by M. P. Embrey. LANCET 2:874-875, October 24, 1970.

"Prostaglandins and abortion," by G. G. Anderson, et al. CLIN OBSTET GYNECOL 14:245-257, March, 1971.

"Prostaglandins and habitual abortion," by M. Bodin. BR MED J 2:587, June 5, 1971.

"Prostaglandins as abortifacients," by S. M. Karim. N ENGL J MED 285:1534-1535, December 30, 1971.

"Prostaglandins as abortion agents," by M. Bygdeman, et al. LAKAR-TIDNINGEN 68:2732-2739, June 2, 1971.

"Prostaglandins in abortion," LANCET 2:536, September 4, 1971.

"Prostaglandins in obstetrics and gynecology," by P. Bersjo, et al. TIDSSKR NOR LAEGEFOREN 91:678-679, March 30, 1971.

"Provincial associations veto Canadian Nurses' Association's abortion statement," CAN NURSE 67:7-8, August, 1971.

"The psyche and abortion. Some psychoanalytical points of view," by H. Carpelan. NORD PSYKIATR TIDSSKR 25:213-225, 1971.

"Psychiatric aspects of therapeutic abortion," by P. H. Linton. SOUTH MED J 64:Suppl:108-110, February, 1971.

"Psychiatric experience of the Abortion Act (1967)," by N. A. Todd. BR J PSYCHIATRY 119:489-495, November, 1971.

"Psychiatric indications for the termination of pregnancy," MED J AUST 1:171, January 16, 1971.

"Psychiatric indications for the termination of pregnancy," by N. Destro. MED J AUST 1:350-351, February 6, 1971.

"Psychiatric indications for the termination of pregnancy," by S. Gold. MED J AUST 1:499-500, February 27, 1971.

"Psychiatric indications for the termination of pregnancy," by B. D. McKie, et al. MED J AUST 1:771-773, April 3, 1971.

"Psychiatric indications for the termination of pregnancy," by J. Simpson. J MED AUST 1:449-450, February 20, 1971.

"Psychiatric indications for the termination of pregnancy," by D. Vann. MED J AUST 1:404, February 13, 1971.

"Psychiatric sequelae of abortion on demand. (Q&A)," by D. Cappon. POSTGRAD MED 49:255-256, March, 1971.

"A psychiatric syndrome in women evaluated for an unwanted pregnancy," by D. A. Kellogg. MD STATE MED J 20:75-78, October, 1971.

"Psychiatrist: abortion should be avoided when the fetus has a 'life of his own'," by K. Ohrberg. LAKARTIDNINGEN 68:5849-5853, December 8, 1971.

"The psychiatrist and therapeutic abortion," by G. C. Sisler. CAN PSYCHIATR ASSOC J 16:275-277, June, 1971.

"Psychiatrist as consultant for therapeutic abortion," by R. L. Sadoff, et al. PENN MED 74:63-64, May, 1971.

"Psychiatry and abortion," by D. S. Heath. CAN PSYCHIATR ASSOC J 16:55-63, February, 1971.

"Psychologic effects of legal abortion," by J. D. Osofsky, et al. CLIN OBSTET GYNECOL 14:215-234, March, 1971; also in MOD TREAT 8:139-158, February, 1971.

"Psychosexual response and attitudes toward family planning. A study of 100 pregnant women," by A. W. Chang-Silva, et al. OBSTET GYNECOL 37:289-296, February, 1971.

"Psychosocial aspects of selective abortion," by E. J. Lieberman. BIRTH DEFECTS 7:20-21, April, 1971.

"Public health and long-term genetic implications of intrauterine diagnosis and selective abortion," by A. G. Motulsky, et al. BIRTH DEFECTS 7:22-32, April, 1971.

"Public policy making: why the churches strike out," by V. C. Blum. AMERICA 124:224-228, March 6, 1971.

"Pulmonary tuberculosis and pregnancy. Indications for therapeutic abortion in patients with pulmonary or extrapulmonary TBC," by C. Fossati. RASS INT CLIN TER 51:159-169, February 15, 1971.

"Qualitative and quantitative problems in generation," by R. H. Williams. NORTHWEST MED 69:497-501, July, 1970.

"Questions about abortion," by P. Jann. LIGUORIAN 59:14-19, October, 1971.

"Questions to ask," ECONOMIST 239:24+, May 1, 1971.

"Removal of barriers to family planning," WIEN MED WOCHENSCHR

120:129, May 2, 1970.

"A rabbi's view," by P. E. Nussbaum. J MISS STATE MED ASSOC 12: 118-120, March, 1971.

"Radiographic study of extra-amniotically injected hypertonic saline in therapeutic abortion," by B. Gustavii, et al. ACTA OBSTET GYNECOL SCAND 50:315-320, 1971.

"Rallies back, oppose abortion," NAT CATH REP 8:3-4, December 3, 1971.

"Rallying Romans to fight abortion," by J. Kavanaugh. NAT CATH REP 7:Suppl:9, September 10, 1971.

"Ramifications of permissive abortion," by J. Fitzgerald. LINACRE 38:102-105, May, 1971.

"A rare complication of cerclage of the uterine cervix," by G. M. Cattaneo, et al. MINERVA GINECOL 21:932-936, July 31, 1969.

"Rationales for feticide," by D. W. Louisell. CATH WORLD 212:318-319, March, 1971.

"Reasons for refusal of ovulation inhibitors," by C. Imle, et al. MUNCH MED WOCHENSCHR 113:159-163, January 29, 1971.

"Recent abortion litigation," by M. F. McKernan, Jr. CATHOLIC LAWYER 17:1-10, Winter, 1971.

"Recent decisions on abortion laws," by A. R. Holder. J AMER MED ASS 216:933-934, May 3, 1971.

"Recommendations of the Swiss Society for Family Planning concerning ovulation inhibitors," by G. A. Hauser, et al. THER UMSCH 27:631-633, October, 1970.

"Recommended standards for abortion services. Adopted by the Executive Board of the APHA at the 98th Annual Meeting in Houston, Texas, October 29, 1970," AM J PUBLIC HEALTH 61:396-398, February, 1971.

"Recurrent abortion. Histoimmunologic findings on maternal IgA, IgM and IgG immunoglobulins in ovular tissue," by U. Montemagno, et al.

MINERVA GINECOL 21:1086-1090, August 31, 1969.

"Recurrent abortion and uterine hypoplasis," by G. Angeli. MINERVA GINECOL 21:1073-1076, August 31, 1969.

"Recurrent abortion caused by Rh isoimmun ization. Histoimmunologic study on Rh antigen in ovular tissue," by U. Montemagno, et al. MINERVA GINECOL 21:1079-1081, August 31, 1969.

"Recurrent vesicular mole abortion," by I. de L. Brunori, et al. MINERVA GINECOL 21:1082-1083, August 31, 1969.

"Reform of the penal code," by C. Mayerhofer. WIEN MED WOCHENSCHR 121:Suppl:2:7-9, November 20, 1971.

"The relation of pesticides to abortion in dairy cattle," by A. W. Macklin, et al. J AM VET MED ASSOC 159:1743-1748, December, 15, 1971.

"Relation of socioeconomic factors to family planning(based on data from the Tselinograd region)," by L. E. Sviridova. SOV ZDRAVOOKHR 29:11-15, 1970.

"Relationship between fetal anomaly and abortion," by H. Nishimura. SANFUJINKA JISSAI 20:821-825, August, 1971.

"Relationship of family planning to pediatrics and child health," by H. M. Wallace, et al. CLIN PEDIATR 9:699-701, December, 1970.

"Religion, morality, and abortion: a constitutional appraisal," by T. C. Clark. LOYOLA U L REV 2:1, April, 1969.

"Religious pacifist looks at abortion," by G. C. Zahn. COMMONWEAL 94:279-282, May 28, 1971; also in LINACRE QUARTERLY pp 247-253, 1971.

"Repeated abortion and toxoplasmosis," by A. D'Alberton, et al. ANN OSTET GINECOL 91:415-419, June, 1969.

"Repeated abortions due to uterine anomaly," by R. Empereur-Buisson. J SCI MED LILLE 89:317-321, August-September, 1971.

"Repeated or habitual abortions," Q MED REV 21:1-30, July, 1970.

"Report on the abortion capital of the country; New York city," by

S. Edmiston. N Y TIMES MAG p 10-11+, April 11, 1971.

"Report on family planning clinics conducted in the Cape Town municipal area from 1960 to 1969," by I. Robertson. S AFR MED J 45:291-292, March 13, 1971.

"Respect de la vie et moralité de l'avortement," by M. Marcotte. RELATIONS 360:132-137, May, 1971.

"Respect for human life," by J. Aurele. OR 19 (163) 9, May 13, 1971.

"Response to the appeal of 343 women for abortion," by N. Jouravleff. PRESSE MED 79:2246-2248, November 20, 1971.

"Results and prospects of study of disturbances of duration of pregnancy," by V. Trnka. CESK GYNEKOL 36:16-17, February, 1971.

"Results in 1,000 cases of therapeutic abortion managed by vacuum aspiration," by K. C. Loung, et al. BR MED J 4:477-479, November 20, 1971.

"Results of gestanon therapy in women with threatened and habitual abortion," by Ts. Despodova. AKUSH GINEKOL (Sofiia) 9:208-213, 1970.

"Results of treatment of septic abortion with carbenicillin," by J. L. de S. Pérez, et al. GINECOL OBSTET MEX 30:31-32, July, 1971.

"Retinal detachment and interruption of pregnancy, " by C. Legerlotz. KLIN MONATSBL AUGENHEILKD 159:827-832, December, 1971.

"A review of therapeutic abortions at a southern university hospital," by G. L. Fields, et al. WOMAN PHYSICIAN 26:414-416, August, 1971.

"RH-immunization after abortion, retrospective study," by S. Jonsson. NORD MED 84:1601-1602, December 10, 1970.

"Rh iso-immunization following abortion," by S. L. Barron. J REPROD FERTIL 27:157, October, 1971.

"Rhesus isoimmunization after abortion," by S. Murray, et al. BR MED J 3:90-92, July 10, 1971.

"Right of equal access to abortion," IA L REV 56:1015, April, 1971.

"Right to abortion. What is the responsibility of society? Social psychiatric study of abortion applying women in the public health district of Umeå," by K. Broström, et al. LAKARTIDNINGEN 68:5133-5139, November 3, 1971.

"Right to life: who is to decide?" by J. L. Arehart. SCI N 100:298-300, October 30, 1971.

"A right to live, and a right to life," by J. Tweedie. GUARDIAN 9, November 8, 1971.

"The rights of the unborn," by A. J. Quinn, et al. JURIST 577-613, 1971.

"Ripostes on abortion," by B. H. Roberts, et al. N ENGL J MED 284: 1444-1446, June 24, 1971.

"RNs react to abortion issue: Agree CNA should take stand," CANAD NURSE 67:7+, February, 1971.

"Role of induced abortion in rhesus immunization," by J. T. Queenan, et al. LANCET 1:815-817, April 24, 1971.

"The role of the law of homicide in fetal destruction," IOWA LAW R 56:658-674, February, 1971.

"Role of mycoplasma infection in the genesis of spontaneous abortion," by M. A. Bashmakova, et al. VOPR OKHR MATERIN DET 16:67-70, February, 1971.

"Role of pediatrician in family planning," by C. C. de Silva. INDIAN PEDIATR 7:167-171, March, 1970.

"The role of the physician in North Carolina family planning programs," by A. R. Measham. NC MED J 32:51-56, February, 1971.

"Role of progesterone in the 1st trimester of pregnancy and in the treatment of threatened abortion," by L. P. Bengtsson. REV FR GYNECOL OBSTET 63:73-81, March, 1968.

"Role of Rho (D) immune globulin in induced abortions," by J. T. Queenan. CLIN OBSTET GYNECOL 14:235-244, March, 1971; also in MOD TREAT 8:159-168, February, 1971.

"The role of toxoplasmosis in abortion," by A. C. Kimball, et al. AM J OBSTET GYNECOL 111:219-226, September 15, 1971.

"Role of toxoplasmosis in the pathogenesis of abortions of unclear etiology," by J. Kicinski, et al. POL TYG LEK 26:1319-1322, August 23, 1971.

"Roselia: alternative to abortion; reprint from Pittsburgh Catholic February 26, 1971," by R. Snyder. C CHAR 55:20-22, April, 1971.

"Roundtable: Legal Abortion," by A. F. Guttmacher, et al. MEDICAL ASPECTS OF HUMAN SEXUALITY 5,8:50-75, August, 1971.

"Roundup on abortion reform," AMERICA 125:134-135, September 11, 1971.

"Rubella infection in pregnancy and abortion," by O. Goetz, et al. MED KLIN 65:1620-1623, September 11, 1970.

"The rules of the game," by C. Derrick. TRIUMPH 6:14-17, March, 1971.

"Rupture of the bladder secondary to uterine vacuum curettage: a case report and review of the literature," by S. N. Rous, et al. J UROL 106:685-686, November, 1971.

"S. dublin abortion in sheep," by M. Gitter, et al. VET REC 87:775-778, December 19, 1970.

"Saline abortion," by L. R. Cronenwett, et al. AM J NURS 71:1754-1757, September, 1971.

"Saline prep induces abortion," AM DRUGGIST 164:83, July 12, 1971.

"Salmonella dublin abortion in cattle: preliminary observations on the serological response," by M. Hinton. VET REC 88:481, May 1, 1971.

"Salmonella dublin as a cause of diarrhea and abortion in ewes," by W. A. Meinershagen, et al. AM J VET RES 31:1769-1771, October, 1970.

"Sanarelli-Shwartzman phenomenon in febrile abortion," by K. Hübschen, et al. ZENTRALBL GYNAEKOL 93:200-204, February 6, 1971.

"Schwangerschaftsbbruch-Bibliographie," by H. Bour. THEOLOGISCHE QUARTALSCHRIFT 254-263, 1971.

"Schwangerschaftsbbruch in der strafrechtlichen Diskussion," by A. Eser. THEOLOGISCHE QUARTALSCHRIFT 238-253, 1971.

"Scottish Catholic abortion guide urges kindness to patients," RN 34:26+, July, 1971.

"Seasonal distribution of abortions," by A. D. McDonald. BR J PREV SOC MED 25:222.224, November, 1971.

"Second trimester abortion with single intra-amniotic injection of prostaglandins E2 or F2 alpha," by S. M. Karim, et al. LANCET 2:47-48, July 3, 1971.

"The second year's experience with Colorado's abortion law," by W. Droegemueller, et al. AM J OBSTET GYNECOL 109:957-958, March 15, 1971.

"Secular case against abortion on demand," by R. Stith. COMMONWEAL 95:151-154, November 12, 1971.

"Segmental uterine rupture after cerclage of the cervix," by M. Dumont, et al. LYON MED 221:937-938, April 20, 1969.

"Semantics of abortion," by S. M. Zimmerman. N ENGL J MED 284:728, April 1, 1971.

"Seminar on abortion. A physician's view," by H. A. Thiede. J MISS STATE MED ASSOC 12:120-121, March, 1971.

"Seminar on moral aspects of abortion," J MISS STATE MED ASS 12: 115-121, March, 1971.

"Semiquantitative immunological determinations of chorionic gonadotropins with the gravimun test in normal pregnancy and in threatened abortion," by J. Nieder, et al. ZENTRALBL GYNAEKOL 92:721-727, June 6, 1970.

"Septic abortion," by A. B. Lorincz. POSTGRAD MED 49:148-153, June, 1971.

"Septic abortion. The scourge of modern obstetrics," by P. Rattakul. J MED ASSOC THAI 54:312-319, May, 1971.

"Septic abortion and sacroiliitis," by I. Watt. PROC R SOC MED 64:55-56, January, 1971.

78

"Septic abortion: diagnosis and treatment," by B. Neme. MATERN INFANC 29:255-278, April-June, 1970.

"Septic abortion masquerading as thrombotic thrombocytopenic purpura," by M. Yudis, et al. AM J OBSTET GYNECOL 111:350-352, October 1, 1971.

"Serologic diagnosis of rickettsian abortion in ewes," by R. Gaumont. BULL OFF INT EPIZOOT 70:271-279, May, 1968.

"Serologic pregnancy tests as a prevention against complications following interruption of pregnancy," by A. Dzioba, et al. WIAD LEK 24:113-115, January 15, 1971.

"Serum lactic acid level in women before and after interruption of pregnancy," by H. Skalba, et al. WIAD LEK 24:109-112, January 15, 1971.

"Serum potassium level before and after termination of pregnancy," by B. Batko, et al. WIAD LEK 24:645-648, April 1, 1971.

"Sex education and family planning advice by South Dakota doctors. II. Family planning advice," by B. Ranney. SD J MED 24:5-11, June, 1971.

"Sexualité et politique," by P. Watte. REVUE NOUVELLE 201-207, September, 1971.

"Should family planning clinics perform abortions?" by E. Fairchild, et al. FAM PLANN PERSPECT 3:15-17, April, 1971.

"Significance in classification of spontaneous abortion for genetic consultation rooms," by P. Dráč, et al. CESK GYNEKOL 36:491-492, October, 1971.

"The significance of fetal death in the mechanism of abortion induced by intra-amniotic injection of hypertonic salt solution," by L. Kovács, et al. ORV HETIL 112:852-854, April 11, 1971.

"Significance of pseudodecidual reconstruction of the endometrial stroma in the etiology and pathogenesis of habitual abortion," by R. K. Ryzhova. VOPR OKHR MATERIN DET 16:59-63, October, 1971.

"Simple technique of uterine evacuation," by R. P. Soonawala. LANCET 2:640-641, September 18, 1971.

"The single instrument abortion during the first 3 months of pregnancy and its quota of disorders with inflammatory complications," by W. Altmann. ZENTRALBL GYNAEKOL 92:984-993, August 1, 1970.

"Skin homograft in prevention of habitual abortion: report of a case and review of the literature," by S. R. Hewitt. J IR MED ASSOC 64:323-325, June 24, 1971.

"Skin-vegetative changes in the anterior abdominal wall in normal pregnancy and threatened abortion," by S. I. Fofanov. AKUSH GINEKOL 44:26-31, October 1968.

"Small vaginal Cesarean section in abortion," by G. Plasse, et al. BULL FED SOC GYNECOL OBSTET LANG FR 21:172-174, April-May, 1969.

"Social aspects of abortion counseling for patients undergoing elective abortion," by E. D. Smith, et al. CLIN OBSTET GYNECOL 14:204-214, March, 1971.

"Socioeconomic outcomes of restricted access to abortion," by C. Muller. AM J PUBLIC HEALTH 61:1110-1118, June, 1971.

"Sociogenic health and disease: planning for abortion services in the Bronx," by V. W. Sidel, et al. NEW PHYSICIAN 20:773-774, December, 1971.

"A sociologic approach to abortion," by G. Texier. GYNECOL PRAT 20:363-373, 1969.

"Sociologic study on factors influencing birth-rate among student families in Sofiia," by G. Kardashev. AKUSH GINEKOL (Sofiia) 10: 106-112, 1971.

"Sociology of human reproduction," by J. Morsa. BRUX MED 49:65-70, February, 1969.

"Some aspects of regulating family size in India," by K. G. Simonian. SOV ZDRAVOOKHR 29:58-63, 1970.

"Some data on the functional state of the adrenal cortex in obstetric sepsis," by I. R. Zak, et al. AKUSH GINEKOL 44:44-47, October, 1968.

"Some effects of prostaglandins E2 and F2 on the pregnant rhesus monkey," by K. T. Kirton, et al. BIOL REPROD 3:163-168, October, 1970.

"Some international aspects of abortion," by M. Fishbein. MED WORLD NEWS 12:68, September 17, 1971.

"Some news just isn't fit to print," by W. Hoffman. TRIUMPH 6:19-23, December, 1971.

"Some notes on the practical use of oestrogens in veterinary obstetrics and gynaecology," by C. H. de Bois. TIJDSCHR DIERGENEESKD 96: 1165-1172, September 1, 1971.

"Some operative and postoperative hazards of legal termination of pregnancy," by S. V. Sood. BR MED J 4:270-273, October 30, 1971.

"Some problems of treating patients with obstetrical pathology and acute renal insufficiency," by V. K. Prorokova, et al. VOPR OKHR MATERIN DET 15:76-80, October, 1970.

"Some psychiatric aspects of abortion," J NURS 18:76-78, January, 1971.

"Some social characteristics of women seeking abortion," by J. Aitken-Swan. J BIOSOC SCI 3:96-100, January, 1971.

"Some thoughts on therapeutic abortion," by A. P. Chatowsky. RI MED J 54:462-466, September, 1971.

"'Spontaneous' abortion and haemorrhage following attempted amniocentesis in a carrier of haemophilia A," by S. D. Cederbaum, et al. LANCET 2:429-430, August 21, 1971.

"Spontaneous abortion and preventive hormone therapy (results in 110 cases)," by D. Antonopoulos, et al. ZENTRALBL GYNAEKOL 92:706-707, May 30, 1970.

"Spontaneous abortion due to luteal insufficiency. Histologic documentation," by P. Hietter, et al. J SCI MED LILLE 87:317-319, April, 1969.

"Spontaneous abortions in Macaca mulatta," by E. J. Andrews. LAB ANIM SCI 21:964, December, 1971.

"Spontaneous and induced abortion," WHO CHRON 25:104-111, March, 1971.

"Spontaneous and septic abortions in the city of Aberdeen, 1958-1968," by G. P. Milne. J BIOSOC SCI 3:93-95, January, 1971.

"Spontaneous interruption of pregnancy during the early period," by V. I. Grishchenko. AKUSH GINEKOL 45:59-62, September, 1969.

"Standards for changing practice in abortion," by L. Breslow. AM J PUBLIC HEALTH 61:215-217, February, 1971.

"The state of play," by J. Gillott, et al. NOVA 38, October, 1971.

"Statement of the Canadian bishops on abortion," CATH HOSP 2:1+, May, 1971.

"A statement on abortion in Victoria," by P. Brett, et al. MED J AUST 2:982-983, November 6, 1971.

"A statement on abortion in Victoria," by L. Hemingway, et al. MED J AUST 2:1203-1204, December 4, 1971.

"Statistical analysis of applicants and of the induced abortion workup. Grady Memorial Hospital--January-December, 1970," by L. D. Baker, et al. J MED ASSOC GA 60:392-396, December, 1971.

"Statistics on abortion in New York State from questionnaire," by G. Schaefer. CLIN OBSTET GYNECOL 14:258-265, March, 1971.

"Status of abortion in the world," by A. Monti. MINERVA MED 62:Suppl: 21-22, June-July, 1971.

"Sterilization. A case of extensive practice in a developing nation," by D. O. Cowgill, et al. MILBANK MEM FUND Q 49:363-378, July, 1971.

"Sterilization and family planning," by M. Elstein. PRACTITIONER 205:30-37, July, 1970.

"Sterilization on abortion," by D. Gudgeon. LANCET 1:1240, June 12, 1971.

"Stiboestrol and cancer," BR MED J 3:593-594, September 11, 1971.

"Stormy aftermath of abortion reform," by C. Remsberg, et al. GOOD H 172:86-87+, February, 1971.

"Studies of the abortive mechanism of intrauterine injection of hypertonic saline," by B. Gustavii. ACTA OBSTET GYNECOL SCAND 9: Suppl:9:43, 1971.

"Studies on fetal circulation in legal abortions," by S. L. Pehrson. ACTA OBSTET GYNECOL SCAND 49:289-292, 1970.

"Study of fetal erythrocytes in metrorrhagias caused by threatened abortion," by F. Pietropaolo, et al. QUAD CLIN OSTET GINECOL 25:39-44, January, 1970.

"Study of the sulfamethoxazole-trimethoprim combination in gynecology and obstetrics," by J. Villard, et al. J MED LYON 52:401-403, March 5, 1971.

"Study of vaginal smears by luminescent microscopy in normal pregnancy and in threatened abortion," by P. S. Badiva. PEDIATR AKUSH GINEKOL 1:44-46, January-February, 1969.

"Study on induced abortion," BULL INFIRM CATHOL CAN 38:141-146, July-September, 1971.

"Study on septic abortion (October 15, 1968 to October 14, 1969," by A. Jubiz, et al. REV COLOMB OBSTET GINECOL 22:233-246, July-August, 1971.

"Suction curettage for early abortion: experience with 645 cases," by B. N. Nathanson. CLIN OBSTET GYNECOL 14:99-106, March, 1971; also in MOD TREAT 8:64-71, February, 1971.

"Suction evacuation of uterus for incomplete abortion," by S. Rashid, et al. J OBSTET GYNAECOL BR COMMONW 77:1047-1048, November, 1970.

"Suffer the little children," by J. Ryder. SOC JUST 64:123-126, July-August, 1971.

"Suggestions on adding family planning to the curriculums of medical schools," by D. T. Rice. PUBLIC HEALTH REP 85:889-895, October, 1970.

"Summarizing paper of the study team 'Pregnancy Interruption'," WIEN MED WOCHENSCHR 121:Suppl:2:14-20, November 20, 1971.

"Supreme court and abortion," AMERICA 124:443, May 1, 1971.

"Supreme Court of the United States: abortion rulings," NEWSLETTER (SOC HOSP ATTORNEYS) 4:various paging, May, 1971.

"Supreme Court upholds abortion law of the District of Columbia," NEWSLETTER (SOC HOSP ATTORNEYS) 4:3, June, 1971.

"Surgeon, sterilization and abortion," by R. M. Soderstrom. NORTHWEST MED 70:167, March, 1971.

"Surgical treatment and prevention of isthmo-cervical insufficiency causing prematurity, habitual abortion and premature delivery," by R. Tokhin. AKUSH GINEKOL (Sofiia) 8:473-481, 1969.

"Surgical treatment of cervico-segmental insufficiency during pregnancy," by G. Taricco. MINERVA GINECOL 21:1121-1127, September 15, 1969.

"Surgical treatment of habitual abortions," by J. Bocev. MED PREGL 24:135-136, 1971.

"Surveillance of abortion program in New York City," by J. Pakter, et al. BULL NY ACAD MED 47:853-874, August, 1971; also in CLIN OBSTET GYNECOL 14:267-299, March, 1971; MOD TREAT 8:169-201, February, 1971.

"Surveillance of abortions in hospitals in the United States, 1970," by J. B. Kahn, et al. HSMHA HEALTH REP 86:423-430, May, 1971.

"Survey finds determinants of attitudes toward abortion," AMER J NURSING 71:1900, October, 1971.

"Survey of abortion 1962-1964. The North-West England Faculty," by R. W. Kennon. J R COLL GEN PRACT 21:311-312, May, 1971.

"Survey of 3,000 unwanted pregnancies," by J. Lambert. BR MED J 4: 156-160, October 16, 1971.

"Survey on induced abortion and use of contraceptives in Bogota. Method of approach," by S. Gómez, et al. REV COLOMB OBSTET GINECOL 21:427-439, July-August, 1970.

"Symptomatology of detergent-poisoning in 'Pril'-induced abortion," by C. Tschakaloff. WIEN KLIN WOCHENSCHR 81:305-307, April 25, 1969.

"Symptoms suggestive of multiple pregnancy in the 1st trimester and the aspect of acceptability of abortion performed for social reasons," by A. Rumprecht. WIAD LEK 24:2315-2318, December 15, 1971.

"Systematic hystero-salpingography in abortion sequelae," by H. Pigeaud, et al. BULL FED SOC GYNECOL OBSTET LANG FR 20:Suppl:479-480, 1968.

"Teacher opinion poll: liberalizing abortion law," TODAYS ED 60:5, May, 1971.

"The teaching of fertility control and population problems in the medical schools of Brazil," by J. Yunes. REV SAUDE PUBLICA 4:79-84, June, 1970.

"The technique of complement fixation test for the diagnosis of equine viral abortion (Rhinopneumonitis)," by K. Petzoldt. DTSCH TIERA-ERZTL WOCHENSCHR 74:252-255, May 15, 1967.

"Technique of dilatation and curettage for abortion," by G. Schaefer. MOD TREAT 8:50-63, February, 1971.

"Termination of pregnancy by the intrauterine insertion of Utus paste," by S. V. Sood. BR MED J 2:315-317, May 8, 1971.

"Termination of pregnancy from the surgical viewpoint," by E. F. Drews, et al. MED KLIN 66:1-8, January 1, 1971.

"Termination of pregnancy in mink by repeated injections during the period preceding implantation," by J. C. Daniel, Jr. J ANIM SCI 33: 659-661, September, 1971.

"Termination of pregnancy refused," by J. M. Beazley, et al. LANCET 1:1059-1061, May 22, 1971.

"Termination of an unwanted pregnancy observed from a medical and socioeconomic aspect," by K. Kuřciev, et al. GOD ZB MED FAK SKOPJE 16:437-440, 1970.

"Testimony in favor of abortion reform hearings before the Michigan State House Committee on Social Services," by C. Raven. WOMAN PHYSI-CIAN 26:584-586, November, 1971.

"Tetracycline-enzymes in septic abortion," by A. Sangines, et al.

GINECOL OBSTET MEX 26:605-611, November, 1969.

"Texas abortion statutes: constitutional issues and the need for reform," BAYLOR L REV 23:605, Fall, 1971.

"Thanatopsis," by J. Fitzgerald. LINACRE 37:254, November 8, 1970.

"Therapeutic abortion," CAN MED ASS J 105:638-639, September 18, 1971.

"Therapeutic abortion," by E. Borreman. CAN MED ASSOC J 104:421, March 6, 1971.

"Therapeutic abortion," by P. G. Coffey. LAVAL MED 42:611-612, June, 1971.

"Therapeutic abortion," by J. R. Dobson, et al. NZ MED J 74:274, October, 1971.

"Therapeutic abortion," by R. W. Elford. CAN MED ASSOC J 105:638-639, September 18, 1971.

"Therapeutic abortion," by C. Heine. CAN MED ASSOC J 104:421, March 6, 1971.

"Therapeutic abortion," by A. C. Keast. S AFR MED J 45:888-891, August 14, 1971.

"Therapeutic abortion," by R. E. Reed. NC MED J 32:287-288, July, 1971.

"Therapeutic abortion," by S. J. Williams, et al. LANCET 2:1197, November 27, 1971.

"Therapeutic abortion and acculturation," by H. M. Donovan. NURS FORUM 10:378-381, 1971.

"Therapeutic abortion and cultural shock," by R. Zahourek. NURS FORUM 10:8-17, 1971.

"Therapeutic abortion and induction of labour by the intravaginal administration of prostaglandins E2 and F2," by S. M. Karim, et al. J OBSTET GYNAECOL BR COMMONW 78:294-300, April, 1971.

"Therapeutic abortion as a possible source of Rh immunization," by S. R. Hollán, et al. ACTA MED ACAD SCI HUNG 27:337-340, 1970.

"Therapeutic abortion at the obstetrical clinic of Clermont-Ferrand from 1958 to 1969. 24 cases," by G. Petit, et al. MED LEG DOMM CORPOR 3:418-422, October-December, 1970.

"Therapeutic abortion: attitudes of medical personnel leading to complications in patient care," by J. R. Wolff, et al. AM J OBSTET GYNECOL 110:730-733, July 1, 1971.

"Therapeutic abortion by intrauterine instillation of prostaglandins," by M. P. Embrey, et al. BR MED J 1:588-590, March 13, 1971.

"Therapeutic abortion by intrauterine instillation of prostaglandin E2," by G. Roberts, et al. J OBSTET GYNAECOL BR COMMONW 78:834-837, September, 1971.

"Therapeutic abortion. Current status of the question," by P. Piraux, et al. BULL FED SOC GYNECOL OBSTET LANG FR 20:454-456, November-December, 1968.

"Threatened abortion. Development and treatment," by M. Maretti, et al. MATERN INFANC 29:71-78, January-March, 1970.

"Therapeutic abortion experience in North Carolina under the liberalized 1967 law," by W. J. May. NC MED J 32:186-187, May, 1971.

"Therapeutic abortion follow-up study," by A. J. Margolis, et al. AM J OBSTET GYNECOL 110:243-249, May 15, 1971.

"Therapeutic abortion follow-up study," by A. J. Margolis, et al. TRANS PAC COAST OBSTET GYNECOL SOC 38:122-128, 1970.

"Therapeutic abortion: a follow-up study," by A. B. Sclare, et al. SCOTT MED J 16:438-442, October, 1971.

"Therapeutic abortion in California. Effects of septic abortion and maternal mortality," by G. K. Stewart, et al. OBSTET GYNECOL 37:510-514, April, 1971.

"Therapeutic abortion in a Canadian city," CAN MED ASSOC J 103:1085 passim, November 1, 1970.

"Therapeutic abortion in a Canadian city," by J. G. Stapleton. CAN MED

ASSOC J 104:70, January 9, 1971.

"Therapeutic abortion in north-east Scotland: introduction," by G. Horobin. J BIOSOC SCI 3:87-88, January, 1971.

"Therapeutic abortion: medical and social sequels," by A. B. Bames, et al. ANN INTERN MED 75:881-886, December, 1971.

"Therapeutic abortion. Nurses' involvement and moral grounds," by G. Mathew. NURS J INDIA 62:305-306, September, 1971.

"Therapeutic abortion: a prospective study. I," by H. Brody, et al. AM J OBSTET GYNECOL 109:347-353, February 1, 1971.

"Therapeutic abortion: The psychiatric nurse as therapist, liaison, and consultant," by R. Zahourek, et al. PERSPECT PSYCHIAT CARE 9: 64-71, March-April, 1971.

"Therapeutic abortion: a psyshiatric view," by J. M. Donahue. J INDIANA STATE MED ASSOC 64:833-834, August, 1971.

"Therapeutic abortion. A social work view," by F. Addelson. AM J OBSTET GYNECOL 111:984-992, December 1, 1971.

"Therapeutic abortion. A study of psychiatric applicants at North Carolina Memorial Hospital," by J. R. Partridge, et al. NC MED J 32:131-136, April, 1971.

"Therapeutic abortion. Who needs a psychiatrist?" by C. V. Ford, et al. OBSTET GYNECOL 38:206-213, August, 1971.

"Therapeutic abortions," by D. R. McCoy. MIDWIVES CHRON 84:376-377, November, 1971.

"Therapeutic abortions at University Hospitals, 1951-1969, with emphasis on current trends," by D. W. Wetrich, et al. J IOWA MED SOC 60:691-696, October, 1970.

"Therapeutic abortions in California," by E. W. Jackson, et al. CALIF MED 115:28-33, July, 1971.

"Therapeutic abortions: National Association for Mental Health position statement," MENT HYG 55:130, January, 1971.

"Therapeutic abortions, A review of 567 cases," by P. H. Brenner, et al. CALIF MED 115:20-27, July, 1971.

"Therapeutic abortions topic of study and discussion at operating room nurses' conference," by I. Adams. HOSP ADMIN CAN 13:38+, September, 1971.

"Therapeutic interruption of pregnancy in the 3rd trimester," by A. L. Castelazo, et al. GINECOL OBSTET MEX 27:661-681, June, 1970.

"Therapy of premature placental separation with subsequent afibrinogenemia," by H. Bayer. ZENTRALBL GYNAEKOL 93:870-871, June 19, 1971.

"Therapy of prematurity," by F. S. Baranovskaia, et al. AKUSH GINEKOL 47:69-72, June, 1971.

"They take care of their own; abortion loan fund of University of Maine students," by E. Scribner. NATION 212:230, February 22, 1971.

"30 bishops attack abortionist profits," NAT CATH REP 7:5, December 11, 1970.

"Thoughts on the legalization of abortion," by G. Malick. PA MED 74: 39, March, 1971.

"Threatened abortions and their prognosis in the light of cytohormonal and enzymatic studies," by A. Dzioba, et al. WIAD LEK 24:649-652, April 1, 1971.

"Threatened and spontaneous abortion. A retrospective study of the disgnosis on admission," by A. Johannsen. ACTA OBSTET GYNECOL SCAND 49:95-99, 1970.

"Three Protestant theologians join in opposing abortion," NAT CATH REP 7:18, February 26, 1971.

"Three years' experience of the Abortion Act," by A. W. Weir. MIDWIVES CHRON 85:232-234, July, 1971.

"To study antiabortion brief," NAT CATH REP 8:1-2, December 10, 1971.

"To teach or not to teach family planning in Kenyan primary schools," by J. B. Maathuis. EAST AFR MED J 47:545-549, November, 1970.

"Topics on the qualitative and quantitative problem in the limitation of births," by L. Bussi. MINERVA MED 62:1592-1593, April 14, 1971.

"Torts--unplanned parenthood and the benefit rule," WAKE FOREST L REV 8:159, December, 1971.

"Toward the reduction of unwanted pregnancy," by F. S. Jaffe. SCIENCE 174,4005:119-127, October, 1971.

"Toxicity of levorin to pregnant rats and their fetus," by N. N. Slonit-skaia. ANTIBIOTIKI 15:1089-1093, December, 1970.

"Training of adscript personnel in Latin American programs of family planning," by C. B. Arnold. EDUC MED SALUD 3:40-55, January-March, 1969.

"Transplacental hemorrhage during voluntary interruption of pregnancy," by K. M. Lakoff, et al. J REPROD MED 6:260-261, June, 1971.

"Transvaginal treatment of uterine perforation," by A. Tsuji. SANFU-JINKA JISSAI 20:519-528, May, 1971.

"Treatment of acute postabortum renal failure," by J. Guedon, et al. THERAPEUTIQUE 47:513-516, May, 1971.

"Treatment of bacterial shock in abortion," by W. Mosier. DTSCH GESUNDHEITSW 26:1356-1360, July 15, 1971.

"Treatment of habitual abortion due to abnormal hormone secretion," by Y. Tanaka. SANFUJINKA JISSAI 20:842-848, August, 1971.

"Treatment of pregnant women with spontaneous abortion of hormonal origin and isthmicocervical insufficiency," by M. P. Chertova, et al. AKUSH GINEKOL 46:48-51, November, 1970.

"Treatment of spontaneous abortion with high doses of sex hormones and the child's state," by V. Sulovic, et al. BULL FED SOC GYNECOL OBSTET LANG FR 20:Suppl:304-306, 1968.

"Treatment of threat of premature labor and miscarriage with Dilatol," by H. Neumann, et al. ZENTRALBL GYNAEKOL 93:849-859, June 19, 1971.

"Treatment of threatened abortion," by P. Magnin. LYON MED 18:Suppl:

27-31, 1971.

"Treatment of threatened abortion and premature labor with Duvadilan," by H. Neumann, et al. ZENTRALBL GYNAEKOL 92:1100-1108, Aug August 22, 1970.

"Trends in pregnancy and fertility in a rural area of East Pakistan," by J. Stoeckel, et al. J BIOSOC SCI 2:329-335, October, 1970.

"Trial of a killed vaccine in the prevention of ovine abortion due to toxoplasmosis," by J. K. Beverley, et al. BR VET J 127:529-535, November, 1971.

"The trump cards of the abortion lobby," by N. St. John-Stevas. TIMES 14, February 18, 1971.

"T-strains of mycoplasma in bronchopneumonic lungs of an aborted fetus," by N. Romano, et al. N ENGL J MED 285:950-952, October 21, 1971.

"Two books on abortion and the questions they raise," by C. B. Luce. NAT R 23:27-28+, January 12, 1971.

"Two California courts issue conflicting opinions on the state's abortion law," HOSPITALS 45:107, August 16, 1971.

"Two condemnations of abortion," C MIND 69:9-11, November, 1971.

"Two pastorals on abortion; October, 1970," by P. O'Boyle. C MIND 69:5-11, March, 1971.

"220 MDs back abortion curbs," AMER MED NEWS 14:3, November 15, 1971.

"Ultrasonic diagnosis: abortions and threatened abortions," by S. Levi. GYNECOL OBSTET 70:333-342, May-June, 1971.

"The unborn child and the constitutional conception of life (United States)," IOWA LAW R 56:994-1014, April, 1971.

"Unborn child in Georgia law: abortion reconsidered," GA L REV 6: 168, Fall, 1971.

"The unclear voice against abortion," by P. Steinfels. NAT CATH REP 7:12, May 14, 1971.

"Underlying sources of agreement and communication between husbands and wives in Dacca, East Pakistan," JOURNAL OF MARRIAGE AND THE FAMILY 33,3:571-583, August, 1971.

"Understanding the abortion argument," by R. Wertheimer. PHIL PUB AFFAIRS 1:67-95, Fall, 1971.

"United States government policy on abortion," by G. Contis, et al. AMER J PUBLIC HEALTH 61:1038-1041, May, 1971.

"Unwanted pregnancy and its prevention," by M. Mall-Haefeli. THER UMSCH 27:693-697, October, 1970.

"Urinary excretion of C21 labeled corticosteroids during early stages of pregnancy and after abortion," by M. G. Simakova. AKUSH GINEKOL 45:21-25, September, 1969.

"The urinary excretion of chorionic gonadotrophins after induced abortion," by M. Sloth, et al. ACTA OBSTET GYNECOL SCAND 50:227-228, 1971.

"Use of an antihemorrhagic factor (AMFAC) in obstetric-gynecologic hemorrhages of various origin," by M. Giaquinto, et al. RIV ITAL GINECOL 53:549-559, August-September, 1969.

"Use of benzlpenicillin in the treatment of Proteus infections," by I. P. Fomina, et al. ANTIBIOTIKI 16:450-454, May, 1971.

"The use of prostaglandin E2 in the management of intrauterine death, missed abortion and hydatidiform mole," by G. M. Filshie. J OBSTET GYNAECOL BR COMMONW 78:87-90, January, 1971.

"Use of prostaglandins for induction of abortion and labor," by A. Gillespie. ANN NY ACAD SCI 180:524-527, April 30, 1971.

"The use of prostaglandins in obstetrics," LOND CLIN MED J 12:9-11, January, 1971.

"The use of prostaglandins in obstetrics and gynaecology," by M. Filshie. MIDWIFE HEALTH VISIT 7:99-102, March, 1971.

"Use of the statistical method of paired combinations in studying aspects of regulating family size," by A. I. Markov. SOV ZDRAVOOKHR 29:43-46, 1970.

"Use of a synthetic progestational hormone, chlormadionone, in obstetrics," by R. Palliez, et al. LILLE MED 659:663, June-July, 1969.

"Use of transcycline in fever states following induced abortion," by J. A. Cacault. BULL FED SOC GYNECOL OBSTET LANG FR 21:116-124, April-May, 1969.

"The use of an 'unnatural' prostaglandin in the termination of pregnancy," by A. Gillespie, et al. J OBSTET GYNAECOL BR COMMONW 78:301-304, April, 1971.

"Uselessness of estrogens in maturation of the cervix and induction of labor," by O. Agüero, et al. GINECOL OBSTET MEX 30:21-29, July, 1971.

"Uterine abortion and the significance of inflammatory diseases of female genitalia," by W. Altmann. ZENTRALBL GYNAEKOL 92:1076-1083, August 15, 1970.

"Uterine malformations in relation to sterility and infertility," by G. Magli, et al. RASS INT CLIN TER 51:1259-1267, October 30, 1971.

"Uterine perforation in artificial abortions," by A. Lazarov, et al. GOD ZB MED FAK SKOPJE 16:429-435, 1970.

"Uterine pregnancy complicated by interligament extra-uterine pregnancy and torsion of the oophoritic cyst," by A. V. Tarkovskaia. PEDIATR AKUSH GINEKOL 5:62, September-October, 1970.

"Uteroplasty in infertility caused by congenital malformations," by C. J. Sánchez, et al. GINECOL OBSTET MEX 26:305-314, September, 1969.

"Utilization of a family planning program by the poor population of a metropolitan area," by J. D. Beasley, et al. MILBANK MEM FUND Q 48:241-281, April, 1970.

"Vacuum aspiration, using pericervical block, for legal abortion as an outpatient procedure up to the 12th week of pregnancy," by B. M. Berić, et al. LANCET 2:619-621, September 18, 1971.

"Vacuum curettage in septic abortion," J REPROD MED 7:198, October, 1971.

"Vacuum extraction in febrile abortion," by G. Göbel. DTSCH GESUNDHEITSW 26:305-308, February 11, 1971.

"Vacuum termination of pregnancy," by S. C. Lewis. BR MED J 4:365, November 6, 1971.

"Vaginal cytology and urinary pregnanediol levels in threatened abortion, actual abortion and missed abortion," by A. Pannain. ARCH OSTET GINECOL 74:14-49, January-February, 1969.

"Vaginal hysterectomy: a modality for therapeutic abortion and sterilization," by L. E. Laufe, et al. AM J OBSTET GYNECOL 110:1096-1099, August 15, 1971.

"Vaginal tubal ligation at time of vacuum curettage for abortion," by S. R. Sogolow. OBSTET GYNECOL 38:888-892, December, 1971.

"Value of external hyterography for the diagnosis of threatened premature labor," by M. Ia. Martynshin. AKUSH GINEKOL 44:46-50, July, 1968.

"Value of uterosedative drug in threatened premature labor," by R. Palliez, et al. PEDIATRIE 26:673-675, September, 1971.

"Very early ovular abortion on the 10th day," by F. De Gennaro. MINERVA GINECOL 21:837-842, July 15, 1969.

"A view on abortion," by H. P. David. J PSYCHIAT NURS 9:30-31, March-April, 1971.

"The vindication of Milan Vuitch," by M. Lawrence. TRIUMPH 6:8-11, July, 1971.

"A voice in the wilderness," by J. Caldwell. NC MED J 32:470-471, November, 1971.

"Voluntary abortion in a municipal hospital," by D. P. Swartz, et al. INT SURG 56:166-171, September, 1971.

"Voluntary male sterilization," MED J AUST 1:455-456, February 27, 1971.

"Voting against motherhood (Abortion in Canada) review article," by R. Evans. CAN FORUM 51:9-11, June, 1971.

"The wages of pluralism," by P. Bozell. TRIUMPH 6:18-20, March, 1971.

"Welcher Weg für die Reform des § 218?" by F. G. von Westphalen. NEUE ORDNUNG pp 443-453, 1971.

"We've had one," ECONOMIST 239:34, April 10, 1971.

"What abortion really is," by M. Mandelin. SAIRAANHOITAJA 47:474-477, June 10, 1971.

"What are the real emotional aspects of abortion?" by R. B. Sloane. MED INSIGHT 3:20-25, September, 1971.

"What every woman should know about abortion," by J. E. Brody. READ DIGEST 98:119-122, February, 1971.

"What every woman should know about abortion," by G. M. Landau. PARENTS 46:42-43+, January, 1971.

"What is an abortion: Variations on a definition," by M. Gaudefroy, et al. J SCI MED LILLE 86:641-645, October, 1968.

"What we do, and don't know about miscarriage," by S. Olds. TODAYS HEALTH 49:42-45, February, 1971.

"What you should know about New York abortions," by H. Eisenberg. HOSP PHYSICIANS 7:37+, February, 1971.

"When you refer abortion patients out of state," MED ECON 48:67+, August 16, 1971.

"Whither IUD? The present and future of intrauterine contraceptives," by C. H. Birnberg, et al. OBSTET GYNECOL 37:861-865, June, 1968.

"Who gets abortions, how, and when," MED WORLD NEWS 12:52, December 3, 1971.

"Who shall live? by K. Vaux. A review," by R. A. McCormick. AMERICA 122:424-425, April 18, 1970.

"Why are nurses shook-up over abortion?" by I. Fischl. LOOK 35:66, February 9, 1971.

"Why not?" ECONOMIST 239:29, June 26, 1971.

"Why repeat legal abortions?" by S. Cullhed. LAKARTIDNINGEN 68: 2716-2718, June 2, 1971.

"Women--the impact of advances in fertility control on their future. A presidential address," by G. S. Jones. FERTIL STERIL 22:347-350, June, 1971.

"Would you leave a child to die on the mountain side?" by M. J. D. Newman. CATH HOSP 2:8, January, 1971.

"Yano explains vote on abortion," by M. Hyer. NAT CATH REP 7:14-15, December 11, 1970.

"Your replies to the abortion quiz," by M. Gillen. CHATELAINE 44: 23, 62-63, March, 1971.

"Zur Diskussion über Schwangerschaftsabbruch: Versuch einer ethischen Orientierung," by A. Auer. THEOLOGISCHE QUARTALSCHRIFT 193-213, 1971.

"Zur Diskussion um den Schwangerschaftsabbruch (9-item symposium)," ARZT UND CHRIST 129-229, 1971.

SUBJECT INDEX

ABNORMALITIES
  see: Complications

ABORTION: AFRICA
  "To teach or not to teach family planning in Kenyan primary schools,"
     by J. B. Maathuis. EAST AFR MED J 47:545-549, November, 1970.

ABORTION: ALASKA
  "Contraception and abortion among Aleuts and Eskimos in Alaska: a
     demographic study," by H. D. Alpern. J REPROD MED 7:239-244,
     November, 1971.

ABORTION: ARGENTINE
  "Family planning in Cordoba (Argentine Republic)," by M. A.
     Agliozzo, et al. GINECOL OBSTET MEX 28:105-110, July, 1970.

ABORTION: AUSTRIA
  "Family planning and present law situation in Austria," by H.
     Husslein. WIEN KLIN WOCHENSCHR 83:141-144, March 5, 1971.

ABORTION: AUSTRALIA
  "Birth control survey in a lower social group in Melbourne," by C.
     Wood, et al. MED J AUST 1:691-696, March 27, 1971.

  "Medical abortion in South Australia. The first 12 months under new
     legislation," by A. F. Connon. MED J AUST 1:608-614, Septem-
     ber 18, 1971.

ABORTION: BRAZIL
  "The teaching of fertility control and population problems in the
     medical schools of Brazil," by J. Yunes. REV SAUDE PUBLICA
     4:79-84, June, 1970.

ABORTION: BULGARIA

"Geographic distribution of legal abortion in Bulgaria," by G. Stoimenov, et al. AKUSH GINEKOL (Sofiia) 10:112-116, 1971.

"Sociologic study on factors influencing birth-rate among student families in Sofia," by G. Kardashev. AKUSH GINEKOL (Sofiia) 10:106-112, 1971.

ABORTION: CANADA

"Abortion statements in Canada: Catholic clarity, Protestant ambivalence," by G. Lane. CHR CENT 88:1303-1304, November 3, 1971.

"Legal abortions in Canada," by L. E. Rozovsky. CAN HOSP 48: 39-41, February, 1971.

"Therapeutic abortion in a Canadian city," CAN MED ASSOC J 103: 1085 passim, November 1, 1970.

"Therapeutic abortion in a Canadian city," by J. G. Stapleton. CAN MED ASSOC J 104:70, January 9, 1971.

ABORTION: CHILE

"Analysis of the contraceptive program and control of abortion in Chile (1964-1969)," by B. Viel, et al. REV MED CHIL 99:486-494, July, 1971.

ABORTION: CHINA

"Family planning in China," by S. Ornstedt. LAKARTIDNINGEN 68:2582-2583, May 26, 1971.

ABORTION: COLOMBIA

"Survey on induced abortion and use of contraceptives in Bogota. Method of approach," by S. Gômez, et al. REV COLOMB OBSTET GINECOL 21:427-439, July-August, 1970.

ABORTION: ENGLAND

"The effects of legalized abortion in England," by J. V. O'Sullivan. HOSP PROGR 52:75-78, June, 1971.

"Legal regulation of abortion in England (Abortion Act 1967)," by K. Händel. BEITR GERICHTL MED 27:72-75, 1970.

ABORTION: ENGLAND

"Official statistics of legal abortions in England," by K. Händel. MED KLIN 65:524-526, March 13, 1971.

"Survey of abortion 1962-1964. The North-West England Faculty," by R. W. Kennon. J R COLL GEN PRACT 21:311-312, May, 1971.

ABORTION: FINLAND
"Legal abortions in Finland," by P. A. Jarvinen. ANN CHIR GYNAECOL FENN 60:65-66, 1971.

ABORTION: FRANCE
"France: free abortions, now!" NEWSWEEK 77:54+, April 19, 1971.

"France: we've had one," ECONOMIST 239:34, April 10, 1971.

"Influenza and rhino-pneumonia in horses in France," by A. Brion. BULL OFF INT EPIZOOT 70:149-169, May, 1968.

"Therapeutic abortion at the obstetrical clinic of Clermont-Ferrand from 1958 to 1969. 24 cases," by G. Petit, et al. MED LEG DOMM CORPOR 3:418-422, October-December, 1970.

ABORTION: GERMANY
"Abortions at the University Gynecological Clinic in Erlangen during 1950-1968," by W. Rummel, et al. MED KLIN 65:1123-1125, June 5, 1970.

"Abschaffung des 218 StGB?" by E. W. Böckenförde. STIMM ZEIT 188:147-167, September, 1971.

"Integration of the family planning in the health care of the German Democratic Republic," by K. H. Mehlan. Z AERZTL FORTBILD 64:429-432, May 1, 1970.

ABORTION: GREAT BRITAIN
"Abortion: 'a woman's right to decide'," by P. Worthington. DAILY TELEGRAPH 11, September 1, 1971.

"The British candidate for termination of pregnancy: a quantified survey of psychiatric referrals," by R. G. Priest. BR J PSYCHI-ATRY 118:579-580, May, 1971.

"The family-size umbrella," by M. Woolacott. GUARDIAN 11,

ABORTION: GREAT BRITAIN

January 11, 1971.

"A population policy for Britain," LANCET 1:534, March 13, 1971.

ABORTION: HUNGARY
"Hungary clamps down on abortions," J AMER MED ASS 215:2122, March 29, 1971.

ABORTION: INDIA
"Literacy and family planning in India," by V. J. Marsick. INDIAN JOURNAL OF ADULT EDUCATION 32,7:8-10,21, July, 1971.

"Memorandum on The Medical Termination of Pregnancy Bill 1971; presented to Shrimati Indira Gandhi, Prime Minister of India, by Archbishop Angelo Fernandes," OR 39(183)4, September 30, 1971.

"Some aspects of regulating family size in India," by K. G. Simonian. SOV ZDRAVOOKHR 29:58-63, 1970.

ABORTION: ITALY
"Morbidity and mortality in the offspring of 300 consanguineous couples in Florence," by U. Bigozzi, et al. ACTA GENET MED GEMELLOL 19:515-528, October, 1970.

ABORTION: JAMAICA
"The Jamaican male and family planning," by B. I. Morgan, et al. WEST INDIAN MED J 20:5-11, March, 1971.

ABORTION: JAPAN
"Abortion in Japan; cond from Family Life December, 1970," by P. Popenoe. C DGST 35:27-29, September, 1971.

"The abortion program in Japan," by T. Wagatsuma. J REHABIL 7: 16-19, July, 1971.

"Japan's 22 year experience with a liberal abortion law," by Y. Hayasaka, et al. LINACRE 38:33-44, February, 1971.

"An outbreak of mare abortion in Japan due to infection with equine rhinopneumonitis virus," by T. Shimizu, et al. BULL OFF INT EPIZOOT 70:251-256, May, 1968.

ABORTION: LATIN AMERICA
"Training of adscript personnel in Latin American programs of family planning," by C. B. Arnold. EDUC MED SALUD 3:40-55, January-March, 1969.

ABORTION: MACEDONIA
"Abortion in SR Macedonia," by A. Lazarov, et al. GOD ZB MED FAK SKOPJE 16:413-428, 1970.

ABORTION: MALAYSIA
"The demand for abortion in an urban Malaysian population," by O. S. Ooi. MED J MALAYA 25:175-181, March, 1971.

ABORTION: NETHERLANDS
"Lettre pastorale de l'episcopat Hollandais sur l'avortement direct," DOC CATH 68:486-489, May 16, 1971.

ABORTION: NICARAGUA
"Analysis of 2,746 abortions treated at their Managua General Hospital," by C. Guido, et al. INT SURG 56:125-127, August, 1971.

ABORTION: PAKISTAN
"The impact of desired family size upon family planning practices in rural East Pakistan," by P. W. Mosena. JOURNAL OF MARRIAGE AND THE FAMILY 33,3:567-570, August, 1971.

"Trends in pregnancy and fertility in a rural area of East Pakistan," by J. Stoeckel, et al. J BIOSOC SCI 2:329-335, October, 1970.

"Underlying sources of agreement and communication between husbands and wives in Dacca, East Pakistan," JOURNAL OF MARRIAGE AND THE FAMILY 33,3:571-583, August, 1971.

ABORTION: POLAND
"Analysis of complications after legal interruption of pregnancy in Poland," by E. Chroscielewski. MED LEG DOMM CORPOR 3:16-17, January-March, 1970.

ABORTION:ROMANIA
"Abortion legislation: the Romanian experience," by H. P. David, et al. STUDIES IN FAMILY PLANNING 2:205-210, October, 1971.

ABORTION: RUSSIA
"Relation of socioeconomic factors to family planning (based on data from the Tselinograd region)," by L. E. Sviridova. SOV ZDRA-VOOKHR 29:11-15, 1970.

ABORTION: SCOTLAND
"Abortion in the north-east of Scotland," by I. MacGillivray. J BIOSOC SCI 3:89-92, January, 1971.

"Scottish Catholic abortion guide urges kindness to patients," RN 34:26+, July, 1971.

"Therapeutic abortion in north-east Scotland: introduction," by G. Horobin. J BIOSOC SCI 3:87-88, January, 1971.

ABORTION: SINGAPORE
"Birth control in Singapore and the IUCD," MED J AUST 1:566, March 13, 1971.

"Changing trends in mortality and morbidity from abortion in Singapore (1964 to 1970)," by M. C. Cheng, et al. SINGAPORE MED J 12: 256-258, October, 1971.

ABORTION: SWEDEN
"Legal abortion in Sweden: thirty years' experience," by J. O. Ottosson. J BIOSOC SCI 3:173-192, April, 1971.

ABORTION: SWITZERLAND
"Abortion situation in Switzerland and the need for sociomedical measures," by H. Stamm. GEBURTSHILFE FRAUENHEILKD 31:241-250, March, 1971.

"Legal and illegal situation in Switzerland," by H. Stamm. BIBL GYNAECOL 55:1-43, 1970.

ABORTION: TAIWAN
"Fertility after insertion of an IUCD in Taiwan's family-planning program," by R. Freedman, et al. SOC BIOL 18:46-54, March, 1971.

ABORTION: YUGOSLAVIA
"Induced abortion and its trends in Yugoslavia," by B. M. Berich. AKUSH GINEKOL 46:67-68, November, 1970.

AMPICILLIN
"Peculiarities of ampicillin use in acute renal failure," by M. I.
Kuzin, et al. ANTIBIOTIKI 16:553-558, June, 1971.

ANESTHESIA
"Anaesthetic practice and pregnancy," by D. D. Moir. LANCET 1:
1027, May 15, 1971.

"Anesthesia in abortions," by B. E. Marbury. CLIN OBSTET
GYNECOL 14:81-84, March, 1971.

"Anesthesia, pregnancy, and miscarriage: a study of operating room
nurses and anesthetists," by E. N. Cohen, et al. ANESTHESI-
OLOGY 35:343-347, October, 1971.

"Anesthetic-induced abortion?" by D. H. Carr. ANESTHESIOLOGY
35:335, October, 1971.

"Experience in the use of the NAPP-1 apparatus for fluothane anesthesia in minor gynecologic surgery," by V. A. Glotova, et al.
NOV MED PRIBOROSTR 2:41-45, 1970.

"500 outpatient abortions performed under local anesthesia," by I. K.
Strausz, et al. OBSTET GYNECOL 38:199-205, August, 1971.

"Paracervical block anesthesia for evacuation of the uterus," by V.
E. Aimakhu. WEST AFR MED J 20:277-279, August, 1971.

ANTIBODIES
"Artificial abortion and immunization with antigens A or B in women
with blood group O," by M. Jakubowska, et al. POL TYG LEK
25:1263-1264, August 17, 1970.

"A field trial of the fluorescence antibody test for toxoplasmosis in
the diagnosis of ovine abortion," by J. F. Archer, et al. VET REC
88:206-208, February 20, 1971.

"The fluorescent antibody technic for the diagnosis of equine herpes
virus abortion in comparison with conventional diagnostic methods,"
by U. Luttmann, et al. DTSCH TIERAERZTL WOCHENSCHR 78:
623-627, December 1, 1971.

"Further field studies on the fluorescent antibody test in the diagnosis of ovine abortion due to toxoplasmosis," by J. F. Archer, et al. VET REC 88:178-180, February 13, 1971.

"Immunoserologic properties of antigens from Vibrio fetus of ovine origin," by L. L. Myers, et al. AM J VET RES 31:1773-1777, October, 1970.

"On the presence of anti-fetal antibodies in women after spontaneous abortion," by G. Gabbrielli, et al. BOLL SOC ITAL BIOL SPER 45:601-602, May 15, 1969.

"Recurrent abortion caused by Rh isoimmunization. Histoimmunologic study on Rh antigen in ovular tissue," by U. Montemagno, et al. MINERVA GINECOL 21:1079-1081, August 31, 1969.

ARTIFICIAL ABORTION
see: Induced Abortion

BEHAVIOR
see: Sociology, Behavior and Abortion

BENZYLPENICILLIN
"Use of benzylpenicillin in the treatment of Proteus infections," by I. P. Fomina, et al. ANTIBIOTIKI 16:450-454, May, 1971.

BIRTH CONTROL
see also: Family Planning

"Abortion: the rearguard in birth control," by J. M. Kummer. J REPROD MED 5:167-174, October, 1970.

"Birth control," by R. S. Kirk, et al. SCIENCE 170:1256 passim, December 18, 1970.

"Birth control," by M. Verhaeghe. LILLE MED 14:924-938, October, 1969.

"Birth control. Future of the different contraceptive and abortion methods," by R. Vokaer. GYNECOL OBSTET 70:15-44, January-February, 1971.

"Birth control. Problem of the gynecologist from the medical, moral and religious point of view," by S. Fossati. MINERVA GINECOL

22:664-668, July 15, 1970.

"Birth control and induced abortion," by E. A. Bendek. REV COLOMB OBSTET GINECOL 21:579-586, November-December, 1970.

"Birth control in Singapore and the IUCD," MED J AUST 1:566, March 13, 1971.

"Birth control survey in a lower social group in Melbourne," by C. Wood, et al. MED J AUST 1:691-696, March 27, 1971.

"Birth control--the views of women," by J. A. Hurst. MED J AUST 2: 835-838, October 31, 1970.

"The demographic effects of birth control and legal abortion," by H. Sjövall. LAKARTIDNINGEN 67:5261-5272, November 4, 1970.

"Experience in education of couples about birth control in under developed countries (Reunion and Maurice islands)," by R. Traissac. BULL FED SOC GYNECOL OBSTET LANG FR 22:187-190, April-May, 1970.

"Juridical and legal-political problems of birth regulation," by G. Kaiser. MED KLIN 63:1526-1530, September 20, 1968.

"Participation of low-income urban women in a public health birth control program," by Z. L. Janus, et al. PUBLIC HEALTH REP 85:859-867, October, 1970.

"Topics on the qualitative and quantitative problem in the limitation of births," by L. Bussi. MINERVA MED 62:1592-1593, April 14, 1971.

CANDIDIASIS
"Double septicemia due to Streptococcus and Candida," by R. Le Lourd, et al. BORD MED 4:3197-3208, November, 1971.

CARBENICILLIN
"Results of treatment of septic abortion with carbenicillin," by J. L. P. de Salazar, et al. GINECOL OBSTET MEX 30:31-32, July, 1971.

CEPHALOSPORINS
"Cephalosporins in the treatment of septic abortion," by R. F. Soto,

et al. REV OBSTET GINECOL VENEZ 30:509-515, 1970.

CERVICAL INCOMPETENCE OR INSUFFICIENCY

"Abortion under paracervical block," by A. J. Penfield. NY STATE J MED 71:1185-1189, June 1, 1971.

"An abortion with an unusual course (cervical pregnancy)," by J. Richon, et al. BULL FED SOC GYNECOL OBSTET LANG FR 22:243-246, April-May, 1970.

"Aspiration abortion without cervical dilation," by S. Goldsmith, et al. AM J OBSTET GYNECOL 110:580-582, June 15, 1971.

"Cerclage in the Gynecologic Department in Kragujevac and Arandelovac," by M. Durić, et al. MED PREGL 23:255-257, 1970.

"Cervical cerclage in the treatment of incompetent cervix. A retrospective analysis of the indications and results of 164 operations," by M. Seppälä, et al. ACTA OBSTET GYNECOL SCAND 49:343-346, 1970.

"Cervical insufficiency in pregnancy," by R. Wawryk, et al. WIAD LEK 24:1513-1519, August 15, 1971.

"Cervico-isthmic gapings and abortions of the 1st trimester," by H. Serment, et al. BULL FED SOC GYNECOL OBSTET LANG FR 23:197-201, April-May, 1971.

"Cervico-segmentary insufficiency in pregnancy," MINERVA GINECOL 21:802-809, July 15, 1969.

"Combination of a surgical and drug treatment in isthmo-cervical insufficiency during pregnancy," by H. Hertel, et al. GEBURTSHILFE FRAUENHEILKD 29:9-15, January, 1969.

"Course of delivery following cerclage for cervical incompetence," by R. Artal, et al. HAREFUAH 81:65-68, July 15, 1971.

"Course of pregnancy following cerclage for cervical incompetence," by R. Artal, et al. HAREFUAH 81:63-65, July 15, 1971.

"Defects and limitations of cervical cerclage," by J. Richon, et al. BULL FED SOC GYNECOL OBSTET LANG FR 23:82-86, January-

March, 1971.

"Experiences with cerclage," by G. Ruzicska, et al. ORV HETIL 112: 1628-1631, July 11, 1971.

"Iatrogenic paracervical implantation of fetal tissue during therapeutic abortion. A case report," by L. R. Ayers, et al. OBSTET GYNECOL 37:755-760, May, 1971.

"Insufficiency of the cervix uteri," by B. Budînská. ACTA UNIV CAROL 16:377-427, 1970.

"A rare complication of cerclage of the uterine cervix," by G. M. Cattaneo, et al. MINERVA GINECOL 21:932-936, July 31, 1969.

"Segmental uterine rupture after cerclage of the cervix," by M. Dumont, et al. LYON MED 221:937-938, April 20, 1969.

"Surgical treatment and prevention of isthmo-cervical insufficiency causing prematurity, habitual abortion and premature delivery," by R. Tokhin. AKUSH GINEKOL (Sofiia) 8:473-481, 1969.

"Surgical treatment of cervico-segmental insufficiency during pregnancy," by G. Taricco. MINERVA GINECOL 21:1121-1127, September 15, 1969.

"Treatment of pregnant women with spontaneous abortion of hormonal origin and isthmicocervical insufficiency," by M. P. Chertova, et al. AKUSH GINEKOL 46:48-51, November, 1970.

CHILDREN

"Acute suppurated thyroiditis in children. Apropos of a case," by P. Beauvais, et al. PEDIATRIE 26:633-641, September, 1971.

"Children of cardiac patients," by J. Palmade. BORD MED 4:1939-1940 passim, June, 1971.

"Family group therapy for children with self-induced seizures," by S. S. Libo, et al. AM J ORTHOPSYCHIATRY 41:506-509, April, 1971.

"Relationship of family planning to pediatrics and child health," by H. M. Wallace. CLIN PEDIATR (Phila) 9:699-701, December, 1970.

CESAREAN SECTION

CESAREAN SECTION
see: Complications

CLINICAL ASPECTS
"Abortion clinics studied in British Columbia to take pressure off hospitals," HOSP ADMIN CAN 13:17, January, 1971.

"Abortion: new restraints on private clinics," LANCET 2:1074, November 13, 1971.

"Case of habitual abortion in a patient with primary hyperparathyroidism (current obstetrical clinico-diagnostico-therapeutic and statistical aspects," by C. Zanoner. FRIULI MED 24:227-240, May-June, 1969.

"Clinical and statistical considerations of recurrent abortion," by G. Pritsivelis, et al. MINERVA GINECOL 21:1067-1069, August 31, 1969.

"Clinical aspects of human reproduction," by P. O. Hubinont. BRUX MED 49:71-75, February, 1969.

"Clinical aspects of poisonings with chemical abortifacients," by M. Canale. MINERVA GINECOL 21:1183-1185, September 30, 1969.

"Clinical attitude towards bleeding in early pregnancy," by P. Järvinen. DUODECIM 87:389-391, 1971.

"Clinical condition of women with pathological development of ovum and fetus," by P. Dráč, et al. CESK GYNEKOL 36:49-50, February, 1971.

"Clinical direction," BR MED J 4:382, November 13, 1971.

"Clinical experience in midwifery. Threatened abortion," by K. Zenki. JAP J MIDWIFE 25:47-49, January, 1971.

"Clinical experience with basal temperature rhythm," by J. P. Durkan. FERTIL STERIL 21:322-324, April, 1970.

"Clinical experiences with pregnancy interruption with a vacuum extractor," by C. Flämig, et al. ZENTRALBL GYNAEKOL 91:1567-1570, November 29, 1969.

CLINICAL ASPECTS

"Clinico-statistical considerations on a second series of cases of premature detachment of the normally inserted placenta (5-year period 1964-1968)," by A. Muziarelli, et al. MINERVA GINECOL 23:657-670, September 15, 1971.

"Criminal abortion. A clinical case and medicolegal aspects," by F. De Gennaro. MINERVA GINECOL 21:1002-1005, August 15, 1969.

"Family planning. Clinical practice and problems," by H. J. Staemmler, et al. DTSCH MED WOCHENSCHR 96:959-964, May 28, 1971.

"Hormonal contraception. Clinical experience, gained up to now and present-day problems," by J. Teter. POL TYG LEK 25:1641-1643, November 2, 1970.

"Hormonal studies and clinical observations in patients with threatening abortion or premature birth, respectively treated with depot-17-alpha-hydroxyprogesterone-caproate," by F. Tóth, et al. Z GEBURTSHILFE GYNAEKOL 175:168-175, October, 1971.

"Midtrimester abortion: clinical experience with amniocentesis and hypertonic instillation in 400 patients," by J. M. Mackenzie, et al. CLIN OBSTET GYNECOL 14:107-123, March, 1971.

"The pharmacodynamic action of caffeine. Deductions in clinical obstetrics," by A. Crainicianu. MINERVA GINECOL 23:984-989, December 15, 1971.

COLLEGE STUDENTS

"Contraceptive practices among college women," by T. Crist. MEDICAL ASPECTS OF HUMAN SEXUALITY 5,11:168-176, November, 1971.

"100 college students form group to oppose abortion," NAT CATH REP 8:5, December 10, 1971.

"Preparing students for abortion care," by D. Malo-Juvera. NURS OUTLOOK 19:347-349, May, 1971.

"Sociologic study on factors influencing birth-rate among student families in Sofia," by G. Kardashev. AKUSH GINEKOL (Sofiia) 10:106-112, 1971.

COLLEGE STUDENTS

"They take care of their own; abortion loan fund of University of Maine students," by E. Scribner. NATION 212:230, February 22, 1971.

COMPLICATIONS
see also: Hemorrhage

"Abortion and maternal Rh immunization," by W. Q. Ascari. CLIN OBSTET GYNECOL 14:625-634, June, 1971.

"Abortion caused by chromosomal abnormalities and estrogen insufficiency of the corpus luteum," by J. Cohen. PRESSE MED 78: 1744, September 26, 1970.

"Abortion caused by chromosome aberration, with special reference to habitual abortion," by K. Watanabe. SANFUJINKA JISSAI 20: 826-832, August, 1971.

"Abortion complicated by Clostridium perfringens infection," by J. A. Pritchard, et al. AM J OBSTET GYNECOL 111:484-492, October 15, 1971.

"Abortion due to C. pyogenes?" by T. J. Smith. VET REC 87:519-520, October 24, 1970.

"Abortion in women with latent toxoplasma infections," by P. Janssen, et al. KLIN WOCHENSCHR 48:25-30, January 1, 1970.

"Abortion sequel--Rh problems," NORTHWEST MED 70:29, January, 1971.

"Abortion with cerebral air embolism after 4 years," by H. Wojahn. BEITR GERICHTL MED 27:97-100, 1970.

"Abortion--with complications," by D. Brett, et al. NURS TIMES 67: 1209-1210, September 30, 1971.

"Abortions and unrecognized trophoblastic disease," by A. H. DeCherney, et al. N ENGL J MED 285:407-408, August 12, 1971.

"Abortions as the cause of ectopic pregnancy," by K. Kurčiev, et al. GOD ZB MED FAK SKOPJE 16:405-411, 1970.

COMPLICATIONS

"Abruptio placenta with renal failure," by S. Johnson. MIDWIVES
CHRON 85:344-345, October, 1971.

"Ace renal insufficiency in obstetrics," by C. Ponticelli, et al.
ARCH ITAL UROL NEFROL 42:142-159, 1969.

"Acute intestinal obstruction caused by lithopaedion," by S. A.
Zaheer. BR J SURG 58:401-402, May, 1971.

"Acute renal failure after septic abortion," by G. Staude, et al.
Z UROL NEPHROL 64:23-28, January, 1971.

"Acute renal insufficiency with diffuse intravascular coagulation in
2 fatal cases of septic abortion," by L. E. Ribeiro, et al. ACTA
OBSTET GINECOL HISP LUSIT 19:215-224, April, 1971.

"Acute suppurated thyroiditis in children. Apropos of a case," by P.
Beauvais, et al. PEDIATRIE 26:633-641, September, 1971.

"Allergic abortions," by A. Burthiault. GYNECOL PRAT 20:123-128,
1969.

"Amniocentesis and abortion: methods and risks," by F. Fuchs.
BIRTH DEFECTS 7:18-19, April, 1971.

"Amnioscopy in patients with bad obstetric history and high risk pregnancies," by K. H. Ng. MED J MALAYA 26:59-61, September,
1971.

"Amniotic fluid volume. A measurement of the amniotic fluid present
in 72 pregnancies during the first half of pregnancy," by D. L.
Smith. AM J OBSTET GYNECOL 110:166-172, May 15, 1971.

"Analysis of complications after legal interruption of pregnancy in
Poland," by E. Chroscielewski. MED LEG DOMM CORPOR 3:16-
17, January-March, 1970.

"Anomaly of the maternal karyotype in 2 cases of habitual abortion and
fetal abnormalities," by M. Vitse, et al. BULL FED SOC GYNECOL
OBSTET LANG FR 20:466-469, November-December, 1968.

"Bacterial infection of the placenta in cases of spontaneous abortion.

Correlation with the histological lesions," by M. Veron, et al. PATHOL BIOL 19:129-138, February, 1971.

"Behavior of maternal antiplacental IgA, IgM and IgG immunoglobulins in recurrent abortion," by U. Montemagno, et al. MINERVA GINE-COL 21:1083-1086, August, 1969.

"Blood alkaline phosphatase activity before and after interruption of pregnancy," by H. Skalba, et al. WIAD LEK 24:1503-1506, August 15, 1971.

"Calcified extra-uterine foetus co-existing with normal intra-uterine pregnancy," by F. M. Bulwa. EAST AFR MED J 48:109-115, March, 1971.

"Case of amniotic fluid embolism and secondary afibrinogenemia in artificial abortion," by V. M. Shikhatova. AKUSH GINEKOL 45: 68, March, 1969.

"A case of latent (subacute) hypofibrinogenemia due to retained dead fetus," by B. Georgiev, et al. AKUSH GINEKOL (Sofiia) 10:165, 1971.

"Case of severe lesion of the urinary bladder in the course of induced abortion," by W. Maternik, et al. POL PRZEGL CHIR 43:1035-1038, June, 1971.

"A cause of reproductive failures," by M. Massobrio, et al. MINERVA GINECOL 23:507-535, June, 1971.

"Children of cardiac patients," by J. Palmade. BORD MED 4:1939-1940 passim, June, 1971.

"Chromosome abnormalities in early spontaneous abortions," by D. T. Arakaki, et al. J MED GENET 7:118-124, June, 1970.

"Chronic typhoid abscess of body wall," by T. A. Stoker, et al. PROC R SOC MED 64:1000-1001, September, 1971.

"Clinical aspects of poisonings with chemical abortifacients," by M. Canale. MINERVA GINECOL 21:1183-1185, September 30, 1969.

"Coagulation failure after vaginal termination of pregnancy," by S. V. Sood. BR MED J 4:724, December 18, 1971.

"Coeliac disease presenting as recurrent abortion," by R. A. Joske, et al. J OBSTET GYNAECOL BR COMMONW 78:754-758, August, 1971.

"Coincidence of a submucous uterine myoma with pregnancy," by I. Philadelphy, et al. ZENTRALBL GYNAEKOL 92:1317-1319, October 3, 1970.

"Complications of abortion," by J. Stallworthy. NURS MIRROR 132: 21-25, January 8, 1971.

"Complications of amnioinfusion with hypertonic saline for midtrimester abortion," by R. C. Goodlin. AM J OBSTET GYNECOL 110: 885-886, July 15, 1971.

"Content of chorionic gonadotropins in urine of women with threatened abortion," by A. T. Berko. PEDIATR AKUSH GINEKOL 1:37-40, January-February, 1971.

"Content of silicon, aluminum, titanium in blood in normal pregnancy and threatened abortion," by L. I. Priakhina. PEDIATR AKUSH GINEKOL 1:35-37, January-February, 1971.

"Content of vitamin E in blood and estriol excretion in women with threatened abortion," by L. Ia. Davidov, et al. PEDIATR AKUSH GINEKOL 1:33-35, January-February, 1971.

"Cytogenetics and malformation in abortion," by D. H. Carr. FED PROC 30:102-103, January-February, 1971.

"Death from sickle-cell crisis after abortion," BR MED J 3:123, July 10, 1971.

"Delayed abortion due to coalescence defect in the decidual," by G. Bruniquel. BULL FED SOC GYNECOL OBSTET LANG FR 21: 469-473, September-October, 1969.

"Difficulties encountered apropos of toxic abortions. Apropos of a case," by C. Vitani, et al. MED LEG DOMM CORPOR 2:153-154,

April-June, 1969.

"Disseminated intravascular coagulation complicating hysterotomy in elderly gravidas," by R. E. Sabbagha, et al. OBSTET GYNECOL 38:844-847, December, 1971.

"Double septicemia due to Streptococcus and Candida," by R. Le Lourd, et al. BORD MED 4:3197-3208, November, 1971.

"The duration of the positive pregnosticon-planotest reaction following evacuation of the uterine cavity," by E. Reinold. Z GEBURT-SHILFE GYNAEKOL 174:75-79, 1971.

"Early complications from artificial abortion," by J. Jurukovski, et al. GOD ZB MED FAK SKOPJE 16:503-507, 1970.

"Early gynecological complications as the result of legal abortion," by E. Lunow, et al. ZENTRALBL GYNAEKOL 93:49-58, January 9, 1971.

"Electrocardiographic abnormalities in the course of induced abortions," by J. Horeau, et al. SEM HOP PARIS 47:2034-2039, July 10, 1971.

"Electrolyte changes and serious complications after hypertonic saline instillation," by R. L. Berkowitz. CLIN OBSTET GYNECOL 14:166-178, March, 1971; also in MOD TREAT 8:114-126, February, 1971.

"Etiologic incidence of rickettsial and coxsackie infection in pregnancy interruptions: serologic study," by J. Y. Gillet, et al. BULL FED SOC GYNECOL OBSTET LANG FR 21:213-216, April-May, 1969.

"Experience and complications with the use of hypertonic intra-amni- amniotic saline solution," by H. Berk, et al. SURG GYNECOL OBSTET 133:955-958, December, 1971.

"Fetal losses in a high prevalence area of chronic Chagas' disease," by J. R. Teruel, et al. REV INST MED TROP SAO PAULO 12: 239-244, July-August, 1970.

"Fever of unknown etiology," by D. B. Louria. DEL MED J 43:343-

348, November, 1971.

"Gaping uterine isthmus (85 cases)," by H. Serment, et al. REV FR GYNECOL OBSTET 64:509.514, October, 1969.

"Hematoma of the broad ligament of the uterus caused by uterine perforation," by H. Murooka, et al. SANFUJINKA JISSAI 20:534-539, May, 1971.

"Human chromosome abnormalities. 2. Occurrence in spontaneous abortion and antenatal detection by amniocentesis," by L. J. Butler. MIDWIFE HEALTH VISIT 7:105-108, March, 1971.

"Human infection by Vibrio fetus," by I. A. Cooper, et al. MED J AUST 1:1263-1267, June 12, 1971.

"Hysteroscopy (preliminary report)," by R. Q. Guerrero, et al. GINE-COL OBSTET MEX 27:683-691, June, 1970.

"Immediate and remote complications of repeated induced abortion," by B. Kh. Aronov. PEDIATR AKUSH GINEKOL 4:53-55, July-August, 1970.

"Immunological rejection as a cause of abortion," by M. G. Kerr. J REPROD FERTIL 3:Suppl:49-55, April, 1968.

"Importance of colposcopic examinations after delivery and intra-uterine interventions," by J. Simon. ZENTRALBL GYNAEKOL 93:1220-1226, August 28, 1971.

"Importance of the uterine anatomic factor in the etiology of recurrent abortion," by C. Orlandi, et al. MINERVA GINECOL 21:1061-1064, August 31, 1969.

"Incidence of uterine perforations in criminal abortions," by E. Rosenzweig, et al. RAD MED FAK ZAGREBU 18:221-224, 1970.

"Infected abortion and disseminated intravascular coagulation (DIC). Heparin prevention and early diagnosis of the DIC," by W. Kuhn, et al. MED WELT 22:1199-1200, July 24, 1971.

"Intra-abdominal chicken-bone abscess," by R. N. Berk, et al.

RADIOLOGY 101:311-313, November, 1971.

"Late abortion and difficulties of evacuation of the uterus," by H. Serment, et al. BULL FED SOC GYNECOL OBSTET LANG FR 21: 174-176, April-May, 1969.

"Legal abortions: Early medical complications. An interim report of the joint program for the study of abortion," by C. Tietze, et al. FAMILY PLANN PERSPECT 3:6-14, October, 1971.

"Leukocytic and thrombocytic isoimmunization in pregnancy," by M. Minev. AKUSH GINEKOL 10:213-218, 1971.

"Luteinizing hormone titration in the anterior pituitary of women who died during pregnancy and the post-abortion period," by M. De la Lastra. REV MED CHIL 98:782-785, November, 1970.

"Maternal herpes-simplex infection causing abortion. Histopathologic study of the placenta," by A. G. Garcia. HOSPITAL 78:1267-1274, November-December, 1970.

"Maternal serologic analysis and histoimmunologic localization of IgG, IgM and IgA immunoglobulins in ovular tissue during the 1st trimester," by U. Montemagno, et al. ARCH OSTET GINECOL 74:58-71, January-February, 1969.

"Meningitis with Escherichia coli (O119B14)," by I. Voiculescu, et al. MED INTERNA 23:1007-1011, August, 1971.

"Morphological abnormalities of the uterus and abortion," by R. Iizuka, et al. SANFUJINKA JISSAI 20:833-841, August, 1971.

"Morphological changes in the kidneys in acute renal insufficiency following an abortion," by N. F. Kan'shina, et al. ARKH PATOL 32:59-64, 1970.

"Morphology of abortive ovum," by P. Dráč, et al. CESK GYNEKOL 36:48-49, February, 1971.

"Morphology of the kidneys in acute post-abortion renal insufficiency," by N. F. Kan'shina, et al. AKUSH GINEKOL 45:36-39, March, 1969.

"Multiple enzyme deficiencies in placental tissue from two blighted-ovum abortions," by J. B. Edlow, et al. AM J OBSTET GYNECOL 111:365-368, October 1, 1971.

"Mycotic abortion in man: a case report," by R. A. Franciosi, et al. J REPROD MED 4:25-28, February, 1970.

"Nidation inhibition and abortion following rape," by E. Böhm, et al. MED KLIN 66:989-996, July 2, 1971.

"Nursing care study: abortion--with complications," by D. Brett, et al. NURS TIMES 67:1209-1210, September 30, 1971.

"Obstetrical complications of uterine malformations," by G. Poizat. REV MED LIEGE 25:763-764, December 1, 1970.

"Occurrence of incompatibility in the ABO and Rh systems following abortion," by A. Jasiewicz. ZENTRALBL GYNAEKOL 93:295-297, February 27, 1971.

"On a case of dicoumarin necrosis," by B. Danilov, et al. REV MED CHIR SOC MED NAT IASI 75:479-483, April-June, 1971.

"100 clinical cases of pregnancy complications treated with a 19-nor-progesterone, registered as 31.458 Ba and followed until term," by M. Lanvin, et al. BULL FED SOC GYNECOL OBSTET LANG FR 20:110-117, April-May, 1968.

"The oxytocic effect of acridine dyes and their use in terminating mid-trimester pregnancies," by B. V. Lewis, et al. J OBSTET GYNAECOL BR COMMONW 78:838-842, September, 1971.

"The oxytocic effect of acridine dyes and their use in the termination of mid-trimester pregnancies," by V. Lewis, et al. J REPROD FERTIL 25:456-457, June, 1971.

"Peculiarities of ampicillin use in acute renal failure," by M. I. Kuzin, et al. ANTIBIOTIKI 16:553-558, June, 1971.

"Pelvic short wave diathermy given inadvertently in early pregnancy," by A. H. Imrie. J OBSTET GYNAECOL BR COMMONW 78:91-92, January, 1971.

"Perinatal risk associated with maternal genital herpes simplex virus infection," by A. J. Nahmias, et al. AM J OBSTET GYNECOL 110:825-837, July 15, 1971.

"Perirenal masses simulating renal tumors," by J. W. Fenlon, et al. J UROL 106:448-450, October, 1971.

"Porcine mycotic abortion caused by Aspergillus fumigatus," by R. W. Mason. AUST VET J 47:18-19, January, 1971.

"Possibility of conservative treatment in uterine perforation from the standpoint of morphology," by K. Kobayashi, et al. SANFUJINKA JISSAI 20:529-533, May, 1971.

"Postabortal and postpartum tetanus," by B. K. Adadevoh, et al. J OBSTET GYNAECOL BR COMMONW 77:1019-1023, November, 1970.

"Postabortion septicemia caused by Clostridium welchii. Report of 4 cases," by J. Cantillo, et al. REV COLOMB OBSTET GINECOL 22:247-255, July-August, 1971.

"Prognostic importance of determining excretion of chorionic gonadotropin in the diagnosis of spontaneous abortion," by A. T. Berko. AKUSH GINEKOL 47:37-41, June, 1971.

"Prolonged amenorrhea after abortion during intensive treatment with progestagens," by J. P. Pundel. GYNECOL PRAT 22:77-85, 1971.

"Pulmonary tuberculosis and pregnancy. Indications for therapeutic abortion in patients with pulmonary or extrapulmonary TBC," by C. Fossati. RASS INT CLIN TER 51:159-169, February 15, 1971.

"A rare complication of cerclage of the uterine cervix," by G. M. Cattaneo, et al. MINERVA GINECOL 21:932-936, July 31, 1969.

"Reasons for refusal of ovulation inhibitors," by C. Imle, et al. MUNCH MED WOCHENSCHR 113:159-163, January 29, 1971.

"Recurrent abortion. Histoimmunologic findings on maternal IgA, IgM and IgG immunoglobulins in ovular tissue," by U. Montemagno, et al. MINERVA GINECOL 21:1086-1090, August 31, 1969.

COMPLICATIONS

"Recurrent abortion and uterine hypoplasia," by G. Angeli. MINERVA
GINECOL 21:1073-1076, August 31, 1969.

"Recurrent abortion caused by Rh isoimmunization. Histoimmunologic
study on Rh antigen in ovular tissue," by U. Montemagno, et al.
MINERVA GINECOL 21:1079-1081, August 31, 1969.

"Repeated abortions due to uterine anomaly," by R. Empereur-Buisson.
J SCI MED LILLE 89:317-321, August-September, 1971.

"Results and prospects of study of disturbances of duration of pregnancy," by V. Trnka. CESK GYNEKOL 36:16-17, February, 1971.

"Retinal detachment and interruption of pregnancy," by C. Legerlotz.
KLIN MONATSBL AUGENHEILKD 159:827-832, December, 1971.

"RH-immunization after abortion, retrospective study," by S. Jonsson.
NORD MED 84:1601-1602, December 10, 1970.

"Rh iso-immunization following abortion," by S. L. Barron. J REPROD
FERTIL 27:157, October, 1971.

"Rhesus isoimmunization after abortion," by S. Murray, et al. BR
MED J 3:90-92, July 10, 1971.

"Role of induced abortion in rhesus immunization," by J. T. Queenan,
et al. LANCET 1:815-817, April 24, 1971.

"Role of mycoplasma infection in the genesis of spontaneous abortion,"
by M. A. Bashmakova, et al. VOPR OKHR MATERIN DET 16:67-
70, February, 1971.

"Role of Rho (D) immune globulin in induced abortions," by J. T.
Queenan. CLIN OBSTET GYNECOL 14:235-244, March, 1971;
also in MOD TREAT 8:159-168, February, 1971.

"Rubella infection in pregnancy and abortion," by O. Goetz, et al.
MED KLIN 65:1620-1623, September 11, 1970.

"Rupture of the bladder secondary to uterine vacuum curettage: a case
report and review of the literature," by S. N. Rous, et al. J UROL
106:685-686, November, 1971.

"Segmental uterine repture after cerclage of the cervix," by M. Dumont, et al. LYON MED 221:937-938, April 20, 1969.

"Semiquantitative immunological determinations of chorionic gonadotropins with the gravimun test in normal pregnancy and in threatened abortion," by J. Nieder, et al. ZENTRALBL GYNAEKOL 92:721-727, June 6, 1970.

"Serologic pregnancy tests as a prevention against complications following interruption of pregnancy," by A. Dzioba, et al. WIAD LEK 24:113-115, January 15, 1971.

"The single instrument abortion during the first 3 months of pregnancy and its quota of disorders with inflammatory complications," by W. Altmann. ZENTRALBL GYNAEKOL 92:984-993, August 1, 1970.

"Small vaginal Cesarean section in abortion," by G. Plasse, et al. BULL FED SOC GYNECOL OBSTET LANG FR 21:172-174, April-May, 1969.

"Some operative and postoperative hazards of legal termination of pregnancy," by S. V. Sood. BR MED J 4:270-273, October 30, 1971.

"Some problems of treating patients with obstetrical pathology and acute renal insufficiency," by V. K. Prorokova, et al. VOPR OKHR MATERIN DET 15:76-80, October, 1970.

"Spontaneous abortion due to luteal insufficiency. Histologic documentation," by P. Hietter, et al. J SCI MED LILLE 87:317-319, April, 1969.

"Suction evacuation of uterus for incomplete abortion," by S. Rashid, et al. J OBSTET GYNAECOL BR COMMONW 77:1047-1048, November, 1970.

"Symptomatology of detergent-poisoning in 'Pril'-induced abortion," by C. Tschakaloff. WIEN KLIN WOCHENSCHR 81:305-307, April 25, 1969.

"Systematic hystero-salpingography in abortion sequelae," by H. Pigeaud, et al. BULL FED SOC GYNECOL OBSTET LANG FR 20:Suppl:479-480, 1968.

"Therapeutic abortion as a possible source of Rh immunization," by S. R. Hollán, et al. ACTA MED ACAD SCI HUNG 27:337-340, 1970.

"Therapeutic abortion: attitudes of medical personnel leading to complications in patient care," by J. R. Wolff, et al. AM J OBSTET GYNECOL 110:730-733, July 1, 1971.

"Therapy of premature placental separation with subsequent afibrino-genemia," by H. Bayer. ZENTRALBL GYNAEKOL 93:870-871, June 19, 1971.

"Treatment of acute postabortum renal failure," by J. Guedon, et al. THERAPEUTIQUE 47:513-516, May, 1971.

"Treatment of bacterial shock in abortion," by W. Mosler. DTSCH GESUNDHEITSW 26:1356-1360, July 15, 1971.

"The urinary excretion of chorionic gonadotrophins after induced abortion," by M. Sloth, et al. ACTA OBSTET GYNECOL SCAND 50:227-228, 1971.

"Urinary excretion of C21 labeled corticosteroids during early stages of pregnancy and after abortion," by M. G. Simakova. AKUSH GINEKOL 45:21-25, September, 1969.

"Use of benzylpenicillin in the treatment of Proteus infections," by I. P. Fomina, et al. ANTIBIOTIKI 16:450-454, May, 1971.

"Use of transcycline in fever states following induced abortion," by J. A. Cacault. BULL FED SOC GYNECOL OBSTET LANG FR 21:116-124, April-May, 1969.

"Uterine abortion and the significance of inflammatory diseases of female genitalia," by W. Altmann. ZENTRALBL GYNAEKOL 92: 1076-1083, August 15, 1970.

"Uterine malformations in relation to sterility and infertility," by G. Magli, et al. RASS INT CLIN TER 51:1259-1267, October 30, 1971.

"Uterine perforation in artificial abortions," by A. Lazarov, et al. GOD ZB MED FAK SKOPJE 16:429-435, 1970.

"Uterine pregnancy complicated by interligament extra-uterine pregnancy and torsion of the oophoritic cyst," by A. V. Tarkovskaia. PEDIATR AKUSH GINEKOL 5:62, September-October, 1970.

"Uteroplasty in infertility caused by congenital malformations," by J. S. Contreras, et al. GINECOL OBSTET MEX 26:305-314, September, 1969.

"Vaginal cytology and urinary pregnanediol levels in threatened abortion, actual abortion and missed abortion," by A. Pannain. ARCH OSTET GINECOL 74:14-49, January-February, 1969.

"Vaginal hysterectomy: a modality for therapeutic abortion and sterilization," by L. E. Laufe, et al. AM J OBSTET GYNECOL 110:1096-1099, August 15, 1971.

"Very early ovular abortion on the 10th day," by F. De Gennaro. MINERVA GINECOL 21:837-842, July 15, 1969.

CONTRACEPTION

"Abortion and contraception in family planning. A commentary," by C. F. Coffelt. J REHABIL 7:13-15, July, 1971.

"Abortion and experiences with 500 Lippes' intrauterine devices," by M. Ribarić. LIJEC VJESN 92:443-450, 1970.

"Abortion or contraception?" BR MED J 3:261-262, July 31, 1971.

"Abortion or contraception?" by W. Wood, et al. BR MED J 3:476-477, August, 1971.

"Adolescent attitudes toward abortion: effects on contraceptive practices," by I. W. Gabrielson, et al. AMER J PUBLIC HEALTH 61:730-738, April, 1971.

"The American Catholic: contraception and abortion," by J. Fitzgerald. LINACRE 38:264-267, November, 1971.

"Analysis of the contraceptive program and control of abortion in Chile (1964-1969)," by B. Viel, et al. REV MED CHIL 99:486-494, July, 1971.

"Attenders at a contraceptive clinic for single women," by M. Wadsworth, et al. J BIOSOC SCI 3:133-143, April, 1971.

"Birth control. Future of the different contraceptive and abortion methods," by R. Vokaer. GYNECOL OBSTET 70:15-44, January-February, 1971.

"Birth control in Singapore and the IUCD," MED J AUST 1:566, March 13, 1971.

"Contraception," by H. Winn. CLIN OBSTET GYNECOL 13:701-712, September, 1970.

"Contraception and abortifacients," by E. Diamond. LINACRE 38: 122-126, May, 1971.

"Contraception and abortion among Aleuts and Eskimos in Alaska: a demographic study," by H. D. Alpern. J REPROD MED 7:239-244, November, 1971.

"Contraception by intra-uterine device," by M. Lancet, et al. HARE-FUAH 78:223-236, March 1, 1970.

"Contraceptive practices among college women," by T. Crist. MEDICAL ASPECTS OF HUMAN SEXUALITY 5,11:168-176, November, 1971.

"Endometritis and abortion by association of Lippes' loop and pregnancy with intraplacental insertion of the apparatus," by A. Notter, et al. BULL FED SOC GYNECOL OBSTET LANG FR 21:460, September-October, 1969.

"An exploratory study of troops and their families practising contraception," by R. N. Varma, et al. INDIAN J MED RES 59:321-329, February, 1971.

"Family planning in a rural area using intrauterine devices," by R. C. Ramirez. REV CHIL OBSTET GINECOL 35:11-13, 1970.

"Family planning with special reference to the intrauterine contraception using intrauterine pessary of the Dana-Super type," by C. Zwahr. ZENTRALBL GYNAEKOL 93:645-650, May 8, 1971.

"Fertility after insertion of an IUCD in Taiwan's family-planning program," by R. Freedman, et al. SOC BIOL 18:46-54, March, 1971.

"Four years' experience with the Lippes Loop as a method of family planning," by L. L. Williams, et al. WEST INDIAN MED J 20:12-16, March, 1971.

"Genetic consequences of contraception in Santiago," by R. Cruz-Coke Coke. REV MED CHIL 99:190-194, February, 1971.

"Hormonal contraception. Clinical experience, gained up to now and present-day problems," by J. Teter. POL TYG LEK 25:1641-1643, November 2, 1970.

"Immediate postpartum IUD insertion," by L. Banharnsupawat, et al. OBSTET GYNECOL 38:276-285, August, 1971.

"Induced abortion--contraception," by O. Koller. TIDSSKR NOR LAEGEFOREN 91:629-632, March 30, 1971.

"The legalizing of contraceptives and abortions," by E. Szabady, IMPACT OF SCIENCE ON SOCIETY 21,3:265-270, July-September, 1971.

"Motivations, acceptance and refusal of contraceptive methods," by F. Jamet. BULL INST NATL SANTE RECH MED 23:1333-1346, November-December, 1968.

"Population, contraception and abortion," J R COLL GEN PRACT 21:377-378, July, 1971.

"Public health and long-term genetic implications of intrauterine diagnosis and selective abortion," by A. G. Motulsky, et al. BIRTH DEFECTS 7:22-32, April, 1971.

"Recommendations of the Swiss Society for Family Planning concerning ovulation inhibitors," by G. A. Hauser, et al. THER UMSCH 27:631-633, October, 1970.

"Survey on induced abortion and use of contraceptives in Bogota. Method of approach," by S. Gómez, et al. REV COLOMB OBSTET GINECOL 21:427-439, July-August, 1970.

CONTRACEPTION

"Whither IUD? The present and future of intrauterine contraceptives," by C. H. Birnberg, et al. OBSTET GYNECOL 37:861-865, June, 1968.

DEMOGRAPHY
see also: Immigration and Emigration
Population

"Assessing the demographic effect of a family planning programme," by W. Brass. PROC R SOC MED 63:1105-1107, November, 1970.

"Contraception and abortion among Aleuts and Eskimos in Alaska: a demographic study," by H. D. Alpern. J REPROD MED 7:239-244, November, 1971.

"Demographic adaptations to urban conditions," by G. M. Korostelev, et al. SOV ZDRAVOOKHR 29:35-36, 1970.

"The demographic effects of birth control and legal abortion," by H. Sjövall. LAKARTIDNINGEN 67:5261-5272, November 4, 1970.

"A demographic study on the relationships of nuptiality, child mortality, and attitude toward fertility to actual fertility in Hsueh-Chia township in Taiwan. I. Relationship of marriage cohort and marriage age to actual fertility," by H. Y. Wu. J FORMOSAN MED ASSOC 69:243-255, May 23, 1970.

"Family planning and demography," by J. Henripin. UNION MED CAN 97:608-612, May, 1968.

DIAGNOSIS
"Application of the randomized response technique in obtaining quantitative data," by B. G. Greenberg, et al. AM STAT ASSN J 66:243-250, June, 1971.

"Colpocytodiagnosis of threatened abortion," by O. I. Lopatchenko. VOPR OKHR MATERIN DET 15:27-30, December, 1970.

"Contribution to the diagnosis of infectious swine abortion," by F. Kemenes, et al. ZENTRALBL VETERINAERMED 18:170-176, March, 1971.

"Determination of C-reactive protein in metrorrhagic blood with special reference to the diagnosis of threatened abortion," by C. Zanoner. FRIULI MED 24:413-421, July-August, 1969.

"Diagnosis and management of internal abortion. Clinico-statistical study on 204 cases," by G. Zucconi, et al. RIV OSTET GINECOL 24:323-333, November, 1969.

"Diagnostic value of combined dynamic tests in corpus luteum deficiency," by P. Kićović. MED PREGL 22:577-580, 1969.

"A field trial of the fluorescence antibody test for toxoplasmosis in the diagnosis of ovine abortion," by J. F. Archer, et al. VET REC 88:206-208, February 20, 1971.

"The fluorescent antibody technic for the diagnosis of equine herpes virus abortion in comparison with conventional diagnostic methods," by U. Luttmann, et al. DTSCH TIERAERZTL WOCHENSCHR 78: 623-627, December 1, 1971.

"Further field studies on the fluorescent antibody test in the diagnosis of ovine abortion due to toxoplasmosis," by J. F. Archer, et al. VET REC 88:178-180, February 13, 1971.

"Hydatidiform mole with a co-existent fetus diagnosed in advance by ultrasound," by P. Jouppila, et al. ANN CHIR GYNAECOL FENN 60:89-91, 1971.

"Identification of meconium by the determination of acid phosphatase and spectrophotometric analysis," by E. Eliakis, et al. MED LEG DOMM CORPOR 4:163-168, April-June, 1971.

"Infected abortion and disseminated intravascular coagulation (DIC). Heparin prevention and early diagnosis of the DIC," by W. Kuhn, et al. MED WELT 22:1199-1200, July 24, 1971.

"Main causes of repetitive abortion revealed by hysterography," by P. Dellenbach, et al. J RADIOL ELECTROL MED NUCL 52:522-523, August-September, 1971.

"Our experience in the diagnosis and therapy of recurrent abortion," by I. Coghi, et al. MINERVA GINECOL 21:1070-1073, August 31, 1969.

"Possibility of prognosis of threatened abortion," by G. P. Mandruzzato, et al. MINERVA GINECOL 22:476-477, May 15, 1970.

"Prenatal diagnosis and the prevention of birth defects," by R. H. Heller. MD STATE MED J 20:59-62, May, 1971.

"The prognosis of threatened abortion," by A. Johannsen. ACTA OBSTET GYNECOL SCAND 49:89-93, 1970.

"Prognosis of threatened abortion," by J. M. Thoulon. LYON MED 18: Suppl:21-25, 1971.

"Prognosis of threatened abortion. A comparative study with the use of vaginal cytology and urinary gonadotropin immunoassay," by A. F. Youssef, et al. AM J OBSTET GYNECOL 109:8-11, January 1, 1971.

"Prognostic importance of determining excretion of chorionic gonadotropin in the diagnosis of spontaneous abortion," by A. T. Berko. AKUSH GINEKOL 47:37-41, June, 1971.

"Prognostic value of vaginal exfoliative cytodiagnosis in habitual abortion," by I. Penev. AKUSH GINEKOL (Sofiia) 8:335-344, 1969.

"Public health and long-term genetic implications of intrauterine diagnosis and selective abortion," by A. G. Motulsky, et al. BIRTH DEFECTS 7:22-32, April, 1971.

"Septic abortion: diagnosis and treatment," by B. Neme. MATERN INFANC 29:255-278, April-June, 1970.

"Septic abortion masquerading as thrombotic thrombocytopenic purpura," by M. Yudis, et al. AM J OBSTET GYNECOL 111:350-352, October 1, 1971.

"Serologic diagnosis of rickettsian abortion in ewes," by R. Gaumont. BULL OFF INT EPIZOOT 70:271-279, May, 1968.

"The technique of complement fixation test for the diagnosis of equine viral abortion (Rhinopneumonitis)," by K. Petzoldt. DTSCH TIERAERZTL WOCHENSCHR 74:252-255, May 15, 1967.

DIAGNOSIS

"Threatened abortions and their prognosis in the light of cytohormonal and enzymatic studies," by A. Dzioba, et al. WIAD LEK 24:649-652, April 1, 1971.

"Threatened and spontaneous abortion. A retrospective study of the diagnosis on admission," by A. Johannsen. ACTA OBSTET GYNECOL SCAND 49:95-99, 1970.

"Ultrasonic diagnosis: abortions and threatened abortions," by S. Levi. GYNECOL OBSTET 70:333-342, May-June, 1971.

"Value of external hysterography for the diagnosis of threatened premature labor," by M. Ia. Martynshin. AKUSH GINEKOL 44:46-50, July, 1968.

DILATOL
"Treatment of threat of premature labor and miscarriage with Dilatol," by H. Neumann, et al. ZENTRALBL GYNAEKOL 93:849-859, June 19, 1971.

DUVADILAN
"Treatment of threatened abortion and premature labor with Duvadilan," by H. Neumann, et al. ZENTRALBL GYNAEKOL 92:1100-1108, August 22, 1970.

DRUG THERAPY
see also: Techniques of Abortion
Under Specific Drugs

"Active management in modern treatment of gestosis," by A. Cretti. GINEKOL POL 42:437-440, April, 1971.

"Changes in uterine volume during hypertonic saline induced abortions," by A. Kivikoski, et al. ACTA OBSTET GYNECOL SCAND 9:Suppl:9:45, 1971.

"Decidual-cell necrosis after injection of hypertonic saline for therapeutic abortion," by B. Gustavil, et al. LANCET 2:826, October 9, 1971.

"Drug-induced arrest of a pathological labor," by J. Huter. BULL FED SOC GYNECOL OBSTET LANG FR 20:Suppl:432-434, 1968.

128

"Effect of therapy in threatened abortion," by F. S. Baranovskaia, et al. PEDIATR AKUSH GINEKOL 1:41-44, January-February, 1971.

"Effect of vitamin E on the placenta and fetus," by L. V. Knysh. AKUSH GINEKOL 44:30-34, September, 1968.

"Electrolyte dynamics in hypertonic saline-induced abortions," by F. D. Frigoletto, et al. OBSTET GYNECOL 38:647-652, November, 1971.

"Experience with the Kovács method of extra-amniotic glucose injection," by I. Kocsis, et al. ORV HETIL 112:1585-1587, July 4, 1971.

"Histochemical studies on the chorion in pregnant women treated with gestanon (preliminary report)," by Ts. Despotova, et al. AKUSH GINEKOL (Sofiia) 8:461-465, 1969.

"Hormonal and placental changes after intra-amniotic injection of hypertonic saline," by R. L. Berkowitz, et al. CLIN OBSTET GYNECOL 14:179-191, March, 1971.

"Hypertonic solutions to induce abortion," by I. L. Craft, et al. BR MED J 2:49, April 3, 1971.

"3. Methotrexate and concentration of chorionic gonadotropin," by L. Lajos, et al. ORV HETIL 112:2077-2080 passim, August 29, 1971.

"Neurovegetative reactivity in women during interruption of unwanted pregnancy in the 2d trimester by intra-amniotic instillation of saline solution," by B. Kiutukchiev, et al. AKUSH GINEKOL (Sofiia) 8:482-485, 1969.

"Outpatient intra-amniotic injection of hypertonic saline," by T. D. Kerenyi. CLIN OBSTET GYNECOL 14:124-140, March, 1971.

"Outpatient saline abortion," by H. Schulman, et al. OBSTET GYNE-COL 37:521-526, April, 1971.

"Oxytocin administration in abortions induced with hypertonic saline," by J. D. Schulman, et al. LANCET 2:606-607, September 11, 1971.

"PGE compounds for induction of labour and abortion," by M. Embrey. ANN NY ACAD SCI 180:518-523, April 30, 1971.

"Pathologic findings after hypertonic saline instillation in midtrimester abortion," by A. Blaustein, et al. CLIN OBSTET GYNECOL 14: 192-203, March, 1971; also in MOD TREAT 8:127-138, February, 1971.

"Plasma progesterone during abortion induced by intra-amniotic hypertonic saline," by T. H. Holmdahl, et al. ACTA OBSTET GYNECOL SCAND 9:Suppl:48, 1971.

"Plasma progesterone in pregnancy interrupted by the intrauterine injection of hypertonic saline," by T. H. Holmdahl, et al. ACTA ENDOCRINOL 66:82-88, January, 1971.

"Prevention of abortion and premature delivery," by K. Watanabe. SANFUJINKA JISSAI 20:428-433, April, 1971.

"Prevention of abortion in hospital personnel," by M. Isokoski, et al. SAIRAANHOITAJA 47:486-488, June 10, 1971.

"Prevention of uterine injury during induced abortion," by S. Sugiyama. SANFUJINKA JISSAI 20:494-495, April, 1971.

"Prevention of uterine perforation," by M. Kusumoto. SANFUJINKA JISSAI 20:540-544, May, 1971.

"Radiographic study of extra-amniotically injected hypertonic saline in therapeutic abortion," by B. Gustavii, et al. ACTA OBSTET GYNECOL SCAND 50:315-320, 1971.

"Saline abortion," by L. R. Cronenwett, et al. AM J NURS 71:1754-1757, September, 1971.

"Saline prep induces abortion," AM DRUGGIST 164:83, July 12, 1971.

"The significance of fetal death in the mechanism of abortion induced by intra-amniotic injection of hypertonic salt solution," by L. Kovács, et al. ORV HETIL 112:852-854, April 11, 1971.

DRUG THERAPY

"Stilboestrol and cancer," BR MED J 3:593-594, September 11, 1971.

"Studies of the abortive mechanism of intrauterine injection of hypertonic saline," by B. Gustavii. ACTA OBSTET GYNECOL SCAND 9:Suppl:43, 1971.

"Study of the sulfamethoxazole-trimethoprim combination in gynecology and obstetrics," by J. Villard, et al. J MED LYON 52:401-403, March 5, 1971.

"Unwanted pregnancy and its prevention," by M. Mall-Haefeli. THER UMSCH 27:693-697, October, 1970.

"The use of prostaglandin E 2 in the management of intrauterine death, missed abortion and hydatidiform mole," by G. M. Filshie. J OBSTET GYNAECOL BR COMMONW 78:87-90, January, 1971.

"Uselessness of estrogens in maturation of the cervix and induction of labor," by O. Agüero, et al. GINECOL OBSTET MEX 30:21-29, July, 1971.

"Value of uterosedative drug in threatened premature labor," by R. Palliez, et al. PEDIATRIE 26:673-675, September, 1971.

EDUCATION AND ABORTION
"Education about abortion," by E. S. Gendel, et al. AM J PUBLIC HEALTH 61:520-529, March, 1971.

"Learning abortion care," by A. Goldmann. NURS OUTLOOK 19:350-352, May, 1971.

"The teaching of fertility control and population problems in the medical schools of Brazil," by J. Yunes. REV SAUDE PUBLICA 4:79-84, June, 1970.

"To teach or not to teach family planning in Kenyan primary schools," by J. B. Maathuis. EAST AFR MED J 47:545-549, November, 1970.

"Suggestions on adding family planning to the curriculums of medical schools," by D. T. Rice. PUBLIC HEALTH REP 85:889-895, October, 1970.

FAMILY PLANNING
  see also: Sociology, Behavior and Abortion

"Abortion and contraception in family planning. A commentary," by C. F. Coffelt. J REHABIL 7:13-15, July, 1971.

"Assessing the demographic effect of a family planning programme," by W. Brass. PROC R SOC MED 63:1105-1107, November, 1970.

"Attendance at family planning centers," by C. Texier. EVOL PSYCHIATR 34:595-637, July-September, 1969.

"Awareness and acceptance of different family planning in a rural population," by H. S. Gandhi, et al. INDIAN J PUBLIC HEALTH 13:130-143, July, 1969.

"Birth planning and eugenics," by J. Benoist. UNION MED CAN 97: 613-616, May, 1968.

"The complete family planning service at King's College Hospital," by P. Newton. NURS TIMES 66:1399-1400, October 29, 1970.

"Evaluation of periodic continence as a family planning method. Acceptance among low socioeconomical levels in Cali, Columbia," by V. R. Guerrero, et al. REV COLOMB OBSTET GINECOL 22:13-18, January-February, 1971.

"Evaluation of periodic continence as a method of family planning," by R. Guerrero, et al. REV COLOMB OBSTET GINECOL 21:545-552, November-December, 1970.

"Family planning," by H. Husslein. WIEN KLIN WOCHENSCHR 82: 553-554, July 31, 1970.

"Family planning. Clinical practice and problems," by H. J. Staemmler, et al. DTSCH MED WOCHENSCHR 96:959.964, May 28, 1971.

"Family planning. Critical review of the Resolution of Family Planning," by B. Stambolovic. LIJEC VJESN 92:493-500, 1970.

"Family planning and conjugal roles in New York City poverty areas," by S. Polgar, et al. SOC SCI MED 4:135-139, July, 1970.

"Family planning and demography," by J. Henripin. UNION MED CAN 97:608-612, May, 1968.

"Family planning and maternal and child health," by J. M. Yang. YONSEI MED J 11:67-76, 1970.

"Family planning and present law situation in Austria," by H. Husslein. WIEN KLIN WOCHENSCHR 83:141-144, March 5, 1971.

"Family planning and the reduction of fertility and illegitimacy: a preliminary report on a rural southern program," by J. D. Beasley, et al. SOC BIOL 16:167-178, September, 1969.

"Family planning Association. Conference on Health Services and Public Health Act 1968," J R COLL GEN PRACT 17:117-119, February, 1969.

"Family planning comes of age," by L. M. Hellman. AM J OBSTET GYNECOL 109:214-224, January 15, 1971.

"Family planning--a health priority," J MED ASSOC STATE ALA 40: 414-415, December, 1970.

"Family planning--how, when and where," by U. Borell. NORD MED 86:840-842, July 15, 1971.

"Family planning in China," by S. Ornstedt. LAKARTIDNINGEN 68: 2582-2583, May 26, 1971.

"Family planning in Cordoba (Argentine Republic)," by M. A. Agliozzo, et al. GINECOL OBSTET MEX 28:105-110, July, 1970.

"Family planning in the developing world," by W. G. Povey. OBSTET GYNECOL 36:948-952, December, 1970.

"Family planning in the Negro ghettos of Chicago," by D. J. Bogue. MILBANK MEM FUND Q 48:283-307, April, 1970.

"Family planning in a rural area using intrauterine devices," by R. C. Ramirez. REV CHIL OBSTET GINECOL 35:11-13, 1970.

"Family planning physicians answer abortion critics," AMER MED

NEWS 14:1+, April 19, 1971.

"Family planning policies and practice in population control," by A. Wiseman. R SOC HEALTH J 91:134-138, May-June, 1971.

"Family planning with special reference to the intrauterine contraception using intrauterine pessary of the Dana-Super type," by C. Zwahr. ZENTRALBL GYNEKOL 93:645-650, May 8, 1971.

"The family-size umbrella," by M. Woolacott. GUARDIAN 11, January 11, 1971.

"Fertility after insertion of an IUCD in Taiwan's family-planning program," by R. Freedman, et al. SOC BIOL 18:46-54, March, 1971.

"Four years' experience with the Lippes Loop as a method of family planning," by L. L. Williams, et al. WEST INDIAN MED J 20:12-16, March, 1971.

"Geographic distribution of need for family planning and subsidized services in the United States," by R. C. Lerne. AM J PUBLIC HEALTH 60:1944-1955, October, 1970.

"The impact of desired family size upon family planning practices in rural East Pakistan," by P. W. Mosena. JOURNAL OF MARRIAGE AND THE FAMILY 33,3:567-570, August, 1971.

"The impact of liberalized abortion laws on family planning," by E. W. Overstreet. J REHABIL 7:20-21, July, 1971.

"Inadequacy of a one-method family-planning program," by R. G. Potter. SOC BIOL 18:1-9, March, 1971.

"Integration of the family planning in the health care of the German Democratic Republic," by K. H. Mehlan. Z AERZTL FORTBILD 64:429-432, May 1, 1970.

"International cooperation in family planning," by M. Strachan. NURS OUTLOOK 19:103, February, 1971.

"The Jamaican male and family planning," by B. I. Morgan, et al. WEST INDIAN MED J 20:5-11, March, 1971.

"Literacy and family planning in India," by V. J. Marsick. INDIAN JOURNAL OF ADULT EDUCATION 32,7:8-10, 21, July, 1971.

"Meeting the needs of the single parent family," FAMILY COORDINATOR 20,4:327-336, October, 1971.

"Meeting the problems of today's families through extension programs," FAMILY COORDINATOR 20,4:337-340, October, 1971.

"National council on family relations: position paper on abortion," FAMILY COORDINATOR 20,4:401-402, October, 1971.

"New national program of family planning in the United States," by S. C. Scheyer. SALUD PUBLICA MEX 12:657-661, September-October, 1970.

"The nurse's role in family planning," by A. Rooke. NURS TIMES 67:727-730, June, 1971.

"Physicians and methods of birth planning," by P. J. Donaldson. RI MED J 53:419-423 passim, August, 1970.

"Planned parenthood 40 years in Alabama," by O. T. Bolding, et al. J MED ASSOC STATE ALA 40:451 passim, January, 1971.

"Postpartal counseling on family planning in the hospital," by D. Langnickel. ARCH GYNAEKOL 211:363-364, June 4, 1971.

"Psychosexual response and attitudes toward family planning. A study of 100 pregnant women," by A. W. Chang-Silva, et al. OBSTET GYNECOL 37:289-296, February, 1971.

"Recommendations of the Swiss Society for Family Planning concerning ovulation inhibitors," by G. A. Hauser, et al. THER UMSCH 27:631-633, October, 1970.

"Relation of socioeconomic factors to family planning (based on data from the Tselinograd region)," by L. E. Sviridova. SOV ZDRAVOOKHR 29:11-15, 1970.

"Relationship of family planning to pediatrics and child health," by H. M. Wallace, et al. CLIN PEDIATR 9:699-701, December, 1970.

"Removal of barriers to family planning," WIEN MED WOCHENSCHR 120:129, May 2, 1970.

"Report on family planning clinics conducted in the Cape Town municipal area from 1960 to 1969," by I. Robertson. S AFR MED J 45: 291-292, March 13, 1971.

"Role of pediatrician in family planning," by C. C. de Silva. INDIAN PEDIATR 7:167-171, March, 1970.

"The role of the physician in North Carolina family planning programs," by A. R. Measham. NC MED J 32:51-56, February, 1971.

"Sex education and family planning advice by South Dakota doctors. II. Family planning advice," by B. Ranney. SD J MED 24:5-11, June, 1971.

"Should family planning clinics perform abortions?" by E. Fairchild, et al. FAM PLANN PERSPECT 3:15-17, April, 1971.

"Some aspects of regulating family size in India," by K. G. Simonian. SOV ZDRAVOOKHR 29:58-63, 1970.

"Sterilization and family planning," by M. Elstein. PRACTITIONER 205:30-37, July, 1970.

"Suggestions on adding family planning to the curriculums of medical schools," by D. T. Rice. PUBLIC HEALTH REP 85:889-895, October, 1970.

"To teach or not to teach family planning in Kenyan primary schools," by J. B. Maathuis. EAST AFR MED J 47:545-549, November, 1970.

"Toward the reduction of unwanted pregnancy," by F. S. Jaffe. SCIENCE 174,4005:119-127, October, 1971.

"Training of adscript personnel in Latin American programs of family planning," by C. B. Arnold. EDUC MED SALUD 3:40-55, January-March, 1969.

"Underlying sources of agreement and communication between husbands and wives in Dacca, East Pakistan," JOURNAL OF

MARRIAGE AND THE FAMILY 33,3:571-583, August, 1971.

"Use of the statistical method of paired combinations in studying aspects of regulating family size," by A. I. Markov. SOV ZDRAVOOKHR 29:43-46, 1970.

"Utilization of a family planning program by the poor population of a metropolitan area," by J. D. Beasley, et al. MILBANK MEM FUND Q 48:241-281, April, 1970.

FAMILY THERAPY
"Family group therapy for children with self-induced seizures," by S. S. Libo, et al. AM J ORTHOPSYCHIATRY 41:506-509, April, 1971.

"Family therapy in the treatment of anorexia nervos," by A. Barcai. AM J PSYCHIATRY 128:286-290, September, 1971.

"Follow-up after abortion," by L. A. Pike. BR MED J 2:767, June 26, 1971.

"Group therapy following abortion," by N. R. Bernstein, et al. J NERV MENT DIS 152:303-314, May, 1971.

"Preoperative instruction for the patient undergoing elective abortion," by D. F. Kallop. CLIN OBSTET GYNECOL 14:60-66, March, 1971.

FERTILITY
see: Sterility

FETUS
"Calcified extra-uterine foetus co-existing with normal intra-uterine pregnancy," by F. M. Bulwa. EAST AFR MED J 48:109-115, March, 1971.

"A case of latent (subacute) hypofibrinogenemia due to retained dead fetus," by B. Georgiev, et al. AKUSH GINEKOL (Sofiia) 10:165, 1971.

"Chromosome findings in women with habitual abortions and fetal malformations," by E. Golob, et al. WIEN KLIN WOCHENSCHR

83:668-670, September 24, 1971.

"Doctor claims hundreds of fetuses die needlessly," NAT CATH REP 7:3, March 15, 1971.

"Effect of vitamin E on the placenta and fetus," by L. V. Knysh. AKUSH GINEKOL 44:30-34, September, 1968.

"Embryonic development in patients with recurrent abortions," by B. J. Poland. FERTIL STERIL 22:325-331, May, 1971.

"Fetal indications for therapeutic abortion," by A. C. Barnes. ANNU REV MED 22:133-144, 1971.

"Fetal losses in a high prevalence area of chronic Chagas' disease," by J. R. Teruel, et al. REV INST MED TROP SAO PAULO 12: 239-244, July-August, 1970.

"A fetal salvage program: the use of plasma diamine oxidase as a fetal monitor," by A. B. Weingold, et al. INT J FERTIL 16: 24-35, January-March, 1971.

"Fetus as a legal entity--facing reality," SANDIEGO L REV 8:126, 1971.

"The foetus began to cry...abortion," NURS J INDIA 62:325+, October, 1971.

"Human infection by Vibrio fetus," by I. A. Cooper, et al. MED J AUST 1:1263-1267, June 12, 1971.

"Hydatidiform mole with a co-existent fetus diagnosed in advance by ultrasound," by P. Jouppila, et al. ANN CHIR GYNAECOL FENN 60:89-91, 1971.

"Immunoserologic properties of antigens from Vibrio fetus of ovine origin," by L. L. Myers, et al. AM J VET RES 31:1773-1777, October, 1970.

"Legal possibilities of pregnancy interruption for eugenic or fetal indications," by D. Krauss. MUNCH MED WOCHENSCHR 113: 1505-1512, November 5, 1971.

FETUS

"Petrified fetus (lithopedion) in a 74-year-old woman," by N. N. Tiraspolskaia, et al. PEDIATR AKUSH GINEKOL 4:61, July-August, 1970.

"Plasma levels of progesterone in early pregnancy after removal of the foetoplacental unit, and following removal of corpus luteum," by P. E. Lebech. ACTA ENDOCRINOL 155:Suppl:134, 1971.

"Relationship between fetal anomaly and abortion," by H. Nishimura. SANFUJINKA JISSAI 20:821-825, August, 1971.

"The significance of fetal death in the mechanism of abortion induced by intra-amniotic injection of hypertonic salt solution," by L. Kovács, et al. ORV HETIL 112:852-854, April 11, 1971.

"Studies on fetal circulation in legal abortions," by S. L. Pehrson. ACTA OBSTET GYNECOL SCAND 49:289-292, 1970.

"Study of fetal erythrocytes in metrorrhagias caused by threatened abortion," by F. Pietropaolo, et al. QUAD CLIN OSTET GINECOL 25:39-44, January, 1970.

"T-strains of mycoplasma in bronchopneumonic lungs of an aborted fetus," by N. Romano, et al. N ENGL J MED 285:950-952, October 21, 1971.

GENETICS

"Abortion caused by chromosomal abnormalities and estrogen insufficiency of the corpus luteum," by J. Cohen. PRESSE MED 78:1744, September 26, 1970.

"Abortion caused by chromosome aberration, with special reference to habitual abortion," by K. Watanabe. SANFUJINKA JISSAI 20:826-832, August, 1971.

"Application of genetics in gynecology and obstetrics," by L. C. Ayala. ENFERMERAS 18:4-11, January-February, 1971.

"Birth planning and eugenics," by J. Benoist. UNION MED CAN 97: 613-616, May, 1968.

"Chromosomal abortion," by M. Massobrio, et al. MINERVA GINECOL 23:443-472, May 31, 1971.

"Chromosomal studies in relation to abortion," by P. Adler, et al. J AM OSTEOPATH ASSOC 70:1319-1323, August, 1971.

"Chromosome aberrations in oogenesis and embryogenesis of mammals and man," by G. Röhrborn. ARCH TOXIKOL 28:115-119, 1971.

"Chromosome abnormalities in early spontaneous abortion," by D. T. Arakaki, et al. J MED GENET 7:118-124, June, 1970.

"Chromosome findings in women with habitual abortions and fetal malformations," by E. Golob, et al. WIEN KLIN WOCHENSCHR 83:668-670, September 24, 1971.

"Chromosome pathology in spontaneous abortions," by C. Zara. ARCH OSTET GINECOL 75:215-225, May-June, 1970.

"Chromosome studies in selected spontaneous abortions. 3 Early pregnancy loss," by D. H. Carr. OBSTET GYNECOL 37:570-574, May, 1971.

"Chromosome studies in selected spontaneous abortions. Polploidy in man," by D. H. Carr. J MED GENET 8:164-174, June, 1971.

"Chromosomic abortions. The value of new data and the interest of further research," by R. Debre. INDIAN J PEDIATR 38:114-118, March, 1971.

"Cultivation of lymphocytes from cord blood, obtained postmortem and from live infants, for chromosome analysis," by Z. Papp, et al. ORV HETIL 112:2287-2288, September 19, 1971.

"Cytogenetic aspects of habitual abortion. 1. Chromosome analysis of couples with history of habitual abortion," by K. Koike. NAGOYA MED J 16:59-72, November, 1970.

"Cytogenetic investigation of spontaneous abortions," by A. M. Kuliev. HUMANGENETIK 12:275-283, 1971.

"Cytogenetics and malformation in abortions," by D. H. Carr. FED

PROC 30:102-103, January-February, 1971.

"Eugenic prophylaxis in the light of international legislation," by R. D'Andrea. ANN SANITA PUBBLICA 32:25-49, January-February, 1971.

"Experiences in the genetic counseling office," by M. Avčin. WIEN MED WOCHENSCHR 120:356-359, May 16, 1970.

"Fertility in balanced heterozygotes for a familial centric fusion translocation, t(DgDg)," by J. A. Wilson. J MED GENET 8:175-178, June, 1971.

"Genetic aspects of spontaneous abortions," by J. Cousin. J SCI MED LILLE 89:313-315, August-September, 1971.

"Genetic consequences of contraception in Santiago," by R. Cruz-Coke. REV MED CHIL 99:190-194, February, 1971.

"Genetics in therapeutic abortion," by A. C. Christakos. SOUTH MED J 64:Suppl:105-108, February, 1971.

"Genome unbalance and reproductive wastage in man and mammals," by C. E. Ford. NORD MED 86:1545, December 16, 1971.

"Human chromosome abnormalities. 2. Occurrence in spontaneous abortion and antenatal detection by amniocentesis," by L. J. Butler. MIDWIFE HEALTH VISIT 7:105-108, March, 1971.

"Prenatal mortality and genetic wastage in man," by M. G. Kerr. J BIOSOC SCI 3:223-237, April, 1971.

"Public health and long-term genetic implications of intrauterine diagnosis and selective abortion," by A. G. Motulsky, et al. BIRTH DEFECTS 7:22-32, April, 1971.

"Significance in classification of spontaneous abortion for genetic consultation rooms," by P. Dráč, et al. CESK GYNEKOL 36:491-492, October, 1971.

GYNAECOLOGY

"Application of genetics in gynecology and obstetrics," by L. C.

Ayala. ENFERMERAS 18:4-11, January-February, 1971.

"Gynecology and obstetrics," by D. N. Danforth. SURG GYNECOL OBSTET 132:221-225, February, 1971.

"Problems of listeriosis in gynecology and obstetrics," by M. Pommier, et al. SEM HOP PARIS 47:2489-2491, November 8, 1971.

"Prostaglandins in obstetrics and gynecology," by P. Bersjo, et al. TIDSSKR NOR LAEGFOREN 91:678-679, March 30, 1971.

"Study of the sulfamethoxazole-trimethoprim combination in gynecology and obstetrics," by J. Villard, et al. J MED LYON 52:401-403, March 5, 1971.

HABITUAL ABORTION

"Abortion caused by chromosome aberration, with special reference to habitual abortion," by K. Watanabe. SANFUJINKA JISSAI 20:826-832, August, 1971.

"Anomaly of the maternal karyotype in 2 cases of habitual abortion and fetal abnormalities," by M. Vitse, et al. BULL FED SOC GYNECOL OBSTET LANG FR 20:466-469, November-December, 1968.

"Case of habitual abortion in a patient with primary hyperparathyroidism (current obstetrical clinico-diagnostico-therapeutic and statistical aspects)," by C. Zanoner. FRIULI MED 24:227-240, May-June, 1969.

"Chromosome findings in women with habitual abortions and fetal malformations," by E. Golob, et al. WIEN KLIN WOCHENSCHR 83:668-670, September 24, 1971.

"Cytogenetic aspects of habitual abortion. 1. Chromosome analysis of couples with history of habitual abortion," by K. Koike. NAGOYA MED J 16:59-72, November, 1970.

"Electrolytes, enzymes and hormones in women with spontaneous and habitual abortions," by B. Kiutukchiev, et al. AKUSH GINEKOL (Sofiia) 10:89-98, 1971.

"Folic acid and habitual abortion," by G. Brigato, et al. MINERVA GINECOL 22:471-474, May 15, 1970.

"Functional studies in women with habitual abortion and premature labor," by B. Kiutukchiev, et al. AKUSH GINEKOL (Sofiia) 9: 461-469, 1970.

"Habitual abortion," by N. Vaglio. MINERVA GINECOL 21:1059-1061, August 31, 1969.

"Iodine salivary clearance in a group of hyperthyroid women with a history of recurrent or habitual abortion," by A. Viglione, et al. MINERVA GINECOL 21:1077-1079, August 31, 1969.

"Medical record of women with habitual abortion," by I. Penev. AKUSH GINEKOL (Sofiia) 9:470-478, 1970.

"Prognostic value of vaginal exfoliative cytodiagnosis in habitual abortion," by I. Penev. AKUSH GINEKOL (Sofiia) 8:335-344, 1969.

"Prostaglandins and habitual abortion," by M. Bodin. BR MED J 2: 587, June 5, 1971.

"Repeated abortions due to uterine anomaly," by R. Empereur-Buisson. J SCI MED LILLE 89:317-321, August-September, 1971.

"Repeated or habitual abortions," Q MED REV 21:1-30, July, 1970.

"Results of gestanon therapy in women with threatened and habitual abortion," by Ts. Despodova. AKUSH GINEKOL (Sofiia) 9:208-213, 1970.

"Significance of pseudodecidual reconstruction of the endometrial stroma in the etiology and pathogenesis of habitual abortion," by R. K. Ryzhova. VOPR OKHR MATERIN DET 16:59-63, October, 1971.

"Skin homograft in prevention of habitual abortion: report of a case and review of the literature," by S. R. Hewitt. J IR MED ASSOC 64:323-325, June 24, 1971.

"Surgical treatment and prevention of isthmo-cervical insufficiency

causing prematurity, habitual abortion and premature delivery,"
by R. Tokhin. AKUSH GINEKOL (Sofiia) 8:473-481, 1969.

"Surgical treatment of habitual abortions," by J. Bocev. MED PREGL
24:135-136, 1971.

"Treatment of habitual abortion due to abnormal hormone secretion,"
by Y. Tanaka. SANFUJINKA JISSAI 20:842-848, August, 1971.

HEMORRHAGE
see also: Complications
Transplacental Hemorrhage

"Accidental haemorrhage. The present position," by A. P. Barry.
J IR MED ASSOC 64:494-497, September 23, 1971.

"Analysis of 480 births after bleeding during pregnancy," by H.
Wallner, et al. MUNCH MED WOCHENSCHR 113:690-695,
April 30, 1971.

"Changes in the thrombelastograph following blood loss during late
spontaneous abortion," by L. V. Terskaia. AKUSH GINEKOL 45:
70-72, September, 1969.

"Clinical attitude towards bleeding in early pregnancy," by P.
Järvinen. DUODECIM 87:389-391, 1971.

"Hemorrhage. A persistent source of obstetrical emergency," by G.
C. Lewis, Jr. J KY MED ASSOC 69:105-109, February, 1971.

"Pregnancy in the 4th month; spontaneous abortion. Acute hemorrhagic
pancreatitis. (Presentation of a clinical case)," by P. Dulea, et
al. MED INTERNA 23:1513-1516, December, 1971.

"'Spontaneous' abortion and haemorrhage following attempted amniocentesis in a carrier of haemophilia A," by S. D. Cederbaum, et
al. LANCET 2:429-430, August 21, 1971.

"Use of an antihemorrhagic factor (AMFAC) in obstetric-gynecologic
hemorrhages of various origin," by M. Giaquinto, et al. RIV ITAL
GINECOL 53:549-559, August-September, 1969.

HISTORY
  "Abortion in the Maori in historical perspective," by L. K. Gluckman. NZ MED J 74:323-325, November, 1971.

  "Abortion in perspective," by R. J. Endres. AM J OBSTET GYNECOL 111:436-439, October 1, 1971.

  "Abortion throughout antiquity and in the books of Hippocrates," by J. P. Pundel. BULL SOC SCI MED GRAND DUCHE LUXEMB 108:19-30, March, 1971.

  "Family planning comes of age," by L. M. Hellman. AM J OBSTET GYNECOL 109:214-224, January 15, 1971.

HORMONES
  "Contractibility of the human uterus and the hormonal situation. Studies on therapy with progesterone in pregnancy," by P. Mentasti, et al. MINERVA GINECOL 21:685-687, May 31, 1969.

  "Cytohormonal studies of vaginal smears performed during the treatment of imminent abortions," by B. Wierstakow, et al. GINEKOL POL 41:977-984, September, 1970.

  "Electrolytes, enzymes and hormones in women with spontaneous and habitual abortions," by B. Kiutukchiev, et al. AKUSH GINEKOL (Sofiia) 10:89-98, 1971.

  "Hormonal and placental changes after intra-amniotic injection of hypertonic saline," by R. L. Berkowitz, et al. CLIN OBSTET GYNECOL 14:179-191, March, 1971.

  "Hormonal contraception. Clinical experience, gained up to now and present-day problems," by J. Teter. POL TYG LEK 25:1641:1643, November 2, 1970.

  "Hormone produces abortion in 9," AM DRUGGIST 162:73, July 13, 1970.

  "Long-term results of treatment with a delayed-action progestational hormone in threatened abortion," by P. Scillieri. MINERVA GINECOL 22:413-416, April 15, 1970.

145

"Luteinizing hormone titration in the anterior pituitary of women who died during pregnancy and the post-abortion period," by M. De la Lastra. REV MED CHIL 98:782-785, November, 1970.

"96% of women abort when given hormone," AM DRUGGIST 162:47, October 19, 1970.

"Pregnancy interruption and its influence on the hormonal activity of the thyroid," by W. Hartwig, et al. REV FR ENDOCRINOL CLIN 12:27-32, January-February, 1971.

"Pregnancy preservation with hormones," by G. A. Hauser. THER UMSCH 28:438-443, 1971.

"Spontaneous abortion and preventive hormone therapy (results in 110 cases)," by D. Antonopoulos, et al. ZENTRALBL GYNAEKOL 92:706-707, May 30, 1970.

"Threatened abortions and their prognosis in the light of cytohormonal and enzymatic studies," by A. Dzioba, et al. WIAD LEK 24:649-652, April 1, 1971.

"Treatment of habitual abortion due to abnormal hormone secretion," by Y. Tanaka. SANFUJINKA JISSAI 20:842-848, August, 1971.

"Treatment of pregnant women with spontaneous abortion of hormonal origin and isthmicocervical insufficiency," by M. P. Chertova, et al. AKUSH GINEKOL 46:48-51, November, 1970.

"Treatment of spontaneous abortion with high doses of sex hormones and the child's state," by V. Sulovic, et al. BULL FED SOC GYNECOL OBSTET LANG FR 20:Suppl:304-306, 1968.

"Use of a synthetic progestational hormone, chlormadinone, in obstetrics," by R. Palliez, et al. LILLE MED 659-663, June-July, 1969.

HOSPITALS AND ABORTION
"Abortion in an upstate community hospital," by R. R. Murray. CLIN OBSTET GYNECOL 14:141-148, March, 1971.

"Abortion: medical aspects in a municipal hospital," by D. P. Swartz, et al. BULL NY ACAD MED 47:845-852, August, 1971.

"Abortion: physician and hospital attitudes," by R. E. Hall. AM J PUBLIC HEALTH 61:517-519, March, 1971.

"Abortions by resident physicians in a municipal hospital center," by J. J. Kopelman, et al. AM J OBSTET GYNECOL 111:666-671, November 1, 1971.

"Black hospital in Kansas ordered to halt abortions: Douglas Hospital, Kansas City," HOSPITALS 45:21, August 16, 1971.

"Coordination of outpatient services for patients seeking elective abortion," by C. H. Siener, et al. CLIN OBSTET GYNECOL 14: 48:59, March, 1971.

"Demand abortions in public hospitals: medicolegal opinion," by H. B. Alsobrook, Jr. J LOUISIANA STATE MED SOC 123:29-30, January, 1971.

"The family enters the hospital," by G. M. Abroms, et al. AM J PSYCHIATRY 127:1363-1370, April, 1971.

"500 outpatient abortions performed under local anesthesia," by I. K. Strausz, et al. OBSTET GYNECOL 38:199-205, August, 1971.

"Hospital streamlines abortion policy: Atlantic City, N. J.," MOD HOSP 117:46, August, 1971.

"Impact on hospital practice of liberalizing abortions and female sterilizations," by A. D. Claman, et al. CAN MED ASSOC J 105: 35-41, July 10, 1971.

"Management of incomplete abortion as an outpatient procedure," by A. Allen, et al. CENT AFR J MED 17:91-96, May, 1971.

"Medicolegal opinion. Re: on demand abortions in public hospitals," by H. B. Alsobrook, Jr. J LA STATE MED SOC 123:29-30, January, 1971.

"Military hospitals struggle to keep balanced approach on abortions," US MED 7:4+, November 1, 1971.

"Model abortion program set up in Wickersham Hospital, New York City," HOSP MANAGE 111:7, May, 1971.

"Occurrence of recurrent abortion among patients in our hospital in the last 3 years," by R. Palagi, et al. MINERVA GINECOL 21: 1064-1066, August 31, 1969.

"Outpatient abortion," by P. Diggory. LANCET 2:767-768, October 2, 1971.

"Outpatient abortion: New York style," by B. L. Shaw. RN 34:44-49, October, 1971.

"Outpatient abortions," LANCET 2:656, September 18, 1971.

"Outpatient intra-amniotic injection of hypertonic saline," by T. D. Kerenyi. CLIN OBSTET GYNECOL 14:124-140, March, 1971.

"Outpatient saline abortion," by H. Schulman, et al. OBSTET GYNE-COL 37:521-526, April, 1971.

"Outpatient termination of pregnancy," by S. C. Lewis, et al. BR MED J 4:606-610, December 4, 1971.

"President on abortion: executive order to military hospitals," NEWSWEEK 77:129+, April 19, 1971.

"Prevention of abortion in hospital personnel," by M. Isokoski, et al. SAIRAANHOITAJA 47:486-488, June 10, 1971.

"Problems diminish as New York City's hospitals perform 165,000 legal abortions in the first year," MOD HOSP 117:46, August, 1971.

"Procedures for abortions at The New York Lying-In Hospital," by R. E. Kaye. CLIN OBSTET GYNECOL 14:153-165, March, 1971; also in MOD TREAT 8:101-113, February, 1971.

"Surveillance of abortions in hospitals in the United States, 1970," by J. B. Kahn, et al. HSMHA HEALTH REP 86:423-430, May, 1971.

"Therapeutic abortions at University Hospitals, 1951-1969, with emphasis on current trends," by D. W. Wetrich, et al. J IOWA MED SOC 60:691-696, October, 1970.

"A review of therapeutic abortions at a southern university hospital," by G. L. Fields, et al. WOMAN PHYSICIAN 26:414-416, August, 1971.

"Vacuum aspiration, using pericervical block, for legal abortion as an outpatient procedure up to the 12th week of pregnancy," by B. M. Berić, et al. LANCET 2:619-621, September 18, 1971.

"Voluntary abortion in a municipal hospital," by D. P. Swartz, et al. INT SURG 56:166-171, September, 1971.

IMMIGRATION AND EMIGRATION
see also: Demography
Population

"Abortion and immigration," by D. C. Wallace. MED J AUST 1:659-660, March 20, 1971.

"Abortion and immigration," by V. H. Wallace. MED J AUST 1:404-405, February 13, 1971.

INDUCED ABORTION
see also: Techniques of Abortion

"Analysis of complications after legal interruption of pregnancy in Poland," by E. Chroscielewski. MED LEG DOMM CORPOR 3: 16-17, January-March, 1970.

"Artificial abortion," by S. Tojo, et al. SHUJUTSU 25:58-65, January, 1971.

"Artificial abortion and immunization with antigens A or B in women with blood group O," by M. Jakubowska, et al. POL TYG LEK 25:1263-1264, August 17, 1970.

"Artificial abortion in women with heart defects," by Z. Piechowiak, et al. GINEKOL POL 42:371-375, 1971.

"Birth control and induced abortion," by E. A. Bendek. REV COLOMB

OBSTET GINECOL 21:579-586, November-December, 1970.

"Blood alkaline phosphatase activity before and after interruption of pregnancy," by H. Skalba, et al. WIAD LEK 24:1503-1506, August 15, 1971.

"Bougie-induced abortion at mid-pregnancy and placental function: histological and histochemical study of the placenta," by Y. Manabe, et al. ENDOKRINOLOGIE 57:389-394, 1971.

"Case of amniotic fluid embolism and secondary afibrinogenemia in artificial abortion," by V. M. Shikhatova. AKUSH GINEKOL 45: 68, March, 1969.

"Case of severe lesion of the urinary bladder in the course of induced abortion," by W. Maternik, et al. POL PRZEGL CHIR 43:1035-1038, June, 1971.

"Causes and sequelae of abortion," by K. I. Zhuravleva, et al. ZDRAVOOKHR ROSS FED 15:22-25, February, 1971.

"Changes in uterine volume during hypertonic saline induced abortions," by A. Kivikoski, et al. ACTA OBSTET GYNECOL SCAND 9:Suppl:45, 1971.

"Chorionic villi and syncytial sprouts in spontaneous and induced abortions," by T. Fujikura, et al. AM J OBSTET GYNECOL 110: 547-455, June 15, 1971.

"Clinical experiences with pregnancy interruption with a vacuum extractor," by C. Flämig, et al. ZENTRALBL GYNAEKOL 91:1567-1570, November 29, 1969.

"Combined use of the aspiration method and abortion forceps in induced abortion between the 13th and 18th week of pregnancy," by A. Atanasov, et al. AKUSH GINEKOL (Sofiia) 9:223-228, 1970.

"Complications of amnioinfusion with hypertonic saline for midtrimester abortion," by R. C. Goodlin. AM J OBSTET GYNECOL 110:885-886, July 15, 1971.

"Consequences of the legalization of induced abortion in Eastern

Europe," by A. Klinger. THER UMSCH 27:681-692, October, 1970.

"Critical study of single-time and double-time methods of artificial pregnancy interruptions," by W. Weise, et al. ZENTRALBL GYNAEKOL 92:841-848, June 27, 1970.

"Decidual-cell necrosis after injection of hypertonic saline for therapeutic abortion," by B. Gustavil, et al. LANCET 2:826, October 9, 1971.

"Dermatological aspects of pregnancy interruption," by G. W. Korting. MED WELT 43:1685-1691, October 22, 1971.

"The dynamics of the Danilin reaction in the artificial interruption of pregnancy," by R. A. Podgurskaia, et al. AKUSH GINEKOL 47:71-73, February, 1971.

"Early complications from artificial abortion," by J. Jurukovski, et al. GOD ZB MED FAK SKOPJE 16:503-507, 1970.

"Effect of criminal and induced abortion on the morbidity and mortality of women," by I. Kiene. Z GESAMTE HYG 16:274-276, April, 1970.

"The effect of induced abortion on fetomaternal transfusion," by I. Cseh, et al. ORV HETIL 112:2763-2764, November 14, 1971.

"Electrocardiographic abnormalities in the course of induced abortions," by J. Horeau, et al. SEM HOP PARIS 47:2034-2039, July 10, 1971.

"Electrolyte changes and serious complications after hypertonic saline instillation," by R. L. Berkowitz. CLIN OBSTET GYNECOL 14: 166-178, March, 1971.

"Electrolyte dynamics in hypertonic saline-induced abortions," by F. D. Frigoletto, et al. OBSTET GYNECOL 38:647-652, November, 1971.

"Estimates of induced abortion in urban North Carolina," by J. R. Abernathy, et al. DEMOGRAPHY 7:19-29, February, 1970.

"Etiologic incidence of rickettsial and coxsackie infection in pregnancy interruptions: serologic study," by J. Y. Gillet, et al.

BULL FED SOC GYNECOL OBSTET LANG FR 21:213-216, April-May, 1969.

"Examination and evaluation of 141 cases with uterine perforation," by S. Sugiyama, et al. SANFUJINKA JISSAI 20:545-551, May, 1971.

"Experience and complications with the use of hypertonic intra-amniotic saline solution," by H. Berk, et al. SURG GYNECOL OBSTET 133:955-958, December, 1971.

"Extra-amniotic instillation of Rivanol and catheterization of the uterus in late legal abortion," by C. A. Ingemanson. LAKARTID-NINGEN 68:2729-2731, June 2, 1971.

"Extraovular transcervical injection of rivanol for interruption of pregnancy," by S. A. Nabriski, et al. AM J OBSTET GYNECOL 110: 54-56, May 1, 1971.

"Failure in interruption of pregnancy and its management," SANFU-JINKA JISSAI 20:610, May, 1971.

"Family group therapy for children with self-induced seizures," by S. S. Libo, et al. AM J ORTHOPSYCHIATRY 41:506-509, April, 1971.

"Hormonal and placental changes after intra-amniotic injection of hypertonic saline," by R. L. Berkowitz, et al. CLIN OBSTET GYNECOL 14:179-191, March, 1971.

"Hypertonic solutions to induce abortion," by I. L. Craft, et al. BR MED J 2:49, April 3, 1971.

"Immediate and remote complications of repeated induced abortion," by B. Kh. Aronov. PEDIATR AKUSH GINEKOL 4:53-55, July-August, 1970.

"Incidence of uterine perforations in criminal abortions," by E. Rosenzweig, et al. RAD MED FAK ZAGREBU 18:221-224, 1970.

"Induced abortion," MED LETT DRUGS THER 12:98-100, November 27, 1970.

"Induced abortion," by A. W. Mante. TIJDSCHR ZIEKENVERPL 24:248-253, March 16, 1971.

"Induced abortion," by A. Sikkel. NED TIJDSCHR GENEESKD 115: 1119-1120, June 26, 1971.

"Induced abortion and its medico-legal aspects," by D. G. Quintero. REV OBSTET GINECOL VENEZ 30:517-523, 1970.

"Induced abortion and its trends in Yugoslavia," by B. M. Berich. AKUSH GINEKOL 46:67-68, November, 1970.

"Induced abortion--contraception," by O. Koller. TIDSSKR NOR LAEGEFOREN 91:629-632, March 30, 1971.

"Induced abortion for psychiatric indication," by S. Meyerowitz, et al. AM J PSYCHIATRY 127:1153-1160, March, 1971.

"Induced abortion in New York City. A report of six separate studies," by R. E. Hall. AM J OBSTET GYNECOL 110:601-611, July 1, 1971.

"Induction of abortion by the intravenous administration of prostaglandin F 2. A critical evaluation," by N .Wiqvist, et al. ACTA OBSTET GYNECOL SCAND 50:381-389, 1971.

"Induction of abortion by prostaglandins E (PGE1 and PGE2)," by M. P. Embery. J REPROD MED 6:256-259, June, 1971.

"The induction of abortion by prostaglandin F 2," by K. Kinoshita, et al. AM J OBSTET GYNECOL 111:855-857, November, 1971.

"Induction of abortion in the rabbit by hydrocortisonacetate," by G. Wagner. ACTA ENDOCRINOL 155:Suppl:89, 1971.

"Induction of lactogenesis and abortion by prostaglandin F2-alpha in pregnant rats," by R. P. Deis. NATURE (London) 229:568, February 19, 1971.

"Induction of midtrimester abortion by intra-amniotic administration of prostaglandin F2. A preliminary report," by M. Bygdeman, et al. ACTA PHYSIOL SCAND 82:415-416, July, 1971.

"Induction of **mid-trimester** therapeutic abortion by intra-amniotic urea and intravenous oxytocin," by I. Craft, et al. LANCET 2:1058-1060, November 13, 1971.

"Induction of therapeutic abortion by intra-amniotic injection of urea," by J. O. Greenhalf, et al. BR MED J 1:28-29, January 2, 1971.

"Induction of therapeutic abortion with urea," by J. O. Greenhalf. BR MED J 2:107, April 10, 1971.

"Induction of therapeutic abortion with urea," by M. Pugh, et al. BR MED J 1:345, February 6, 1971.

"Interruption of pregnancy by the abdominal route," by M. Blazek, et al. CESK GYNEKOL 36:342-343, July, 1971.

"Interruption of pregnancy by various steroids," by H. Selye, et al. FERTIL STERIL 22:735-740, November, 1971.

"Interruption of pregnancy from the legal viewpoint," by W. Becker. THER GGW 110:1362-1376, September, 1971.

"Intra-amnial introduction of hypertonic solutions--a method for interruption of pregnancy," by I. Atanasov, et al. AKUSH GINEKOL (Sofiia) 10:155-158, 1971.

"Intrauterine injection of hypertonic solutions," by L. P. Bengtsson. LAKARTIDNINGEN 68:2721-2722, June 2, 1971.

"Intrauterine injection of 20 per cent saline for inducing abortion," by M. C. Cheng, et al. SINGAPORE MED J 12:259-263, October, 1971.

"Legal interruption of pregnancy," GYNECOL OBSTET 70:127-132, January-February, 1971.

"Legal possibilities of pregnancy interruption for eugenic or fetal indications," by D. Krauss. MUNCH MED WOCHENSCHR 113:1505-1512, November 5, 1971.

"Legal reforms on pregnancy interruption," by A. Eser. MED WELT 17:721-729, April 24, 1971.

"Life our greatest asset? Moralistic and theologic discussion of pregnancy interruption," by A. Ziegler. WIEN MED WOCHENSCHR 121:Suppl:2:9-13, November 20, 1971.

"Menstrual disturbances after interruption," by D. Andreev. FOLIA MED 12:263-269, 1970.

"Mid-trimester abortion by extra-ovular catheter stimulation of the uterus," by W. H. Godsick. J REPROD MED 7:281, December, 1971.

"Midtrimester abortion: clinical experience with amniocentesis and hypertonic instillation in 400 patients," by J. M. Mackenzie, et al. CLIN OBSTET GYNECOL 14:107-123, March, 1971.

"Neurovegetative reactivity in women during interruption of unwanted pregnancy in the 2nd trimester by intra-amniotic instillation of saline solution," by B. Kiutukchiev, et al. AKUSH GINEKOL (Sofiia) 8:482-485, 1969.

"Nurses opinion on induced abortion," by C. P. Sporken. TIJDSCHR ZIEKENVERPL 24:242-247, March 16, 1971.

"Outpatient intra-amniotic injection of hypertonic saline," by T. D. Kerenyi. CLIN OBSTET GYNECOL 14:124-140, March, 1971.

"Outpatient saline abortion," by H. Schulman, et al. OBSTET GYNE-COL 37:521-526, April, 1971.

"Oxytocin administration in abortions induced with hypertonic saline," by J. D. Schulman, et al. LANCET 2:606-607, September 11, 1971.

"Pathologic findings after hypertonic saline instillation i n midtri-mester abortion," by A. Blaustein, et al. CLIN OBSTET GYNECOL 14:192-203, March, 1971.

"PGE compounds for induction of labour and abortion," by M. Embrey. ANN NY ACAD SCI 180:518-523, April 30, 1971.

"Plasma progesterone during abortion induced by intra-amniotic hyper-tonic saline," by T. H. Holmdahl, et al. ACTA OBSTET GYNECOL SCAND 9:Suppl:48, 1971.

"Plasma progesterone in pregnancy interrupted by the intrauterine injection of hypertonic saline," by T. H. Holmdahl, et al. ACTA ENDOCRINOL 66:82-88, January, 1971.

"Pregnancy interruption and its influence on the hormonal activity of the thyroid," by W. Hartwig, et al. REV FR ENDOCRINOL CLIN 12:27-32, January-February, 1971.

"Pregnancy interruption during toxoplasmosis," by P. Hengst. DTSCH GESUNDHEITSW 26:1611-1614, August 19, 1971.

"Pregnancy interruption from the infant health viewpoint," by G. Krebs. ARCH GYNAEKOL 211:361, June 4, 1971.

"Prevention of uterine injury during induced abortion," by S. Sugiyama. SANFUJINKA JISSAI 20:494-495, April, 1971.

"Problems of termination of pregnancy in European socialistic countries," by J. Koubek. CESK ZDRAV 19:413-419, October, 1971.

"Psychiatric indications for the termination of pregnancy," MED J AUST 1:171, January 16, 1971.

"Psychiatric indications for the termination of pregnancy," by N. Destro. MED J AUST 1:350-351, February 6, 1971.

"Psychiatric indications for the termination of pregnancy," by S. Gold. MED J AUST 1:499-500, February 27, 1971.

"Psychiatric indications for the termination of pregnancy," by B. D. McKie, et al. MED J AUST 1:771-773, April 3, 1971.

"Psychiatric indications for the termination of pregnancy," by J. Simpson. MED J AUST 1:449-450, February 20, 1971.

"Psychiatric indications for the termination of pregnancy," by D. Vann. MED J AUST 1:404, February 13, 1971.

"Retinal detachment and interruption of pregnancy," by C. Legerlotz. KLIN MONATSBL AUGENHEILKD 159:827-832, December, 1971.

"Role of induced abortion in rhesus immunization," by J. T. Queenan, et al. LANCET 1:815-817, April 24, 1971.

"Role of Rho (D) immune globulin in induced abortions," by J. T. Queenan. CLIN OBSTET GYNECOL 14:235-244, March, 1971.

"Saline abortion," by L. R. Cronenwett, et al. AMER J NURS 71:1754-1757, September, 1971.

"Saline prep induces abortion," AM DRUGGIST 164:83, July 12, 1971.

"Serologic pregnancy tests as a prevention against complications following interruption of pregnancy," by A. Dzioba, et al. WIAD LEK 24:113-115, January 15, 1971.

"Serum lactic acid level in women before and after interruption of pregnancy," by H. Skalba, et al. WIAD LEK 24:109-112, January 15, 1971.

"Serum potassium level before and after termination of pregnancy," by B. Batko, et al. WIAD LEK 24:645-648, April 1, 1971.

"The significance of fetal death in the mechanism of abortion induced by intra-amniotic injection of hypertonic salt solution," by L. Kovács, et al. ORV HETIL 112:852-854, April 11, 1971.

"Social aspects of abortion counseling for patients undergoing elective abortion," by E. D. Smith, et al. CLIN OBSTET GYNECOL 14:204-214, March, 1971.

"Spontaneous and induced abortion," WHO CHRON 25.104-111, March, 1971.

"Statistical analysis of applicants and of the induced abortion work-up. Grady Memorial Hospital--January-December, 1970," by L. D. Baker, et al. J MED ASSOC GA 60:392-396, December, 1971.

"Studies of the abortive mechanism of intrauterine injection of hypertonic saline," by B. Gustavii. ACTA OBSTET GYNECOL SCAND 9:Suppl:43, 1971.

"Study on induced abortion," BULL INFIRM CATHOL CAN 38:141-146, July-September, 1971.

"Summarizing paper of the study team 'Pregnancy Interruption'," WIEN MED WOCHENSCHR 121:Suppl:2:14-20, November 20, 1971.

"Survey on induced abortion and use of contraceptives in Bogota. Method of approach," by S. Gómez, et al. REV COLOMB OBSTET GINECOL 21:427-439, July-August, 1970.

"Symptomatology of detergent-poisoning in 'Pril'-induced abortion," by C. Tschakaloff. WIEN KLIN WOCHENSCHR 81:305-307, April 25, 1969.

"Termination of pregnancy by the intrauterine insertion of Utus paste," by S. V. Sood. BR MED J 2:315-317, May 8, 1971.

"Termination of pregnancy from the surgical viewpoint," by E. F. Drews, et al. MED KLIN 66:1-8, January 1, 1971.

"Termination of pregnancy in mink by repeated injections during the period preceding implantation," by J. C. Daniel, Jr. J ANIM SCI 33:659-661, September, 1971.

"Termination of pregnancy refused," by J. M. Beazley, et al. LANCET 1:1059-1061, May 22, 1971.

"Termination of an unwanted pregnancy observed from a medical and socioeconomic aspect," by K. Kurčiev, et al. GOD ZB MED FAK SKOPJE 16:437-440, 1970.

"Transvaginal treatment of uterine perforation," by A. Tsuji. SANFU-JINKA JISSAI 20:519-528, May, 1971.

"The urinary excretion of chorionic gonadotrophins after induced abortion," by M. Sloth, et al. ACTA OBSTET GYNECOL SCAND 50: 227-228, 1971.

"Use of prostaglandins for induction of abortion and labor," by A. Gillespie. ANN NY ACAD SCI 180:524-527, April 30, 1971.

"Use of transcycline in fever states following induced abortion," by J. A. Cacault. BULL FED SOC GYNECOL OBSTET LANG FR 21:116-124, April-May, 1969.

"The use of an 'unnatural' prostaglandin in the termination of pregnancy," by A. Gillespie, et al. J OBSTET GYNAECOL BR COMMONW 78:301-304, April, 1971.

INDUCED ABORTION

"Uselessness of estrogens in maturation of the cervix and induction of labor," by O. Agüero, et al. GINECOL OBSTET MEX 30:21-29, July, 1971.

"Uterine perforation in artificial abortions," by A. Lazarov, et al. GOD ZB MED FAK SKOPJE 16:429-435, 1970.

INFECTION:
see: Complications

ISOXYSUPRINE
"On the use of isoxysuprine in threatened abortion," by A. Julitta, et al. MINERVA GINECOL 21:867-868, July 15, 1969.

IUCD
see: Contraception

LAW ENFORCEMENT
see: Laws and Legislation

LAWS AND LEGISLATION
"The Abortion Act after three years," by M. Simms. POLITICAL QUARTERLY 42:269-286, July-September, 1971.

"The Abortion Act, 1969--a review of the first year's experience," by S. B. Kwa, et al. SINGAPORE MED J 12:250-255, October, 1971.

"The Abortion Act 1967. (b). The social aspects," by N. M. Cogan. R SOC HEALTH J 90:295-298, November-December, 1970.

"The Abortion Act 1967. (c). Implications for the family," by J. Kemp. R SOC HEALTH J 90:299-301 passim, November-December, 1970.

"The Abortion Act: a reply," by M. Simms. CRIMINAL LAW R 86-88, February, 1971.

"The Abortion Act: what has changed?" by J. M. Finnis. CRIMINAL LAW R 3-12, January, 1971.

"Abortion: allegations, actions, and ad interim," by D. S. Wert. PENN MED 74:59-62, May, 1971.

"Abortion and the courts," by B. Roberts, et al. ENVIRONMENTAL LAW 1:225-237, Spring, 1971.

"Abortion and the law," CHRIST NURSE 238:9, December, 1971.

"Abortion and the law," TABLET 225:218-219, March 6, 1971.

"Abortion and the law," by B. A. Brody. J PHILOS 68:357-369, June 17, 1971.

"Abortion and the law," by O. Dijkstra. CLERGY MONTHLY 409-422; 478-485, 1971.

"Abortion and the law," by O. Dijkstra. SOCIAL ACTION 324-340, 1971.

"Abortion and the law. (interviews)," by R. Lucas, et al. AMER MED NEWS 14:10+, April 19, 1971.

"Abortion and public policy: what are the issues?" by E. C. Moore. NY L F 17:411, 1971.

"Abortion and the reverence for life," by P. W. Rahmeier. CHR CENT 88:556-560, May 5, 1971; Reply by R. H. Hamill. 88:957-958, August 11, 1971.

"Abortion battle," NEWSWEEK 77:110, May 3, 1971.

"Abortion: the burden of proof has been reversed," by L. Myers. J AMER MED ASS 217:215, July 12, 1971.

"Abortion: Canada Medical Association prepares Members of Parliament for anticipated Commons debate with reminder of current policy," CAN MED ASS J 105:522-523, September 4, 1971.

"Abortion committee 1965: woman's right to abortion as considerate and early as possible," by G. Bergström, et al. LAKARTIDNINGEN 68:4137-4150, September 8, 1971.

"Abortion--constitutional law--a law prohibiting all abortions except those performed 'for the purpose of saving the life of the mother,' which does not augment a compelling state interest, unconstitutionally infringes on the mother's ninth amendment right to choose whether to bear children," TEX L REV 49:537, March, 1971.

"The abortion controversy," by E. B. Smith. J NATL MED ASSOC 62:379, September, 1970.

"The abortion decision," by D. W. Millard. BRITISH J OF SOCIAL WORK 1:131-148, Summer, 1971.

"Abortion: an environmental convenience or a constitutional right?" by M. J. Sikora, Jr. ENVIRONMENTAL AFFAIRS 1:469-527, November, 1971.

"Abortion games," by D. Baird. LANCET 2:1145, November 20, 1971.

"Abortion games," by I. M. Ingram. LANCET 2:1197, November 27, 1971.

"Abortion games: an inquiry into the working of the act," by I. M. Ingram. LANCET 2:969-970, October 30, 1971.

"Abortion: high court showdown," MED WORLD NEWS 12:5-6, April 9, 1971.

"Abortion: how it's working," NEWSWEEK 78:50-52, July 19, 1971.

"Abortion in Hawaii: the first 124 days," by R. G. Smith, et al. AM J PUBLIC HEALTH 61:530-542, March, 1971.

"Abortion in New York City. Prelininary experience with a permissive abortion statute," by J. J. Rovinsky. OBSTET GYNECOL 38:333-342, September, 1971.

"Abortion in New York City: the first nine months," by J. Pakter, et al. FAM PLANN PERSPECT 3:5-12, July, 1971.

"Abortion in New York State since July 1970," by H. S. Ingraham, et al. MOD TREAT 8:7-26, February, 1971.

"Abortion in the north-east of Scotland," by I. MacGillivray. J BIOSOC SCI 3:89-92, January, 1971.

"Abortion in SR Macedonia," by A. Lazarob, et al. GOD ZB MED FAK SKOPJE 16:413-428, 1970.

"Abortion in U.S.A.," by H. C. McLaren. LANCET 2:713, September 25, ber 25, 1971.

"Abortion issue," by D. Kucharsky. CHR TODAY 15:36, April 23, 1971.

"Abortion law in the supreme court," by W. J. Curran. N ENGL J MED 285:30-31, July, 1971.

"Abortion law reform," by F. Rosner. JAMA 216:147, April 15, 1971.

"Abortion law reform and repeal: legislative and judicial developments," by R. Roemer. AM J PUBLIC HEALTH 61:500-509, March, 1971.

"Abortion-law reform is inevitable, even in Texas," by J. C. Evans. CHR CENT 88:548-549, May 5, 1971; Discussion 88:1051-1052, September 8, 1971.

"Abortion law still binding," NAT CATH REP 7:16, February 19, 1971.

"Abortion laws," SOC JUST 63:374-376, February, 1971.

"Abortion laws: a constitutional right to abortion," NC L REV 49: 487, April, 1971.

"Abortion laws (in the various states): a constitutional right to abortion," by R. L. Welborn. N C LAW R 49:487-502, April, 1971.

"The abortion laws: A severe case of resistance to change," by R. A. Schwartz. OHIO STATE MED J 67:33-38, January, 1971.

"Abortion: laws which legislate morality should be eliminated," by J. A. Merrill. J OKLA STATE MED ASS 64:295-296, July, 1971.

"Abortion: the legal ramifications in Illinois," by F. M. Pfiefer. ILL MED J 139:273, March, 1971.

"Abortion legislation and right to life," by H. Medeiros. SOC JUST 64:84-86, June, 1971; also in OR 149,5:7, February 4, 1971.

"Abortion legislation in North Carolina," by A. Mandetta. TAR HEEL

NURSE 33:8-11, March, 1971.

"Abortion legislation: the Romanian experience," by H. P. Davie, et al. STUDIES IN FAMILY PLANNING 2:205-210, October, 1971.

"Abortion: litigative and legislative processes," by R. Lucas, et al. HUMAN RIGHTS 1:23-53, July, 1971.

"Abortion-on-demand a boon to moonlighting doctors," by M. J. Connor. MED TIMES 99:155 passim, October, 1971.

"Abortion on request: it it really 'liberal'?" by W. K. Kimble. TEX SO INTRA L REV 1:173, 1971.

"Abortion or no abortion--what decides?" by C. McCance, et al. J BIOSOC SCI 3:116-120, January, 1971.

"Abortion: parameters for decision," by R. Gerber IPQ 11:561-584, December, 1971.

"The abortion program in Japan," by T. Wagatsuma. J REHABIL 7: 16-19, July, 1971.

"Abortion referral services: New York State," by L. S. Goldsmith. PHYSICIANS MANAGE 11:36, September, 1971.

"Abortion referral services--profiteers under fire," by T. W. Welch. NEW PHYSICIAN 20:571-575, September, 1971.

"Abortion reform," by R. D. Lamm, et al. YALE REVIEW OF LAW AND SOCIAL ACTION 1:5-63, Spring, 1971.

"Abortion reform and the courts; Florida and Michigan Supreme court decisions," AMERICA 125:52, August 7, 1971.

"Abortion repeal in Hawaii: an unexpected crisis in patient care," by J. F. McDermott, Jr., et al. AM J ORTHOPSYCHIATRY 41:620-626, July, 1971.

"Abortion requests at District of Columbia General Hospital," HSMHA (HEALTH SERV MENT HEALTH ADMIN) HEALTH REP 86:698, August, 1971.

"Abortion revolution: inconsistent change," J MISS STATE MED

ASS 12:129-130, March, 1971.

"Abortion: rhetoric and reality," CHR CENT 88:871, July 21, 1971; Discussion 88:1052-1053, September 8, 1971.

"Abortion--the S.A. scene," by J. H. Hagger. AUSTRALAS NURSES J 5:17, October, 1971.

"Abortion standards, New York City Board of Health," by M. C. McLaughlin. CLIN OBSTET GYNECOL 14:25-35, March, 1971; also in MOD TREAT 8:27-37, February, 1971.

"Abortion: a survey of current legislation," WHO (WORLD HEALTH ORGAN) CHRON 25:328-333, July, 1971.

"Abortion tangle in New York," by A. Bosco. MARRIAGE 53:28-32+, July, 1971.

"Abortion techniques and services: a review and critique," by D. Harting, et al. AM J PUBLIC HEALTH 61:2085-2105, October, 1971.

"Abortion: two opposing legal philosophies," by R. J. Gerber. AM J JURIS 15:1, 1970.

"Abortion U.S.A.--1971," by A. F. Guttmacher. RESIDENT STAFF PHYSICIAN 17:114+, September, 1971.

"Abortion: woman's right and legal problem," by H. Moody. CHRISTIANITY AND CRISIS 31:27-32, March 8, 1971.

"Abortions and the law," by C. C. Copenhaver. MED LEG BULL 219:1-7, July, 1971.

"Abortions for poor and nonwhite women: a denial of equal protection," by A. Charles, et al. HASTINGS L J 23:147, November, 1971.

"Abortions performed in New York State from July 1-October 31, 1970: a preliminary report," HOSP FORUM 39:10-14, March, 1971.

"The act 4 years after (operation of the Abortion act, 1967; Great Britain)," by D. Steel. MENTAL HEALTH 6-9, Summer, 1971.

"Ambivalence on abortion," TIME 97:40, May 3, 1971.

LAWS AND LEGISLATION

"American Psychiatric Association joins others in high court abortion
case," PSYCHIAT NEWS 6:1+, September 15, 1971.

"Anti-abortion campaign," TIME 97:70+, March 29, 1971.

"Attitudes and practices of North Carolina obstetricians: the impact
of the North Carolina Abortion Act of 1967," by W. B. Walker, et
al. SOUTH MED J 64:441-445, April, 1971.

"Attitudes toward Michigan's abortion law and experience of Michigan
physicians with requests for abortion," by B. Serena, et al. MICH
MED 70:309-316, April, 1971.

"California's 1967 therapeutic abortion act: abridging a fundamental
right to abortion," PACIFIC L J 2:186, January, 1971.

"California's Therapeutic Abortion Act upheld and struck down,"
NEWSLETTER (SOC HOSP ATTORNEYS) 4:1-2, August, 1971.

"Cardinal Cooke condemns State's abortion law," OR 53(144)11,
December 31, 1970.

"Catholics and liberalized abortion laws," by N. J. Rigali. CATH
WORLD 213:283-285, September, 1971; Discussion 214:101-102,
December, 1971.

"Cause and effect; decline in birthrate with new abortion law," SCI
AM 225:42, October, 1971.

"Change in attitudes about illegal abortion," by G. Dotzauer. BEITR
GERICHTL MED 27:45-60, 1970.

"Christian values in the legislative process in Britain in the sixties,"
by F. Dowrick. AMER J JURIS 16:156-183, 1971.

"Civil liability for abortion," by A. R. Holder. J AMER MED ASS
215:355-356, January 11, 1971.

"Civil rights in the United States and abortion," by D. Wuerl. OR
2(146)9-10, January 14, 1971.

"The concept of necessity in the laws and deontology," by C.
Palenzona. MINERVA GINECOL 23:917-920, November 15, 1971.

"Concept of relationship between law and deontology," by C. Palenzona. MINERVA MED 40:Suppl:19+, May, 1971.

"Concerning the journal's abortion issue," by V. J. Freda. AM J
PUBLIC HEALTH 61:1284-1285, July, 1971.

"Consequences of the legalization of induced abortion in Eastern
Europe," by A. Klinger. THER UMSCH 27:681-692, October, 1970.

"Consequences of a liberalization of the abortion laws," by Gunnar,
et al. LAKARTIDNINGEN 68:2714-2715, June 2, 1971.

"Constitutional law--abortion--statutory limitation on reasons for abortion is violation of fundamental right to privacy," MERCER L REV
22:461, Winter, 1971.

"Constitutional law--abortions: abortion as a ninth amendment right,"
WASH L REV 46:565, May, 1971.

"Constitutional law--due process and abortion," NEB L REV 51:340,
Winter, 1971.

"Constitutional law--mother's right to abort is greater than unquickened
child's right to live," J URBAN L 48:969, June, 1971.

"Contrasts in world abortion laws," by P. Brookes. DAILY TELE-
GRAPH 12, May 18, 1971.

"Court strikes antiabortion law in Illinois," by J. DeMuth. NAT CATH
REP 7:16, February 12, 1971.

"Criminal abortion. A clinical case and medicolegal aspects," by F.
De Gennaro. MINERVA GINECOL 21:1002-1005, August 15, 1969.

"Criminal law: a call for statutory abortion law reform in Oklahoma,"
OKLA L REV 24:243, May, 1971.

"Criminal law--the Iowa abortion statute is not unconstitutionally
vague and does not deny equal protection," DRAKE L REV 20:666,
June, 1971.

"Criminal liability for abortion," by A. R. Holder. J AMER MED ASS
215:175-176, January 4, 1971.

"D.C. abortion law is upheld," NAT CATH REP 7:3-4, April 30, 1971.

"Debate at the Abortion Meeting," by H. Bengtsson. LAKARTIDNIN-GEN 68:5863-5871, December 8, 1971.

"Debate: should abortion be available on request?" by B. Nathanson. SEXUAL BEHAVIOR 1,7:64-81, October, 1971.

"Declaration du Secretariat de l'episcopat Francais sur l'avortement; July 2, 1970," DOC CATH 67:729, August 2-16, 1970.

"The Declaration of Oslo," S AFR MED J 44:1281, November 14, 1970.

"A defense of abortion," by J. J. Thomson. PHIL PUB AFFAIRS 1: 47-66, Fall, 1971.

"The demand for abortion in an urban Malaysian population," by O. S. Ooi. MED J MALAYA 25:175-181, March, 1971.

"The demographic effects of birth control and legal abortion," by H. Sjövall. LAKARTIDNINGEN 67:5261-5272, November 4, 1970.

"Divorce et avortement; interview," by A. Renard. DOC CATH 67: 1088-1089, December 6, 1970.

"Dr. Daly says law prohibiting abortion should be repealed," NAT CATH REP 7:8, April 2, 1971.

"Effects of the abortion law, 1967, on a gynaecological unit," by E. E. Rawlings, et al. LANCET 2:1249-1251, December 4, 1971.

"The effects of legalized abortion in England," by J. V. O'Sullivan. HOSP PROGR 52:75-78, June, 1971.

"Elective abortions available under New York Medicaid," NEWS-LETTER (SOC HOSP ATTORNEYS) 4:1, July, 1971.

"Eugenic prophyiaxis in the light of international legislation," by R. D'Andrea. ANN SANITA PUBBLICA 32:25-49, January-February, 1971.

"Family planning and present law situation in Austria," by H. Husslein. WIEN KLIN WOCHENSCHR 83:141-144, March 5, 1971.

"Faut-il légaliser l'avortement?" by R. Troisfontaines. NRT 93:489-512, May, 1971.

"Feticide: mens rea with partial immunity?" WASHBURN L J 10:403, Spring, 1971.

"Fetus as a legal entity - facing reality," SAN DIEGO L REV 8:126, 1971.

"Free abortions, now! proposed reforms," NEWSWEEK 77:54+, April 19, 1971.

"Further comment on People v. Belous," CATHOLIC LAW 16:92, Winter, 1970.

"A general-practitioner survey of the Abortion Act 1967," by J. R. Eames, et al. PRACTITIONER 207:227-230, August, 1971.

"Geographic distribution of legal abortion in Bulgaria," by G. Stoimenov, et al. AKUSH GINEKOL (Sofiia) 10:112-116, 1971.

"Guide to abortion laws in the United States," by L. Lader. RED-BOOK 137:51-58, June, 1971.

"Guidelines for therapeutic abortion in Oregon: adopted September 26, 1971 by the Oregon Medical Association House of Delegates," NORTHWEST MED 70:854, December, 1970.

"Gynaecologist and patient alone should be allowed to determine legal abortions," by E. Sjövall. LAKARTIDNINGEN 68:4150-4151, September 8, 1971.

"Health legislation. Abortion: a survey of current legislation," WHO CHRON 25:328-333, July, 1971.

"High court abortion debate relaxed, decorous," AMER MED NEWS 14:9, December 20, 1971.

"High court hears abortion cases," by J. McLellan. NAT CATH REP 8:4, December 24, 1971.

"Illinois court holds abortion 'on demand' legal," HOSPITALS 45:29, February 16, 1971; Supreme Court temporarily stays ruling 17,

March 1, 1971.

"3. The impact of a liberalized abortion law on the medical schools," by M. L. Stone, et al. AM J OBSTET GYNECOL 111:728-735, November 1, 1971.

"The impact of liberalized abortion laws on family planning," by E. W. Overstreet. J REHABIL 7:20-21, July, 1971.

"In what measure should abortion be penalized," by P. DeBoeck. NURSING 43:15-21, July-August, 1971.

"The incidence of illegal abortion (Great Britain)," by W. H. James. POPULATION STUDIES 25:327-339, July, 1971.

"Induced abortion and its medico-legal aspects," by D. G. Quintero. REV OBSTET GINECOL VENEZ 30:517-523, 1970.

"Interruption of pregnancy from the legal viewpoint," by W. Becker. THER GGW 110:1362-1376, September, 1971.

"Is abortion on demand good medicine?" by E. G. Kilroy. OHIO STATE MED J 67:39-46, January, 1971.

"Japan's 22 year experience with a liberal abortion law," by Y. Hayasaka. LINACRE 38:33-44, February, 1971.

"Juridical and legal-political problems of birth regulation," by G. Kaiser. MED KLIN 63:1526-1530, September 20, 1968.

"The Kings County Abortion story," by L. A. Walton. CLIN OBSTET GYNECOL 14:149-152, March, 1971; also in MOD TREAT 8:97-100, February, 1971.

"Law and the unborn child: the legal and logical inconsistencies," NOTRE DAME LAW 46:349, Winter, 1971.

"Law on abortion as it may appear to the layman," by C. P. Harrison. CAN DOCTOR 37:82-83, June, 1971.

"Law professor named special guardian of unborn children in New York City," HOSPITALS 45:27, December 16, 1971.

"Legal abortion and mental health," by C. Thonet. REV CHIL OBSTET GINECOL 35:209-213, 1970.

"Legal abortion in Sweden: thirty years' experience," by J. O. Ottosson. J BIOSOC SCI 3:173-192, April, 1971.

"Legal abortion in the U.S.A. A prelinimary assessment," by M. Potts, et al. LANCET 2:651-653, September 18, 1971.

"Legal abortion mess; Women's medical group, New York," by A. Barry. MCCALLS 98:30+, January, 1971.

"Legal abortion: who, why and where," TIME 98:67-70, September 27, 1971.

"Legal abortions: Early medical complications. An interim report of the joint program for the study of abortion," by C. Tietze. FAMILY PLANN PERSPECT 3:6-14, October, 1971.

"Legal abortions in Canada," by L. E. Rozovsky. CAN HOSP 48: 39-41, February, 1971.

"Legal abortions in Finland," by P. A. Jarvinen. ANN CHIR GYNAECOL FENN 60:65-66, 1971.

"Legal abortions--a social problem," by E. Sjövall. LAKARTIDNINGEN 68:5279-5285, November 10, 1971.

"Legal abortions, socioeconomic status, and measured intelligence in the United States," by J. E. Cohen. SOC BIOL 18:55-63, March, 1971.

"Legal and illegal situtation in Switzerland," by H. Stamm. BIBL GYNAECOL 55:1-43, 1970.

"Legal authority of health departments to regulate abortion practice," by W. J. Curran. AMER J PUBLIC HEALTH 61:621-626, March, 1971.

"Legal interruption of pregnancy," GYNECOL OBSTET 70:127-132, January-February, 1971.

"Legal possibilities of pregnancy interruption for eugenic or fetal indications," by D. Krauss. MUNCH MED WOCHENSCHR 113: 1505-1512, November 5, 1971.

"Legal reforms on pregnancy interruption," by A. Eser. MED WEIT 17:721-729, April 24, 1971.

"Legal regulation of abortion in England (Abortion Act 1967)," by K. Händel. BEITR GERICHTL MED 27:72-75, 1970.

"Legal theory of value assessment and medical aspects of the need to protect the beginning of life," by J. Gerchow, et al. BEITR GERICHTL MED 27:61-71, 1970.

"Legal view of abortion," by C. A. Gravenor, Jr. CAN DOCTOR 37: 44+, March, 1971.

"Legalized abortion: the conscience clause and coercion," by D. Cavanagh. HOSP PROGR 52:86-90, August, 1971.

"Legalized abortion is not 'progress'," by A. Nowlan. ATLAN ADV 61:64-65, March, 1971.

"The legalizing of contraceptives and abortions," by E. Szabady. IMPACT OF SCIENCE ON SOCIETY 21,3:265-270, July-September, 1971.

"Liberal abortion policy upheld in California by the California Medical Association," AMER MED NEWS 14:6, March 29, 1971.

"A liberal law does not include 'abortion on request'," by R. Gillon. LAKARTIDNINGEN 68:3560-3563, August 4, 1971.

"Liberalizing abortion laws; teacher opinion poll. National education association, research division," TODAYS ED 60:5, May, 1971.

"Lineup on abortion: experts see Supreme Court closely divided," AMER MED NEWS 14:12-13, December 6, 1971.

"Live abortion to be investigated," NAT CATH REP 7:7, May 7, 1971.

"Logistic problems of legal abortion," by E. W. Overstreet. AM J PUBLIC HEALTH 61:496-499, March, 1971.

"The logistics of abortion services in the absence of restrictive criminal legislation in the United States," by C. W. Tyler, Jr., et al. AM J PUBLIC HEALTH 61:489-495, March, 1971.

"MDs, legislature act to curb New York abortion agencies," AMER MED NEWS 14:3, June 7, 1971.

"Marshall's ruling ripped," NAT CATH REP 7:14, February 26, 1971.

"Medical abortion in South Australia. The first 12 months under new legislation," by A. F. Connon. MED J AUST 2:608-614, September 18, 1971.

"A medical case for abortion liberalization," by M. L. Taymor. ARCH SURG 102:235, March, 1971.

"Medical-legal considerations of abortion in New York State under the new abortion law," by L. Holtzman. CLIN OBSTET GYNECOL 14:36-47, March, 1971; also in MOD TREAT 8:39-49, February, 1971.

"Medical pressures to tighten the Abortion Act," by N. Hagger. TIMES 14, June 17, 1971.

"Medical records aren't fishing grounds: court," MOD HOSP 116:68-70, March, 1971.

"Medicolegal opinion. Re: on demand abortions in public hospitals," by H. B. Alsobrook, Jr. J LA STATE MED SOC 123:29-30, January, 1971.

"Memorandum on The Medical Termination of Pregnancy Bill 1971; presented to Shrimati Indira Gandhi, Prime Minister of India, by Archbishop Angelo Fernandes," OR 39(183)4, September 30, 1971.

"Moonlighting medics: liberal abortion law proves to be a bonanza for New York (N.Y.) doctors," by M. J. Connor. WALL ST J 177:1+, June 1, 1971.

"More on rights," LANCET 1:791-792, April 17, 1971.

"The new abortion law and problems caused by it," by I. Kettunen. KATILOLEHTI 76:505-510, November, 1971.

"The new abortion laws and practical-vocational nursing education," J PRACT NURS 1:27 passim, January, 1971.

"New abortion laws: how are they working?" by T. Irwin. TODAYS HEALTH 48:20-23+, March, 1970.

"New liberal abortion laws, issues and problems," by H. Freilich. HOSP MANAGE 111:1+, May, 1971.

"New York abortion reform and conflicting municipal regulations: a question of home rule," BUFFALO L REV 20:524, Winter, 1971.

"New York abortion reform law: considerations, application and legal consequences--more than we bargained for?" ALBANY L REV 35: 644, 1971.

"New York State Department of Health; report on abortions," by H. Ingraham. SOC JUST 63:377-384, February, 1971.

"Nixon takes stand against abortion," NAT CATH REP 7:5, April 16, 1971.

"No new abortion laws, checks show," NAT CATH REP 7:5, September 10, 1971.

"Nurses' feelings a problem under new abortion law," AMER J NURS 71:350+, February, 1971.

"On legal abortion," by I. K. Furler. MED J AUST 1:489-496, February 27, 1971.

"An open letter on the abortion problem," SOC JUST 64:86-93, June, 1971.

"Opposition to eased abortions seen mounting," HOSP PROGRESS 52:24-25, February, 1971.

"Parental consent for abortion is appealed to Supreme Court," AMER MED NEWS 14:8, August 2, 1971.

"The Parliament requested overhaul in sterilization law," LAKARTID-NINGEN 67:5732, December 2, 1970.

"Phoenix of abortional freedom: is a penumbral or ninth-amendment right about to arise from the nineteenth-century legislative ashes of a fourteenth-century common-law liberty?" by C. C. Means, Jr. NY L F 17:335, 1971.

"Physician attitudes on abortion and the Kansas abortion law," by R. Bettis, et al. J KANS MED SOC 72:344-349, August, 1971.

"Pilot study of single women requesting a legal abortion," by J. F. Pearson. J BIOSOC SCI 3:417-448, October, 1971.

"Politics of social change: abortion reform. The role of health professionals in the legislative process," by M. A. Pond. AMER J PUBLIC HEALTH 61:904-909, May, 1971.

"The present seriousness of criminal abortion," by M. Monrozies. GYNECOL OBSTET 70:79-94, January-February, 1971.

"President Nixon issues statement," by R. Nixon. OR 18(162)5, May 6, 1971.

"President on abortion; executive order to military hospitals," NEWS-WEEK 77:129+, April 19, 1971.

"Presidential morality, abortion, and federal-state law," by W. J. Curran. AMER J PUBLIC HEALTH 61:1042-1043, May, 1971.

"Prevention of abortion and premature delivery," by K. Watanabe. SANFUJINKA JISSAI 20:428-433, April, 1971.

"Problems diminish as New York City's hospitals perform 165,000 legal abortions in the first year," MOD HOSP 117:46, August, 1971.

"Provinical associations veto Canadian Nurses' Association's abortion statement," CAN NURSE 67:7-8, August, 1971.

"Psychiatric experience of the Abortion Act (1967)," by N. A. Todd. BR J PSYCHIATRY 119:489-495, November, 1971.

"Recent abortion litigation," by M. F. McKernan, Jr. CATHOLIC LAWYER 17:1-10, Winter, 1971.

"Recent decisions on abortion laws," by A. R. Holder. J AMER MED ASS 216:933-934, May 3, 1971.

"Recommended standards for abortion services. Adopted by the Executive Board of the APHA at the 98th Annual Meeting in Houston, Texas, October 29, 1970," AM J PUBLIC HEALTH 61:396-398, February, 1971.

"Reform of the penal code," by C. Mayerhofer. WIEN MED WOCHEN-SCHR 121:Suppl:2:7-9, November 20, 1971.

"Religion, morality, and abortion: a constitutional appraisal," by T. C. Clark. LOYOLA U L REV 2:1, April, 1969.

"Right of equal access to abortions," IA L REV 56:1015, April, 1971.

"Right to abortion. What is the responsibility of society? Social psychiatric study of abortion applying women in the public health district of Umea," by K. Broström, et al. LAKARTIDNINGEN 68: 5133-5139, November 3, 1971.

"The role of the law of homicide in fetal destruction," IOWA LAW R 56:658-674, February, 1971.

"Report on the abortion capital of the country; New York city," by S. Edmiston. N Y TIMES MAG 10-11+, April 11, 1971.

"Roundtable: legal abortion," by A. F. Guttmacher, et al. MEDICAL ASPECTS OF HUMAN SEXUALITY 5,8:50-75, August, 1971.

"Roundup on abortion reform," AMERICA 125:134-135, September 11, 1971.

"The second year's experience with Colorado's abortion law," by W. Droegemueller, et al. AM J OBSTET GYNECOL 109:957-958, March 15, 1971.

"Secular case against abortion on demand," by R. Stith. COMMON-WEAL 95:151-154, November 12, 1971.

"Standards for changing practice in abortion," by L. Breslow. AM J PUBLIC HEALTH 61:215-217, February, 1971.

"Stormy aftermath of abortion reform," by C. Remsberg, et al. GOOD H 172:86-87+, February, 1971.

"Supreme court and abortion," AMERICA 124:443, May 1, 1971.

"Supreme Court of the United States: abortion rulings," NEWSLETTER (SOC HOSP ATTORNEYS) 4:various paging, May, 1971.

"Supreme Court upholds abortion law of the District of Columbia," NEWSLETTER (SOC HOSP ATTORNEYS) 4:3, June, 1971.

"Teacher opinion poll: liberalizing abortion law," TODAYS ED 60: 5, May, 1971.

"Testimony in favor of abortion reform hearings before the Michigan State House Committee on Social Services," by C. Raven. WOMAN PHYSICIAN 26:584-586, November, 1971.

"Texas abortion statutes: constitutional issues and the need for reform," BAYLOR L REV 23:605, Fall, 1971.

"Therapeutic abortion experience in North Carolina under the liberalized 1967 Law," by W. J. May. NC MED J 32:186-187, May, 1971.

"Thoughts on the legalization of abortion," by G. Malick. PA MED 74:39, March, 1971.

"Three years' experience of the Abortion Act," by A. W. Weir. MIDWIVES CHRON 85:232-234, July, 1971.

"Torts--unplanned parenthood and the benefit rule," WAKE FOREST L REV 8:159, December, 1971.

"The trump cards of the abortion lobby," by N. St. John-Stevas. TIMES 14, February 18, 1971.

"Two California courts issue conflicting opinions on the state's abortion law," HOSPITALS 45:107, August 16, 1971.

"The unborn child and the constitutional conception of life (United States)," IOWA LAW R 56:994-1014, April, 1971.

"Unborn child in Georgia law: abortion reconsidered," GA L REV 6:168, Fall, 1971.

"Understanding the abortion argument," by R. Wertheimer. PHIL PUB AFFAIRS 1:67-95, Fall, 1971.

"United States government policy on abortion," by G. Contis, et al. AMER J PUBLIC HEALTH 61:1038-1041, May, 1971.

"The vindication of Milan Vuitch," by M. Lawrence. TRIUMPH 6:8-11, July, 1971.

"Voting against motherhood (Abortion in Canada) review article," by R. Evans. CAN FORUM 51:9-11, June, 1971.

"Welcher Weg für die Reform des §218?" by F. G. von Westphalen. NEUE ORDNUNG 443-453, 1971.

"What you should know about New York abortions," by H. Eisenberg. HOSP PHYSICIAN 7:37+, February, 1971.

"When you refer abortion patients out of state," MED ECON 48:67+, August 16, 1971.

"Yano explains vote on abortion," by M. Hyer. NAT CATH REP 7:14-15, December 11, 1970.

MALE ATTITUDES
see: Sociology, Behavior and Abortion

MENSTRUATION
see: Complications
Induced Abortion

METHOTREXATE
"3. Methotrexate and concentration of chorionic gonadotropin," by L. Lajos, et al. ORV HETIL 112:2077-2080 passim, August 29, 1971.

METHOXYFLURANE
"Methoxyflurane in therapeutic abortion," by M. H. Lawrence. BR J CLIN PRACT 25:414-416, September, 1971.

MICROBIOLOGY
"Attempts to isolate H-1 virus from spontaneous human abortions: a negative report," by S. J. Newman, et al. TERATOLOGY 3:279-281, August, 1970.

"Biological properties of Escherichia coli isolated from pathological material," by M. S. Venugopal, et al. PATHOL MICROBIOL 37: 420-424, 1971.

"Clostridium welchii septicotoxemia. A review and report of 3 cases," by L. P. Smith, et al. AM J OBSTET GYNECOL 110:135-149, May 1, 1971.

"Content of microelements in blood and placental tissue in normal pregnancy and abortion," by P. I. Fogel. PEDIATR AKUSH GINE-KOL 2:33-37, 1971.

"Pathological structures of the placenta examined under the electron microscope. 1st observations of villi of aborted human ova," by R. Herbst, et al. GYNECOL OBSTET 70:369-376, August-October, 1971.

"Study of vaginal smears by luminescent microscopy in normal pregnancy and in threatened abortion," by O. S. Badiva. PEDIATR AKUSH GINEKOL 1:44-46, January-February, 1969.

"T-strains of mycoplasma in bronchopneumonic lungs of an aborted fetus," by N. Romano, et al. N ENGL J MED 285:950-952, October 21, 1971.

MISCARRIAGES
"Anesthesia, pregnancy, and miscarriage: a study of operating room nurses and anesthetists," by E. N. Cohen, et al. ANESTHESIOL-OGY 35:343-347, October, 1971.

"Miscarriages, premature birth and perinatal death of infants in employed and unemployed women," by N. Aresin, et al. ZENTRALBL GYNAEKOL 93:441-444, April 3, 1971.

"Treatment of threat of premature labor and miscarriage with Dilatol," by H. Neumann, et al. ZENTRALBL GYNAEKOL 93:849-859, June 19, 1971.

MISCARRIAGES

"What we do, and don't know about miscarriage," by S. Olds. TO-
DAYS HEALTH 49:42-45, February, 1971.

MORBIDITY
"Changing trends in mortality and morbidity from abortion in Singapore
(1964 to 1970)," by M. C. Cheng, et al. SINGAPORE MED J 12:
256-258, October, 1971.

"Effect of criminal and induced abortion on the morbidity and mortality
of women," by I. Kiene. Z GESAMTE HYG 16:274-276, April, 1970.

"Morbidity and mortality in the offspring of 300 consanguineous couples
in Florence," by U. Bigozzi, et al. ACTA GENET MED GEMELLOL
19:515-528, October, 1970.

"Morbidity and mortality of abortions," by H. Arthure. LANCET 2:
310-311, August 7, 1971.

"Mortality and morbidity of abortion," by P. Huntingford. LANCET 1:
1012-1013, May 15, 1971.

"Mortality and morbidity of legal abortion," by A. Czeizel, et al.
LANCET 2:209-210, July 24, 1971.

MORTALITY
see also: Complications
Sepsis
Septic Abortion and Septic Shock

"Abortion mortality statistics," by R. L. Burt. OBSTET GYNECOL
38:950-951, December, 1971.

"Abortions under the N.H.S.," by H. G. Arthure. BR MED J 4:617,
December 5, 1970.

"Abortions under the N.H.S.," by M. Simms. BR MED J 1:52, January 2, 1971.

"Avoidable factors in maternal deaths," by H. Arthure. MIDWIFE
HEALTH VISIT 7:381+, October, 1971.

"Changes of panorama in the abortion mortality," by O. Pribilla, et
al. BEITR GERICHTL MED 27:76-85, 1970.

"Changing trends in mortality and morbidity from abortion in Singapore (1964 to 1970)," by M. C. Cheng, et al. SINGAPORE MED J 12:256-258, October, 1971.

"Death from sickle-cell crisis after abortion," BR MED J 3:125, July 10, 1971.

"Effect of criminal and induced abortion on the morbidity and mortality of women," by I. Kiene. Z GESAMTE HYG 16:274-276, April, 1970.

"Morbidity and mortality in the offspring of 300 consanguineous couples in Florence," by U. Bigozzi, et al. ACTA GENET MED GEMELLOL 19:515-528, October, 1970.

"Morbidity and mortality of abortions," by H. Arthure. LANCET 2:310-311, August 7, 1971.

"Mortality and morbidity of abortion," by P. Huntingford. LANCET 1: 1012-1013, May 15, 1971.

"Mortality and morbidity of legal abortion," by A. Czeizel, et al. LANCET 2:209-210, July 24, 1971.

"Mortality of abortion," by M. D. Buckley-Sharp. LANCET 2:490-491, August 28, 1971.

"Mortality of abortion," by M. R. Henzl. LANCET 2:368, August 14, 1971.

"Mortality of abortion," by P. Kestelman. LANCET 2:607, September 11, 1971.

"Prenatal mortality and genetic wastage in man," by M. G. Kerr. J BIOSOC SCI 3:223-237, April, 1971.

"Therapeutic abortion in California. Effects of septic abortion and maternal mortality," by G. K. Stewart, et al. OBSTET GYNECOL 37:510-514, April, 1971.

MYCOPLASMA

"Role of mycoplasma infection in the genesis of spontaneous abortion," by M. A. Bashmakova, et al. VOPR OKHR MATERIN DET 16:67-70, February, 1971.

MYCOPLASMA

"T-strains of mycoplasma in bronchopneumonic lungs of an aborted fetus," by N. Romano, et al. N ENGL J MED 285:950-952, October 21, 1971.

NURSES AND ABORTION
"Abortion and one nurse's conscience," NURS TIMES 67:680-681, June 3, 1971.

"Anesthesia, pregnancy and miscarriage: a study of operating room nurses and anesthetists," by E. N. Cohen, et al. ANESTHESIOL-OGY 35:343-347, October, 1971.

"Canadian Nurses' Association board rescinds all statements on abortion," CAN NURSE 67:5, November, 1971.

"A guide for the Catholic nurse on abortion," IR NURS NEWS 5, Spring, 1971.

"How do nurses feel about euthanasia and abortion," by N. K. Brown, et al. AM J NURS 71:1413-1416, July, 1971.

"Massachusetts RN's do not have to help with abortions," HOSP MANAGE 112:17, August, 1971.

"The nurse and the abortion patient," by H. Virjo. SAIRAANHOITAJA 47:478-480, June 10, 1971.

"The nurse and placenta praevia and abruptio. Her function in protecting both mother and child," by G. Rosenheim, et al. BEDSIDE NURSE 3:31-32, December, 1970.

"Nurses and abortion," TIME 97:60, May 31, 1971.

"Nurses' feelings a problem under new abortion law," AMER J NURS 71:350+, February, 1971.

"Nurses opinion on induced abortions," by C. P. Sporken. TIJDSCHR ZIEKENVERPL 24:242-247, March 16, 1971.

"Nursing care in an abortion unit," by B. Yaloff, et al. CLIN OBSTET GYNECOL 14:67-80, March, 1971.

NURSES AND ABORTION

"Nursing care study: abortion--with complications," by D. Brett, et al.
NURS TIMES 67:1209-1210, September 30, 1971.

"Nursing interviews helpful at abortion clinic: New York," AMER J
NURSING 71:352-353, February, 1971.

"Provincial associations veto Canadian Nurses' Association's abortion statement," CAN NURSE 67:7-8, August, 1971.

"RNs react to abortion issue: Agree CNA should take stand," CANAD
NURSE 67:7+, February, 1971.

"Therapeutic abortion. Nurses' involvement and moral grounds," by
G. Mathew. NURS J INDIA 62:305-306, September, 1971.

"Therapeutic abortions topic of study and discussion at operating room
nurses' conference," by I. Adams. HOSP ADMIN CAN 13:38+,
September, 1971.

"Why are nurses shook-up over abortion?" by I. Fischl. LOOK 35:66,
February 9, 1971.

OBSTETRICS
"Abortion and obstetrical shock," by J. C. Lagorce, et al. BULL FED
SOC GYNECOL OBSTET LANG FR 23:245-246, April-May, 1971.

"Ace renal insufficiency in obstetrics," by C. Ponticelli, et al. ARCH
ITAL UROL NEFROL 42:142-159, 1969.

"Application of genetics in gynecology and obstetrics," by L. C.
Ayala. ENFERMERAS 18:4-11, January-February, 1971.

"Enzymatic activity of the blood and obstetrical physiopathology.
I. Serum glutamic-oxalacetic (SGOT) and glutamic-pyruvic (SGPT)
transaminases in normal pregnancy and in some pathological
obstetrical conditions," by A. Valsecchi, et al. MINERVA
GINEKOL 22:943-949, October 15, 1970.

"Gynecology and obstetrics," by D. N. Danforth. SURG GYNECOL
OBSTET 123:221-225, February, 1971.

"Obstetrical complications of uterine malformations," by G. Poizat.

OBSTETRICS

REV MED LIEGE 25:763-764, December 1, 1970.

"Problem of listeriosis in gynecology and obstetrics," by M. Pommier, et al. SEM HOP PARIS 47:2489-2491, November 8, 1971.

"Prostaglandins in obstetrics and gynecology," by P. Bersjo, et al. TIDSSKR NOR LAEGEFOREN 91:678-679, March 30, 1971.

"Septic abortion. The scourge of modern obstetrics," by P. Rattakul. J MED ASSOC THAI 54:312-319, May, 1971.

"Some data on the functional state of the adrenal cortex in obstetric sepsis," by I. R. Zak, et al. AKUSH GINEKOL 44:44-47, October, 1968.

"Study of the sulfamethoxazole-trimethoprim combination in gynecology and obstetrics," by J. Villard, et al. J MED LYON 52:401-403, March 5, 1971.

"The use of prostaglandins in obstetrics," LOND CLIN MED J 12:9-11, January, 1971.

"Use of a synthetic progestational hormone, chlormadinone, in obstetrics," by R. Palliez, et al. LILLE MED 659:63, June-July, 1969.

OUTPATIENT ABORTION
 see: Hospitals and Abortion

OXYTOCIN
 "Induction of mid-trimester therapeutic abortion by intra-amniotic urea and intravenous oxytocin," by I. Craft, et al. LANCET 2:1058-1060, November 13, 1971.

"Medicolegal problems caused by the use of oxytocics," by R. C. Cingolani. MINERVA MEDICOLEG 90:5-10, January-June, 1970.

"Oxytocin administration in abortions induced with hypertonic saline," by J. D. Schulman, et al. LANCET 2:606-607, September 11, 1971.

PHYSICIANS AND ABORTION
 see also: Psychology
        Sociology, Behavior and Abortion

"Abortion and the obstetrician," by I. Donald. LANCET 1:1233, June 12, 1971.

"Abortion and sterilization: an insight into obstetrician-gynecologists' attitudes and practices," by A. T. Fort. SOC BIOL 18:192-194, June, 1971.

"Abortion: physician and hospital attitudes," by R. E. Hall. AM J PUBLIC HEALTH 61:517-519, March, 1971.

"The abortion problem from the medical viewpoint," by H. Husslein. WIEN MED WOCHENSCHR 121:Suppl 2:3-7, November 20, 1971.

"Abortion screening and counseling: a brief guideline for physicians," by J. C. Butler, et al. POSTGRAD MED 50:208-212, October, 1971.

"Abortions by resident physicians in a municipal hospital center," by J. J. Kopelman, et al. AM J OBSTET GYNECOL 111:666-671, November 1, 1971.

"Assumption of attitudes toward abortion during physician education," by S. R. Wolf, et al. OBSTET GYNECOL 37:141-147, January, 1971.

"Attitudes and practices of North Carolina obstetricians: the impact of the North Carolina Abortion Act of 1967," by W. B. Walker, et al. SOUTH MED J 64:441-445, April, 1971.

"Attitudes toward Michigan's abortion law and experience of Michigan physicians with requests for abortion," by B. Serena, et al. MICH MED 70:309-316, April, 1971.

"Doctor Hodgson's choice," by E. Kiester. FAMILY HEALTH 3:14-17, June, 1971.

"Doctors and the population problem," by J. Briggs. LANCET 1:805, April 17, 1971.

"Don't blame the doctors," by J. R. Wilson. SPECTATOR 51, July 10, 1971.

"A general practitioner survey of the Abortion Act 1967," by J. R. Eames, et al. PRACTITIONER 207:227-230, August, 1971.

PHYSICIANS AND ABORTION

"Gynecologist: abortion--a decision between the woman and her
physician," by N. G. Holmberg. LAKARTIDNINGEN 68:5845-
5848, December 8, 1971.

"Let's look at abortion (discussion of the issues from the points of
view of a physician, a pastor, an ethicist and a young woman who
underwent the experience)," SOCIAL ACTION 37:3-39, March, 1971.

"Letter from doctor will do for abortion: Vancouver General Hospital,"
CAN HOSP 48:18, April, 1971.

"Medical obligations imposed by abortion," by F. J. Ingelfinger.
N ENGL J MED 284:727, April 1, 1971.

"Medical responsibility," by K. Chaturachinda. J MED ASSOC THAI
54:149-152, March, 1971.

"New York obstetricians' abortion stand," MED WORLD NEWS 12:12G,
April 2, 1971.

"New York's obstetricians surveyed on abortion," by R. C. Lerner, et
al. FAM PLANN PERSPECT 3:56, January, 1971.

"Opinions on abortion from medical practitioners," by G. A. Gregson,
et al. NZ MED J 73:267-273, May, 1971.

"Physician attitudes on abortion and the Kansas abortion law," by R.
Bettis, et al. J KANS MED SOC 72:344-349, August, 1971.

"Physician's association abortion meeting. Conclusions of the presiding committee," by U. Borell, et al. LAKARTIDNINGEN 68:
5842-5844, December 8, 1971.

"Physician's viewpoint," by K. Neumann. AM DRUGGIST 164:8,
December 13, 1971.

"Role of pediatrician in family planning," by C. C. de Silva. INDIAN
PEDIATR 7:167-171, March, 1970.

"The role of the physician in North Carolina family planning programs," by A. R. Measham. NC MED J 32:51-56, February, 1971.

185

"Seminar on abortion. A physician's view," by H. A. Thiede. J MISS STATE MED ASSOC 12:120-121, March, 1971.

"Surgeon, sterilization and abortion," by R. M. Soderstrom. NORTH-WEST MED 70:167, March, 1971.

"220 MDs back abortion curbs," AMER MED NEWS 14:3, November 15, 1971.

"Termination of an unwanted pregnancy observed from a medical and socioeconomic aspect," by K. Kurciev, et al. GOD ZB MED FAK SKOPJE 16:437-440, 1970.

POPULATION
see also: Demography
Immigration and Emigration

"Cause and effect; decline in birth rate with new abortion law," SCIENTIFIC AMERICAN 225:42, October, 1971.

"Current status of the qualitative and quantitative problem of the limitation of births," by L. Bussi. MINERVA MED 62:1592-1593, April 14, 1971.

"Doctors and the population problem," by J. Briggs. LANCET 1:805, April 17, 1971.

"Family planning policies and practice in population control," by A. Wiseman. R SOC HEALTH J 91:134-138, May-June, 1971.

"Is reaction to the population problem misplaced?" by R. L. Day. PEDIATRICS 47:952-955, May, 1971.

"Malthus on population quality," by E. Cocks. SOC BIOL 18:84-87, March, 1971.

"Population, contraception and abortion," J R COLL GEN PRACT 21:377-378, July, 1971.

"A population policy for Britain," LANCET 1:534, March 13, 1971.

"The teaching of fertility control and population problems in the

medical schools of Brazil," by J. Yunes. REV SAUDE PUBLICA
4:79-84, June, 1970.

POTASSIUM PERMANGANATE
"Attempt at abortion with potassium permanganate tablets," by A.
Le Coz, et al. BULL FED SOC GYNECOL OBSTET LANG FR
20:190-191, April-May, 1968.

"Considerations on 200 cases of vaginal burns by potassium permanganate," by J. A. Guerrero, et al. GINECOL OBSTET MEX 29:
275-279, March, 1971.

POVERTY
"Abortions for poor and nonwhite women: a denial of equal protection?" by A. Charles, et al. HASTINGS L J 23:147, November,
1971.

"Birth control survey in a lower social group in Melbourne," by C.
Wood, et al. MED J AUST 1:691-696, March 27, 1971.

"Evaluation of periodic continence as a family planning method.
Acceptance among low socioeconomical levels in Cali, Colombia," by V. R. Guerrero, et al. REV COLOMB OBSTET GINECOL
22:13-18, January-February, 1971.

"Family planning and conjugal roles in New York City poverty
areas," by S. Polgar, et al. SOC SCI MED 4:135-139, July, 1970.

"Family planning in the Negro ghettos of Chicago," by D. J. Bogue.
MILBANK MEM FUND Q 48:283-307, April, 1970.

"Morbidity and mortality in the offspring of 300 consanguineous
couples in Florence," by U. Bigozzl, et al. ACTA GENET MED
GEMELLOL 19:515-528, October, 1970.

"Participation of low-income urban women in a public health birth control program," by Z. L. Janus, et al. PUBLIC HEALTH REP 85:
859-867, October, 1970.

"Relation of socioeconomic factors to family planning (based on data
from the Tselinograd region)," by L. E. Sviridova. SOV ZDRAVO-
OKHR 29:11-15, 1970.

"Socioeconomic outcomes of restricted access to abortion," by C. Muller. AM J PUBLIC HEALTH 61:1110-1118, June, 1971.

"Therapeutic abortion. A social work view," by F. Addelson. AM J OBSTET GYNECOL 111:984-992, December 1, 1971.

"Utilization of a family planning program by the poor population of a metropolitan area," by J. D. Beasley, et al. MILBANK MEM FUND Q 48:241-281, April, 1970.

PREGNANCY INTERRUPTION
see: Induced Abortion

PROGESTERONE
"Abnormal progesterone synthesis in placental tissue from a spontaneous abortion," by M. Wiener, et al. AM J OBSTET GYNECOL 111: 942-946, December 1, 1971.

"Contractibility of the human uterus and the hormonal situation. Studies on therapy with progesterone in pregnancy," by P. Mentasti, et al. MINERVA GINECOL 21:685-687, May 31, 1969.

"Gynecological indications of a new progestationsl agent with prolonged action," by M. Goisis, et al. MINERVA GINECOL 22:339-367, March 31, 1970.

"Hormonal studies and clinical observations in patients with threatening abortion or premature birth, respectively treated with depot-17-alpha-hydroxyprogesterone-caproate," by F. Tóth, et al. Z GEBURTSHILFE GYNAEKOL 175:168-175, October, 1971.

"Increase in plasma progestrone caused by undernutrition during early pregnancy in the ewe," by I. A. Cumming, et al. J REPROD FERTIL 24:146-147, January, 1971.

"100 clinical cases of pregnancy complications treated with a 19-nor-progesterone, registered as 31.458 Ba and followed until term," by M. Lanvin, et al. BULL FED SOC GYNECOL OBSTET LANG FR 20:110-117, April-May, 1968.

"Plasma levels of progesterone in early pregnancy after removal of the foetoplacental unit, and following removal of corpus luteum," by

PROGESTERONE

P. E. Lebech. ACTA ENDOCRINOL 155:Suppl:134, 1971.

"Plasma progesterone during abortion induced by intra-amniotic hypertonic saline," by T. H. Holmdahl, et al. ACTA OBSTET GYNECOL
SCAND 9:Suppl:48, 1971.

"Plasma progesterone in pregnancy interrupted by the intrauterine
injection of hypertonic saline," by T. H. Holmdahl, et al. ACTA
ENDOCRINOL 66:82-88, January, 1971.

"Progesterone depot in threatened abortion," by A. P. Camilleri, et al.
OBSTET GYNECOL 38:893-895, December, 1971.

"Role of progesterone in the 1st trimester of pregnancy and in the
treatment of threatened abortion," by L. P. Bengtsson. REV FR
GYNECOL OBSTET 63:73-81, March, 1968.

PROSTAGLANDINS
"Action of prostaglandin in the pregnant woman," by S. Karim. ANN NY
ACAD SCI 180:483-498, April 30, 1971.

"The effects of prostaglandins E 2 and F 2 alpha administered by
different routes on uterine activity and the cardiovascular system
in pregnant and non-pregnant women," by S. M. Karim, et al.
J OBSTET GYNAECOL BR COMMONW 78:172-179, February, 1971.

"The efficacy and acceptability of intravenously administered prostaglandin F as an abortifacient," by A. I. Csapo, et al. AM J OBSTET
GYNECOL 111:1059-1063, December 15, 1971.

"Efficacy and tolerance of intravenous prostaglandins F 2 and E 2,"
by C. H. Hendricks, et al. AM J OBSTET GYNECOL 111:564-579,
October 15, 1971.

"Induction of abortion by the intravenous administration of prostaglandin F2. A critical evaluation," by N. Wiqvist, et al. ACTA
OBSTET GYNECOL SCAND 50:381-389, 1971.

"The induction of abortion by prostaglandin F2," by K. Kinoshita, et
al. AM J OBSTET GYNECOL 111:855-857, November, 1971.

"Induction of abortion by prostaglandins E (PGE1 and PGE2)," by

M. P. Embery. J REPROD MED 6:256-259, June, 1971.

"Induction of lactogenesis and abortion by prostaglandin F2-alpha in pregnant rats," by R. P. Deis. NATURE (London) 229:568, February 19, 1971.

"Induction of midtrimester abortion by intra-amniotic administration of prostaglandin F2. A preliminary report," by M. Bygdeman, et al. ACTA PHYSIOL SCAND 82:415-416, July, 1971.

"Inhibition of prostaglandin release and the control of threatened abortion," by A. Tothill, et al. LANCET 2:381, August 14, 1971.

"Present indications of prostaglandins," by P. Thibault. PRESSE MED 79:400, February 20, 1971.

"Prostaglandins," by M. P. Embrey. LANCET 2:874-875, October 24, 1970.

"Prostaglandins and abortion," by G. G. Anderson, et al. CLIN OBSTET GYNECOL 14:245-257, March, 1971.

"Prostaglandins and habitual abortion," by M. Bodin. BR MED J 2: 587, June 5, 1971.

"Prostaglandins as abortifacients," by S. M. Karim. N ENGL J MED 285:1534-1535, December 30, 1971.

"Prostaglandins as abortion agents," by M. Bygdeman, et al. LAKARTIDNINGEN 68:2732-2739, June 2, 1971.

"Prostaglandins in abortion," LANCET 2:536, September 4, 1971.

"Prostaglandins in obstetrics and gynecology," by P. Bersjo, et al. TIDSSKR NOR LAEGFOREN 91:678-679, March 30, 1971.

"Second trimester abortion with single intra-amniotic injection of prostaglandins E2 or F2 alpha," by S. M. Karim, et al. LANCET 2:47-48, July 3, 1971.

"Some effects of prostaglandins E 2 and F 2 on the pregnant rhesus monkey," by K. T. Kirton, et al. BIOL REPROD 3:163-168, October, 1970.

"Therapeutic abortion and induction of labour by the intravaginal administration of prostaglandins E2 and F2," by S. M. Karim, et al. J OBSTET GYNAECOL BR COMMONW 78:294-300, April, 1971.

"Therapeutic abortion by intrauterine instillation of prostaglandin E2," by G. Roberts, et al. J OBSTET GYNAECOL BR COMMONW 78:834-837, September, 1971.

"Therapeutic abortion by intrauterine instillation of prostaglandins," by M. P. Embrey, et al. BR MED J 1:588-590, March 13, 1971.

"The use of prostaglandin E2 in the management of intrauterine death, missed abortion and hydatidiform mole," by G. M. Filshie. J OBSTET GYNAECOL BR COMMONW 78:87-90, January, 1971.

"Use of prostaglandins for induction of abortion and labor," by A. Gillespie. ANN NY ACAD SCI 180:524-527, April 30, 1971.

"The use of prostaglandins in obstetrics," LOND CLIN MED J 12:9-11, January, 1971.

"The use of prostaglandins in obstetrics and gynaecology," by M. Filshie. MIDWIFE HEALTH VISIT 7:99-102, March, 1971.

"The use of an 'unnatural' prostaglandin in the termination of pregnancy," by A. Gillespie, et al. J OBSTET GYNAECOL BR COMMONW 78:301-304, April, 1971.

PSYCHOLOGY

"Abortion. Is it a therapeutic procedure in psychiatry?" by C. V. Ford, et al. JAMA 218:1173-1178, November 22, 1971.

"Abortion and the psychiatrist," by W. Burke. HPR 71:100-207, December, 1970.

"Abortion and suicidal behaviors: observations on the concept of 'endangering the mental health of the mother'," by H. L. Resnik, et al. MENT HYG 55:10-20, January, 1971.

"Abortion: is it a therapeutic procedure in psychiatry?" by C. V. Ford, et al. J AMER MED ASS 218:1173-1178, November 22, 1971.

"Abortion's psychological price," by K. J. Sharp. CHR TODAY 15: 4-6, June 4, 1971.

"The British candidate for termination of pregnancy: a quantified survey of psychiatric referrals," by R. G. Priest. BR J PSYCHIATRY 118:579-580, May, 1971.

"Court denies abortion for mental patient," PSYCHIAT NEWS 6:9, December 15, 1971.

"The emotional scars of abortion," by H. S. Arnstein. LADIES HOME J 88:121+, May, 1971.

"Induced abortion for psychiatric indication," by S. Meyerowitz, et al. AM J PSYCHIATRY 127:1153-1160, March, 1971.

"Legal abortion and mental health," by C. Thonet. REV CHIL OBSTET GINECOL 35:209-213, 1970.

"The psyche and abortion. Some psychoanalytical points of view," by H. Carpelan. NORD PSYKIATR TIDSSKR 25:213-225, 1971.

"Psychiatric aspects of therapeutic abortion," by P. H. Linton. SOUTH MED J 64:Suppl 1:108-110, February, 1971.

"Psychiatric experience of the abortion Act (1967)," by N. A. Todd. BR J PSYCHIATRY 119:489-495, November, 1971.

"Psychiatric indications for the termination of pregnancy," MED J AUST 1:171, January 16, 1971.

"Psychiatric indications for the termination of pregnancy," by N. Destro. MED J AUST 1:350-351, February 6, 1971.

"Psychiatric indications for the termination of pregnancy," by S. Gold. MED J AUST 1:499-500, February 27, 1971.

"Psychiatric indications for the termination of pregnancy," by B. D. McKie, et al. MED J AUST 1:771-773, April 3, 1971.

"Psychiatric indications for the termination of pregnancy," by J. Simpson. MED J AUST 1:449-450, February 20, 1971.

"Psychiatric indications for the termination of pregnancy," by D. Vann. MED J AUST 1:404, February 12, 1971.

"Psychiatric sequelae of abortion on demand," by D. Cappon. POST-GRAD MED 49:255-256, March, 1971.

"A psychiatric syndrome in women evaluated for an unwanted pregnancy," by D. A. Kellogg. MD STATE MED J 20:75-78, October, 1971.

"The psychiatrist and therapeutic abortion," by G. C. Sisler. CAN PSYCHIATR ASSOC J 16:275-277, June, 1971.

"Psychiatrist as consultant for therapeutic abortion," by R. L. Sadoff, et al. PENN MED 74:63-64, May, 1971.

"Psychiatry and abortion," by D. S. Heath. CAN PSYCHIATR ASSOC J 16:55-63, February, 1971.

"Psychologic effects of legal abortion," by J. D. Osofsky, et al. CLIN OBSTET GYNECOL 14:215-234, March, 1971; also in MOD TREAT 8:139-158, February, 1971.

"Some psychiatric aspects of abortion," J NURS 18:76-78, January, 1971.

"Therapeutic abortion. A study of psychiatric applicants at North Carolina Memorial Hospital," by J. R. Partridge, et al. NC MED J 32:131-136, April, 1971.

"Therapeutic abortion. Who needs a psychiatrist?" by C. V. Ford, et al. OBSTET GYNECOL 38:206-213, August, 1971.

"Therapeutic abortion: the psychiatric nurse as therapist, liaison, and consultant," by R. Zahourek, et al. PERSPECT PSYCHIATR CARE 9:64-71, 1971.

"Therapeutic abortion: a psychiatric view," by J. M. Donahue. J INDI-
ANA STATE MED ASSOC 64:833-834, August, 1971.

"What are the real emotional aspects of abortion?" by R. B. Sloane.
MED INSIGHT 3:20-25, September, 1971.

RELIGION, ETHICS AND ABORTION
see also: Sociology, Behavior and Abortion

"Abortion and euthanasia: a reply," by R. D. Lamm, et al. ROCKY
MT MED J 68:40-42, February, 1971.

"Abortion and morality," by P. R. Ehrlich, et al. SAT R 54:58, September 4, 1971.

"Abortion and normative ethics," by S. Hauerwas. CROSS CURR 21:
399-414, Fall, 1971.

"Abortion and pluralist society," by C. F. Magistro. NAT R 23:476-
478+, May 4, 1971.

"Abortion: the Catholic presentation," AMERICA 124:62, January 23,
1971.

"Abortion, death, and the sanctity of life," by H. L. Smith. SOCIAL
SCIENCE AND MEDICINE 5:211-218, June, 1971.

"Abortion kills unborn baby," by P. O'Boyle. SOC JUST 63:372-373+,
February, 1971.

"Abortion: a question of right or wrong?" by R. W. Fox. ABA J 57:
667, July, 1971.

"Abortion: a theological judgment," by J. Dedek. CHICAGO STDS
10:313-333, Fall, 1971.

"Alerte au traducianisme," by A. Ple. SUPPLEMENT 96:59-71,
February, 1971.

"The American Catholic: contraception and abortion," by J. Fitzgerald. LINACRE 38:264-267, November, 1971.

"Birth control. Problem of the gynecologist from the medical, moral and religious point of view," by S. Fossati. MINERVA GINECOL 22:664-668, July, 15, 1970.

"Cardinal Cooke condemns State's abortion law," OR 53(144)11, December 31, 1970.

"Cardinal Terence Cooke launches new service; birthright for mothers," OR 17(161)4, April 29, 1971.

"Cardinals condemn abortion; pastoral letters," by P. O'Boyle, et al. OR 4(148)4, January 28, 1971.

"A Catholic abortion," TRIUMPH 6:7-12, April, 1971.

"Catholics and liberalized abortion laws," by N. J. Rigali. CATH WORLD 213:283-285, September, 1971; Discussion 214:101-102, December, 1971.

"Catholics against the Vatican," by C. Goodhart. SPECTATOR 274, August 21, 1971.

"Chaplains condemn abortion," C MIND 69:4, February, 1971.

"A clergyman's view," by J. G. Chatham. J MISS STATE MED ASSOC 12:116-117, March, 1971.

"De bisschoppelijke verklaring in verband met abortus: Een vraagges-prek met Mgr. Heuschen," COLLATIONES 220-228, 1971.

"Der medizinische Umgang mit dem praenatalen Leben," by W. Mende. THEOLOGISCHE QUARTALSCHRIFT 214-221, 1971.

"Die deutschen Bischöfe über die Verantwortung für das menschliche Leben," HERDER KORRESPONDENZ 544-545, 1971.

"Eine pastoralmedizinische Anmerkung zum Problem der Humanonto-genese," by M. Vodopivec. THEOLOGISCHE QUARTALSCHRIFT 222-227, 1971.

"Erklärung der skandinavischen Bischöfe über die Abtreibung," HERDER KORRESPONDENZ 478-485, 1971.

"Ethical issues in community and research medicine," by A. J. Dyck. N ENGL J MED 284:725-726, April 1, 1971.

"The ethics of a cottage industry in an age of community and research medicine," by P. Ramsey. N ENGL J MED 284:700-706, April 1, 1971.

"A guide for the Catholic nurse on abortion," IR NURS NEWS 5, Spring, 1971.

"How do nurses feel about euthansaia and abortion?" by N. K. Brown, et al. AM J NURS 71:1413-1416, July, 1971.

"Human life and abortion," by P. Harrington. C LAWYER 17:11-44, Winter, 1971.

"The humanity of the unborn child," by E. Diamond. C LAWYER 17:174-180, September, 1971.

"Illinois Catholic Conference on Abortion," SOC JUST 63:414, March, 1971.

"Individuation und Personalisation: Die anthropologische Relevanz embryonalbiologischer Entwicklungsphasen," by A. van Melsen. THEOLOGISCHE QUARTALSCHRIFT 228-237, 1971.

"La escalada del aborto," CHRISTUS 36:29, February, 1971.

"L'avortement et la responsabilité du chrétien; declaration des évêques catholiques des pays nordiques, Goeteborg, juillet, 1971," DOC CATH 68:1076-1084, December 5, 1971.

"Lettre pastorale de l'episcopat Hollandais sur l'avortement direct," DOC CATH 68:486-489, May 16, 1971.

"Life our greatest asset? Moralistic and theologic discussion of pregnancy interruption," by A. Ziegler. WIEN MED WOCHENSCHR 121:Suppl 2 :9-13, November 20, 1971.

"Locums for God," by C. Storr. NEW STATESMAN 78, July 16, 1971.

"Mid-trimester abortions, fetal weight and ethics," by R. C. Goodlin.

CALIF MED 114:85-86, March, 1971.

"Missouri Catholic bishops' statement on abortion," OR 29(173)11,
July 22, 1971.

"Note doctrinale sur l'avortement," DOC CATH 68:285-290,
March 21, 1971.

"Now-generation churchmen and the unborn," by H. B. Kuhn. CHR
TODAY 15:38, January 29, 1971.

"1,000 mourn innocents slain by abortion," NAT CATH REP 7:12,
January 15, 1971.

"Papal fallibility," CHR CENT 87:1309, November 4, 1970; Discussion
88:21, January 6, 1971.

"Politics of death," by R. Kirk. NAT R 23:315, March 23, 1971.

"Practitioner in social medicine: why has the fetus been forgotten?"
by B. Lindegard. LAKARTIDNINGEN 68:5854-5858, December 8,
1971.

"Priest asks study of fetuses' rights," NAT CATH REP 7:3, April 23,
1971.

"Psychiatrist: abortion should be avoided when the fetus has a 'life
of his own'," by K. Ohrberg. LAKARTIDNINGEN 68:5849-5853,
December 8, 1971.

"Public policy making: why the churches strike out," by V. C. Blum.
AMERICA 124:224-228, March 6, 1971.

"A rabbi's view," by P. E. Nussbaum. J MISS STATE MED ASSOC
12:118-120, March, 1971.

"Rallies back, oppose abortion," NAT CATH REP 8:3-4, December 3,
1971.

"Rallying Romans to fight abortion," by J. Kavanaugh. NAT CATH REP
7:Suppl:9, September 10, 1971.

"Rationales for feticide," by D. W. Louisell. CATH WORLD 212:318-319, March, 1971.

"Religious pacifist looks at abortion," by G. C. Zahn. COMMONWEAL 94:279-282, May 28, 1971; also in LINACRE QUARTELY 247-253, 1971.

"Respect de la view et moralité de l'avortement," by M. Marcotte. RELATIONS 360:132-137, May, 1971.

"Schwangerschaftsabbruch-Bibliographie," by H. Bour. THEOLOG-ISCHE QUARTALSCHRIFT 254-263, 1971.

"Schwangerschaftsabbruch in der strafrechtlichen Diskussion," by A. Eser. THEOLOGISCHE QUARTALSCHRIFT 238-253, 1971.

"Scottish Catholic abortion guide urges kindness to patients," RN 34: 26+, July, 1971.

"Seminar on moral aspects of abortion," J MISS STATE MED ASS 12: 115-121, March, 1971.

"Some news just isn't fit to print," by W. Hoffman. TRIUMPH 6:19-23, December, 1971.

"Statement of the Canadian bishops on abortion," CATH HOSP 2:1+, May, 1971.

"30 bishops attack abortionist profits," NAT CATH REP 7:5, December 11, 1970.

"Three Protestant theologians join in opposing abortion," NAT CATH REP 7:18, February 26, 1971.

"To study antiabortion brief," NAT CATH REP 8:1-2, December 10, 1971.

"Two condemnations of abortion," C MIND 69:9-11, November, 1971.

"Two pastorals on abortion; October, 1970," by P. O'Boyle, et al. C MIND 69:5-11, March, 1971.

RELIGION, ETHICS AND ABORTION

"The unclear voice against abortion," by P. Steinfels. NAT CATH REP 7:12, May 14, 1971.

"Zur Diskussion über Schwangerschaftsabbruch: Versuch einer ethischen Orientierung," by A. Auer. THEOLOGISCHE QUARTAL-SCHRIFT 193-213, 1971.

"Zur Diskussion um den Schwangerschaftsabbruch" ARZT UND CHRIST 129-229, 1971.

RESEARCH AND ABORTION

"Abortion associated with mycotic infection in a cow in Hyderabad," by Z. Ahmed, et al. INDIAN VET J 48:446-449, May, 1971.

"Abortion due to Pseudomonas aeruginosa. Protection of the pregnant guinea pig by vaccination," by R. Durieux, et al. GYNECOL OBSTET 69:301-308, August-October, 1970.

"Abortion following ultra-short-wave hyperthermia. Animal experiment studies," by F. Dietzel, et al. ARCH GYNAEKOL 209:237-255, 1970.

"Abortion in mice induced by ellagic acid," by N. Moe. ACTA PATHOL MICROBIOL SCAND 79:487-490, 1971.

"Abortion in neural tube defect fraternities," by A. D. McDonald. BR J PREV SOC MED 25:220-221, November, 1971.

"Abortions of cows after invasion by Theileria annulata (Dschunkow-sky and Luhs, 1904)," by J. Waltschowski, et al. ZENTRALBL VETERINAERMED 17:895-903, September, 1970.

"Abortive effects and comparative metabolism of chlorcyclizine in various mammalian species," by A. J. Steffek, et al. TERATOLOGY 1:399-406, November, 1968.

"Analysis of human chorionic gonadotropin: comparison between the biologic test in frogs and the immunologic pregnancy test," by G. Cobellis, et al. RIV ANAT PATOL ONCOL 33:857-863, 1968.

"The biologist's dilemma," by C. B. Goodhart. NATURE (London)

229:213, January 15, 1971.

"The concept of necessity in the laws and deontology," by C. Palenzona. MINERVA GINECOL 23:917-920, November 15, 1971.

"Concept of relationship between law and deontology," by C. Palenzona. MINERVA MED 40:Suppl:19+, May, 1971.

"Contribution to the diagnosis of infectious swine abortion," by F. Kemenes, et al. ZENTRALBL VETERINAERMED 18:170-176, March, 1971.

"Demonstration of one of the early symptoms of abortion caused by biovariectomy in the pregnant female rat," by M. Clabaut, et al. C R SOC BIOL 164:1958-1962, 1970.

"Efficacy of combined bacterins for experimental immunization of sheep against ovine vibriosis and chlamydial abortion of ewes," by W. A. Meinershagen, et al. AM J VET RES 32:51-57, January, 1971.

"Enzootic abortion of ewes," by W. O. Neitz. BULL OFF INT EPIZOOT 70:367-372, May, 1968.

"Enzootic 'viral' (Rakeia) abortion in goats," by J. Lecoanet, et al. BULL ACAD VET FR 44:61-64, January, 1971.

"Ethical issues in community and research medicine," by A. J. Dyck. N ENGL J MED 284:725-726, April 1, 1971.

"Erthropoetic activity of placental and abortion blood serum and the preparations obtained from them," by V. I. Gudim, et al. PROBL GEMATOL PERELIV KROVI 16:27-32, June, 1971.

"Experimental action of a strain of trachoma agent on the gestation in rats," by P. Giroud. REV INT TRACH 46:113-116, 1969-1970.

"Experimental findings on the effects of administration of fluorouracil in pregnancy. II. Treatment of mice and rabbits with FU," by V. Lauro, et al. MINERVA GINECOL 22:281-285, March 15, 1970.

"Fetal death in the cow, with observations from a practice," by W.

Zindel. SCHWEIZ ARCH TIERHEILKD 112:130-138, March, 1970.

"The function of glucocorticoids of the adrenal cortex in pregnancy and in abortion," by M. I. Zhiliaev. PEDIATR AKUSH GINEKOL 4:33-35, July-August, 1968.

"Increase in plasma progesterone caused by undernutrition during early pregnancy in the ewe," by I. A. Cumming, et al. J REPROD FERTIL 24:146-147, January, 1971.

"Induction of abortion in the rabbit by hydrocortisonacetate," by G. Wagner. ACTA ENDOCRINOL 155:Suppl:89, 1971.

"Induction of lactogenesis and abortion by prostaglandin F2-alpha in pregnant rats," by R. P. Deis. NATURE (London) 229:568, February 19, 1971.

"Influenza and rhino-pneumonia in horses in France," by A. Brion. BULL OFF INT EPIZOOT 70:149-169, May 1968.

"1st experiments concerning the vaccination of horses against rhino-pneumonia (viral abortion of mares) with a live vaccine from cell cultures," by A. Mayr, et al. BULL OFF INT EPIZOOT 70:133-140, May, 1968.

"Isolation of a herpesvirus from the canine genital tract: association with infertility, abortion and stillbirths," by G. Poste, et al. VET REC 88:229-233, February 27, 1971.

"Isolation of V. fetus from aborted sows," by V. F. Shatalov. VETERINARIIA 3:49-50, March, 1971.

"Noise induced lesions with special reference to abortions in cattle," by E. Aehnelt. DTSCH TIERAERZTL WOCHENSCHR 77:543-547, contd, October 15, 1970.

"Noise induced lesions with special reference to abortions in cattle," by R. Kramer. DTSCH TIERAERZTL WOCHENSCHR 77:568-571 concl, November 1, 1970.

"Observations on the anti-gestation effect of Aimax (methallibure) in recently bred gilts," by J. U. Akpokodje, et al. CAN VET J 12: 110-114, May, 1971.

"An outbreak of bovine abortions associated with leptospirosis," by S. G. Knott, et al. AUST VET J 46:385-386, August, 1970.

"An outbreak of mare abortion in Japan due to infection with equine rhinopneumonitis virus," by T. Shimizu, et al. BULL OFF INT EPIZOOT 70:251-256, May, 1968.

"Pathogenesis of abortion in acute nitrite toxicosis in guinea pigs," by D. P. Sinha, et al. TOXICOL APPL PHARMACOL 18:340-347, February, 1971.

"Recurrent vesicular mole abortion," by I. de L. Brunori, et al. MINERVA GINECOL 21:1082-1083, August 31, 1969.

"The relation of pesticides to abortion in dairy cattle," by A. W. Macklin, et al. J AM VET MED ASSOC 159:1743-1748, December 15, 1971.

"S. dublin abortion in sheep," by M. Gitter, et al. VET REC 87:775-778, December 19, 1970.

"Salmonella dublin abortion in cattle: preliminary observations on the serological response," by M. Hinton. VET REC 88:481, May 1, 1971.

"Salmonella dublin as a cause of diarrhea and abortion in ewes," by W. A. Meinershagen. AM J VET RES 31:1769-1771, October, 1970.

"Sanarelli-Shwartzman phenomemon in febrile abortion," by K. Hübschen, et al. ZENTRALBL GYNAEKOL 93:200-204, February 6, 1971.

"Serologic diagnosis of rickettsian abortion in ewes," by R. Gaumont. BULL OFF INT EPIZOOT 70:271-279, May, 1968.

"Some effects of prostaglandins E2 and F2 on the pregnant rhesus monkey," by K. T. Kirton, et al. BIOL REPROD 3:163-168, October, 1970.

"Some notes on the practical use of oestrogens in veterinary obstetrics and gynaecology," by C. H. de Bois. TIJDSCHR DIERGENEESKD 96:1165-1172, September 1, 1971.

"Spontaneous abortions in Macaca mulatta," by E. J. Andrews. LAB ANIM SCI 21:964, December, 1971.

"The technique of complement fixation test for the diagnosis of equine viral abortion (Rhinopneumonitis)," by K. Petzoldt. DTSCH TIERAERZTL WOCHENSCHR 74:252-255, May 15, 1967.

"Termination of pregnancy in mink by repeated injections during the period preceding implanatation," by J. C. Daniel, Jr. J ANIM SCI 33:659-661, September, 1971.

"Toxicity of levorin to pregnant rats and their fetus," by N. N. Slonitskaia. ANTIBIOTIKI 15:1089-1093, December, 1970.

SEPSIS

"Intra-abdominal sepsis," by W. A. Altemeier, et al. ADV SURG 5: 281-333, 1971.

"Some data on the functional state of the adrenal cortex in obstetric sepsis," by I. R. Zak, et al. AKUSH GINEKOL 44:44-47, October, 1968.

SEPTIC ABORTION AND SEPTIC SHOCK

see also: Complications
           Sepsis

"Abortion and obstetrical shock," by J. C. Lagorce, et al. BULL FED SOC GYNECOL OBSTET LANG FR 23:245-246, April-May, 1971.

"Abortion complicated by Clostridium perfringens infection," by J. A. Pritchard, et al. AM J OBSTET GYNECOL 111:484-492, October 15, 1971.

"Acute renal failure after septic abortion," by G. Staude, et al. Z UROL NEPHROL 64:23-28, January, 1971.

"Acute renal insufficiency with diffuse intravascular coagulation in 2 fatal cases of septic abortion," by L. E. Ribeiro, et al. ACTA OBSTET GINECOL HISP LUSIT 19:215-224, April, 1971.

"Aggressive management of incomplete or inevitable abortion. Report of 1002 septic and aseptic patients," by J. L. Breen, et al. J MED SOC NJ 67:711-715, November, 1970.

"Aggressive treatment of septic abortion," by L. G. Keith, et al. AM FAM PHYSICIAN 3:98-103, June, 1971.

"Bacterial abortion and shock," by H. Franke. ZENTRALBL GYNAE-KOL 92:385-391, March 28, 1970.

"Cephalosporins in the treatment of septic abortion," by R. F. Soto, et al. REV OBSTET GINECOL VENEZ 30:509-515, 1970.

"Clostridium welchii septicotoxemia. A review and report of 3 cases," by L. P. Smith, et al. AM J OBSTET GYNECOL 110:135-149, May 1, 1971.

"Double septicemia due to Streptococcus and Candida," by R. Le Lourd, et al. BORD MED 4:3197-3208, November, 1971.

"Endotoxin shock in septic abortions," by E. Hirvonen. ANN CHIR GYNAECOL FENN 60:196-201, 1971.

"Heparin for septic abortion and the prevention of endotoxic shock," by R. R. Margulis, et al. OBSTET GYNECOL 37:474-483, March, 1971.

"Level of histamine in peripheral blood in patients with bacterial shock," by A. D. Makatsariia, et al. AKUSH GINEKOL 46:40-43, October, 1970.

"Modern therapy of endotoxic shock in septic abortion," by B. Krznar, et al. ACTA MED IUGOSL 25:23-36, 1971.

"Postabortal and postpartum tetanus," by B. K. Adadevoh, et al. J OBSTET GYNAECOL BR COMMONW 77:1019-1023, November, 1970.

"Postabortion septicemia caused by Clostridium welchii. Report of 4 cases," by J. Cantillo, et al. REV COLOMB OBSTET GINECOL 22:247-255, July-August, 1971.

"Post abortum bacteremic shock and coagulopathies of consumption," by M. Dumont, et al. GYNECOL OBSTET 70:109-123, January-February, 1971.

"Results of treatment of septic abortion with carbenicillin," by J. L. P. de Salazar, et al. GINECOL OBSTET MEX 30:31-32, July, 1971.

"Septic abortion," by A. B. Lorincz. POSTGRAD MED 49:148-150, June, 1971.

"Septic abortion and sacroiliitis," by I. Watt. PROC R SOC MED 64: 55-56, January, 1971.

"Septic abortion. The scourge of modern obstetrics," by P. Rattakul. J MED ASSOC THAI 54:312-319, May, 1971.

"Septic abortion: diagnosis and treatment," by B. Neme. MATERN INFANC 29:255-278, April-June, 1970.

"Septic abortion masquerading as thrombotic thrombocytopenic purpura," by M. Yudis, et al. AM J OBSTET GYNECOL 111:350-352, October 1, 1971.

"Spontaneous and septic abortions in the city of Aberdeen, 1958-1968," by G. P. Milne. J BIOSOC SCI 3:93-95, January, 1971.

"Study on septic abortion (October 15, 1968 to October 14, 1969)," by A. Jubiz, et al. REV COLOMB OBSTET GINECOL 22:233-246, July-August, 1971.

"Tetracycline-enzymes in septic abortion," by A. Sangines, et al. GINECOL OBSTET MEX 26:605-611, November, 1969.

"Therapeutic abortion in California. Effects of septic abortion and maternal mortality," by G. K. Stewart, et al. OBSTET GYNECOL 37:510-514, April, 1971.

"Treatment of bacterial shock in abortion," by W. Mosier. DTSCH GESUNDHEITSW 26:1356-1360, July 15, 1971.

"Vacuum curettage in septic abortion," J REPROD MED 7:198, October, 1971.

SMOKING AND ABORTION
"Cigarette smoking and abortion. Consecutive prospective study of 4,312 pregnancies," by B. Palmgren, et al. LAKARTIDNINGEN 68:2611-2616, May 26, 1971.

"The injurious effects of smoking on gestation," by L. Vértes. ZENTRALBL GYNAEKOL 92:1395-1398, October 17, 1970.

SOCIOLOGY, BEHAVIOR AND ABORTION
see also: Family Planning
Religion, Ethics and Abortion

"Abortion ads rapped by NAB president," BROADCASTING 80:26, February 1, 1971.

"'Abortion airlift' in the military?" MED WORLD NEWS 12:4-5, June 11, 1971.

"Abortion and the argument from innocence," by M. Kohl. INQUIRY 14:147-151, Summer, 1971.

"Abortion and public opinion: the 1960-1070 decade," by J. Blake. SCIENCE 171:540-549, February 12, 1971.

"Abortion as a public health problem," KATILOLEHTI 76:234-237, May, 1971.

"Abortion: a changing scene," by J. Cottam. LANCET 2:1193-1194, November 27, 1971.

"Abortion: the counterattack," MED WORLD NEWS 12:4-5, April 30, 1971.

"Abortion: the crunch; How to protest abortion," by W. F. Buckley, Jr. NAT R 23:444-445, April 20, 1971.

"Abortion in perspective," by D. Ball. NEW SOCIETY 244, August 5, 1971.

"Abortion investigation: one year leave of absence for bearing a child," TIDSKR SVER SJUKSKOT 38:12, September 22, 1971.

"Abortion is not the answer," by A. I. Weisman. JAMA 217:1553-1554, September 13, 1971.

"Abortion; old figures, new facts," ECONOMIST 236:19, August 15, 1970.

"Abortion: pro and con," by T. I. Steinman. N ENGL J MED 284:728-729, April 1, 1971.

"Abortion problems," by C. B. Goodhart. ROYAL INST. OF GREAT BRITAIN PROC 43:378-393, December, 1970.

"Abortion: a profitable business," by S. Beauman. DAILY TELEGRAPH MAG 20+, November 26, 1971.

"Abortion: public health concerns and needed psychosocial research," by H. P. David. AM J PUBLIC HEALTH 61:510-516, March, 1971.

"Abortion: questions to ask," ECONOMIST 239:24+, May 1, 1971.

"Abortion rap," by D. Schulder, et al. NATION 213:342-343, October ber 11, 1971.

"The abortion situation," CAN MED ASSOC J 104:941, May 22, 1971+.

"Abortion situation in Switzerland and the need for sociomedical measures," by H. Stamm. GEBURTSHILFE FRAUENHEILKD 31:241-250, March, 1971.

"Abortion statements in Canada: Catholic clarity, Protestant ambivalence," by G. Lane. CHR CENT 88:1303-1304, November 3, 1971.

"Abortion throughout the world," by J. De Moerloose. NURS TIMES 67:678-680, June, 1971.

"Abortion throughout the world," by A. Monti. MINERVA GINECOL 23:764-765, September 30, 1971.

"Abortion: what you should know," by P. M. Sarrel, et al. VOGUE 158:93-94, August 1, 1971.

"Abortion: where have we been? Where are we going?" by T. Crist

NC MED J 32:347-351, August, 1971.

"Abortion: why not?" ECONOMIST 239:29, June 26, 1971.

"Abortions at the University Gynecological Clinic in Erlangen during 1950-1968," by W. Rummel, et al. MED KLIN 65:1123-1125, June 5, 1970.

"Abortive confusion," ECONOMIST 239:61, May 15, 1971.

"The alternative abortion," by B. N. Branch, et al. MED ANN DC 40: 691-696, November, 1971.

"Alternative to abortion," by L. N. Bell. CHR TODAY 15:17-19, June 18, 1971.

"Are abortions really necessary?" by R. J. Pion. ANN INTERN MED 75:961-962, December, 1971.

"The biggest killer," DIST NURS 14:186, December, 1971.

"Birth control survey in a lower social group in Melbourne," by C. Wood, et al. MED J AUST 1:691-696, March 27, 1971.

"Birthright," by V. Dillon. SIGN 50:27-29, July, 1971.

"Birthright: alternative to abortion," by J. B. Breslin. AMERICA 125: 116-119, September 4, 1971; Discussion 125:217, 273, October 2, 16, 1971.

"Birthright: a better answer," by I. Critelli, et al. ST ANTH 79:12-18, November, 1971.

"Birthright's goal: stop 100,000 abortions," NAT CATH REP 7:6, September 10, 1971.

"Cardinal Terence Cooke launches new service; birthright for mothers," OR 17(161)4, April 29, 1971.

"Changing attitudes and practices concerning abortion: a sociomedical revolution," by A. F. Guttmacher. MARYLAND STATE MED J 20:59-63, December, 1971.

"Claim abortion can eliminate stress," NAT CATH REP 8:5, December 17, 1971.

"A clearing house for abortion appointments," by E. F. Daily. FAM PLANN PERSPECT 3:12-14, July, 1971.

"Counseling women who are considering abortion," by J. M. Kummer. J PASTORAL CARE 25:233-240, December, 1971.

"Counsellor: threatening risks for practically **indefensible solutions**," by I. Cedermark. LAKARTIDNINGEN 68:5859-5862, December 8, 1971.

"Demographic adaptations to urban conditions," by G. M. Korostelev, et al. SOV ZDRAVOOKHR 29:35-36, 1970.

"Dial for abortion," TIME 97:64, March 15, 1971.

"Drug store: abortion information center?" AM DRUGGIST 162:12-14, August 24, 1970.

"Early abortion in the human," by M. Bygdeman, et al. ANN NY ACAD SCI 180:473-482, April 30, 1971.

"Easy abortion: who's to blame?" US CATH 36:39-40, February, 1971.

"83% in ob-gyn poll take liberal abortion view," AMER MED NEWS 14:3, May 17, 1971.

"En marge du rapport Bird: la femme devant l'avortement," by M. Marcotte. F RELATIONS 358:81-85, March, 1971.

"An epidemiological analysis of abortion in Georgia," by R. W. Rochat, et al. AM J PUBLIC HEALTH 61:543-552, March, 1971.

"Evaluation of periodic continence as a family planning method. Acceptance among low socioeconomical levels in Cali, Columbia," by V. R. Guerrero, et al. REV COLOMB OBSTET GINECOL 22: 13-18, January-February, 1971.

"For direct words on abortion," by P. Ramsey. N ENGL J MED 285: 1541-1542, December 30, 1971.

"France: free abortions, now!" NEWSWEEK 77:54+, April 19, 1971.

"France: we've had one," ECONOMIST 239:34, April 10, 1971.

"From womb into tomb," by R. Engel. LIGUORIAN 59:22-24, December, 1971.

"Guide for women," by A. J. Margolis, et al. REDBOOK 136:26, January, 1971.

"Gynecologist: abortion--a decision between the woman and her physician," by N. G. Holmberg. LAKARTIDNINGEN 68:5845-5848, December 8, 1971.

"Gynaecologist and patient alone should be allowed to determine legal abortions," by E. Sjovall. LAKARTIDNINGEN 68:4150-4151, September 8, 1971.

"Has abortion become all to easy?" by L. Edmunds. DAILY TELE-GRAPH 11, August 20, 1971.

"How safe is abortion?" by H. Price. LANCET 2:1419, December 25, 1971.

"The human person: experimental laboratory or privileged sanctuary?" by C. Carroll. HOSP PROGR 52:35-41, June, 1971.

"Hungary clamps down on abortions," J AMER MED ASS 215:2122, March 29, 1971.

"In defense of human life," by P. O'Boyle. COLUMBIA 50:5, December, 1970.

"In defense of unborn human life," SOC JUST 64:54-55, May, 1971.

"In defense of unborn human life; pastoral letter," OR 18(162)5, May 6, 1971.

"In a permissive society: defense of life," OR 29(173)3-4, July 22, 1971.

"Inaugural address: 7th National Conference of the Indian Academy of

Pediatrics,'' by S. K. Shah. INDIAN PEDIATR 7:1-3, January, 1970.

"International discussion on abortion," SAIRAANHOITAJA 47:484-486, June 10, 1971.

"An invitational symposium," J REPROD MED 6:274-301, June, 1971.

"It's a new game," TRIUMPH 6:46, March, 1971.

"Killing the problem even if it is human," by B. Daly. MARRIAGE 53:72, February, 1971.

"Legal abortions--a social problem," by E. Sjöball. LAKARTIDNINGEN 68:5279-5285, November 10, 1971.

"Legal abortions, socioeconomic status, and measured intelligence in the United States," by J. E. Cohen. SOC BIOL 18:55-63, March, 1971.

"Let us be born, by R. Joyce, et al. A Review," by P. Marx. CATH WORLD 212:218, January, 1971.

"Let's look at abortion (discussion of the issues from the points of view of a physician, a pastor, an ethicist and a young woman who underwent the experience)," SOCIAL ACTION 37:3-39, March, 1971.

"Letter on abortion morality," by M. Hurley. SOC JUST 64:241-242, November, 1971.

"Letters to editor," CATH WORLD 212:173-174, January, 1971.

"Letters to John and Mary Ann, preamble to an exodus," by L. Gilbert. TRIUMPH 6:24-26, October, 1971.

"Life and living it," by Y. Cross, et al. NURS MIRROR 133:49-51, October 15, 1971.

"Life or death, maturity or decline," by M. S. Roach. INFIRM CAN 13:17, July, 1971.

"Mad scramble for abortion money," by H. Eisenberg. MED ECON

48:35+, January 4, 1971.

"Marriage and child care in those classified as mentally retarded," by J. B. Fotheringham. CAN MED ASSOC J 104:813-816, May 8, 1971.

"The morality of abortion," by M. O'Brien. FURROW 21:762-769, December, 1970.

"New York City abortions nearly equal births," AMER MED NEWS 14:9, July 12, 1971.

"New wave of abortion," by J. Kettle. CAN DOCTOR 37:61-62, July, 1971.

"On being reviewed," by M. Simms. HUMANIST 86:336-337, November, 1971.

"1,452 cases," by S. Lee, et al. AM J OBSTET GYNECOL 108:1294-1297, December 15, 1970.

"Parting shots: well-kept-secret weapon in the sexual revolution," by W. A. McWhirter. LIFE 71:69, July 9, 1971.

"Perspectives of abortion," by T. Glenister. TABLET 225:300+, March 27, 1971; 326-327, April 3, 1971; 350-351, April 10, 1971.

"Plain meaning of abortion," by G. L. Hallett. AMERICA 124:632-633, June 19, 1971.

"The politics of abortion," by R. Taylor. TABLET 225:568-569, June 12, 1971.

"The politics of abortion," by C. Goodhart. SPECTATOR 484, April 10, 1971.

"Pre-pregnancy care--a logical extension of prenatal care," by R. F. Friesen. CAN MED ASSOC J 103:495-497, September 12, 1970.

"Presidential address: 7th National Conference of the Indian Academy of Pediatrics," by J. N. Pohowalla. INDIAN PEDIATR 7:4-7, January, 1970.

"The price of a child," by M. Chartier, et al. BULL FED SOC GYNE-COL OBSTET LANG FR 22:506-510, November-December, 1970.

"Progress against abortion," by N. St. John-Stevas. TABLET 225: 1022, October 23, 1971.

"Psychosocial aspects of selective abortion," by E. J. Lieberman. BIRTH DEFECTS 7:20-21, April, 1971.

"Qualitative and quantitative problems in generation," by R. H. Williams. NORTHWEST MED 69:497-501, July, 1970.

"Questions about abortion," by P. Jann. LIGUORIAN 59:14-19, October, 1971.

"Questions to ask," ECONOMIST 239:24+, May 1, 1971.

"Ramifications of permissive abortion," by J. Fitzgerald. LINACRE 38:102-105, May, 1971.

"Religion, morality, and abortion: a constitutional appraisal," by T. C. Clark. LOYOLA U L REV 2:1, April, 1969.

"Respect for human life," by J. Auréle. OR 19(163)9, May 13, 1971.

"Right to abortion. What is the responsibility of society? Social psychiatric study of abortion applying women in the public health district of Umea," by K. Broström, et al. LAKARTIDNINGEN 68: 5133-5139, November 3, 1971.

"Right to life: who is to decide?" by J. L. Arehart. SCI N 100:298-300, October 30, 1971.

"A right to live, and a right to life," by J. Tweedie. GUARDIAN 9, November 8, 1971.

"The rights of the unborn," by A. J. Quinn, et al. JURIST 577-613, 1971.

"Ripostes on abortion," by B. H. Roberts, et al. N ENG J MED 284: 1444-1446, June 24, 1971.

"Roselia: alternative to abortion; reprint from Pittsburgh Catholic February 26, 1971," by R. Snyder. C CHAR 55:20-22, April, 1971.

"The rules of the game," by C. Derrick. TRIUMPH 6:14-17, March, 1971.

"Seasonal distribution of abortions," by A. D. McDonald. BR J PREV SOC MED 25:222-224, November, 1971.

"Semantics of abortion," by S. M. Zimmerman. N ENGL J MED 284: 728, April 1, 1971.

"Sexualité et politique," by P. Watté. REVUE NOUVELLE 201-207, September, 1971.

"Social aspects of abortion counseling for patients undergoing elective abortion," by E. D. Smith, et al. CLIN OBSTET GYNECOL 14: 204-214, March, 1971.

"Socioeconomic outcomes of restricted access to abortion," by C. Muller. AM J PUBLIC HEALTH 61:1110-1118, June, 1971.

"Sociogenic health and disease: planning for abortion services in the Bronx," by V. W. Sidel, et al. NEW PHYSICIAN 20:773-774, December, 1971.

"A sociologic approach to abortion," by G. Texier. GYNECOL PRAT 20:363-373, 1969.

"Sociologic study on factors influencing birthrate among student families in Sofia," by G. Kardashev. AKUSH GINEKOL (Sofiia) 10:106-112, 1971.

"Sociology of human reproduction," by J. Morsa. BRUX MED 49:65-70, February, 1969.

"Some international aspects of abortion," by M. Fishbein. MED WORLD NEWS 12:68, September 17, 1971.

"Some social characteristics of women seeking abortion," by J. Aitken-Swan. J BIOSOC SCI 3:96-100, January, 1971.

"The state of play," by J. Gillott, et al. NOVA 38⁺, October, 1971.

"A statement on abortion in Victoria," by P. Brett, et al. MED J AUST 2:882-983, November 6, 1971.

"A statement on abortion in Victoria," by L. Hemingway, et al. MED J AUST 2:1203-1204, December 4, 1971.

"Status of abortion in the world," by A. Monti. MINERVA MED 62: Suppl:21-2, June-July, 1971.

"Suffer the little children," by J. Ryder. SOC JUST 64:123-126, July-August, 1971.

"Surveillance of abortion program in New York City," by J. Pakter, et al. BULL NY ACAD MED 47:853-874, August, 1971; CLIN OBSTET GYNECOL 14:267-299, March, 1971; MOD TREAT 8:169-201, February, 1971.

"Survey finds determinants of attitudes toward abortion," AMER J NURSING 71:1900, October, 1971.

"Survey of abortion 1962-1964. The Northwest England Faculty," by R. W. Kennon. J R COLL GEN PRACT 21:311-312, May, 1971.

"Survey of 3,000 unwanted pregnancies," by J. Lambert, BR MED J 4:156-160, October 16, 1971.

"Survey on induced abortion and use of contraceptives in Bogota. Method of approach," by S. Gómez, et al. REV COLOMB OBSTET GINECOL 21:427-439, July-August, 1970.

"Symptoms suggestive of multiple pregnancy in the 1st trimester and the aspect of acceptability of abortion performed for social reasons," by A. Rumprecht. WIAD LEK 24:2315-2318, December 15, 1971.

"Termination of an unwanted pregnancy observed from a medical and socioeconomic aspect," by K. Kurciev, et al. GOD ZB MED FAK SKOPJE 16:437-440, 1970.

"Thanatopsis," by J. Fitzgerald. LINACRE 37:254-258, November 8, 1970.

"Therapeutic abortion, A social work view," by F. Addelson. AM J OBSTET GYNECOL 111:984-992, December 1, 1971.

"Therapeutic abortion: medical and social sequels," by A. B. Bames, et al. ANN INTERN MED 75:881-886, December, 1971.

"Therapy of prematurity," by F. S. Baranovskaia, et al. AKUSH GINEKOL 47:69-72, June, 1971.

"Two books on abortion and the questions they raise," by C. B. Luce. NAT R 23:27-28+, January 12, 1971.

"A view on abortion," by H. P. David. J PSYCHIAT NURS 9:30-31, March-April, 1971.

"A voice in the wilderness," by J. Caldwell. NC MED J 32:470-471, November, 1971.

"The wages of pluralism," by P. Bozell. TRIUMPH 6:18-20, March, 1971.

"We've had one," ECONOMIST 239:34, April 10, 1971.

"What abortion really is," by M. Mandelin. SAIRAANHOITAJA 47: 474-477, June 10, 1971.

"What is an abortion: Variations on a definition," by M. Gaudefroy, et al. J SCI MED LILLE 86:641-645, October, 1968.

"Who gets abortions, how, and when," MED WORLD NEWS 12:52, December 3, 1971.

"Who shall live? ed. by K. Vaux. A review," by R. A. McCormick. AMERICA 122:424-425, April 18, 1970.

"Would you leave a child to die on the mountain side?" by M. J. D. Newman. CATH HOSP 2:8, January, 1971.

"Why not?" ECONOMIST 239:29, June 26, 1971.

"Why repeat legal abortions?" by S. Cullhed. LAKARTIDNINGEN 68: 2716-2718, June 2, 1971.

"Your replies to the abortion quiz," by M. Gillen. CHATELAINE 44: 23, 62-63, March, 1971.

SODIUM CHLORIDE
"Accidental intravenous injection in extra-amniotic sodium chloride abortion," by B. Gustavii. LAKARTIDNINGEN 68:2723-2728, June 2, 1971.

SPONTANEOUS ABORTION
see *also:* Threatened Abortion

"Abnormal progesterone synthesis in placental tissue from a spontaneous abortion," by M. Wiener, et al. AM J OBSTET GYNECOL 111:942-946, December 1, 1971.

"Age distribution of 715 mothers having had an early spontaneous abortion," by P. Lazar, et al. C R ACAD SCI 272:2852-2855, June 2, 1971.

"Attempts to isolate H-1 virus from spontaneous human abortions: a negative report," by S. J. Newman, et al. TERATOLOGY 3:279-281, August, 1970.

"Bacterial infection of the placenta in cases of spontaneous abortion. Correlation with the histological lesions," by M. Veron, et al. PATHOL BIOL 19:129-138, February, 1971.

"Changes in the thrombelastograph following blood loss during last late spontaneous abortion," by L. V. Terskaia. AKSUH GINEKOL 45:70-72, September, 1969.

"Chorionic villi and syncytial sprouts in spontaneous and induced abortions," by T. Fujikura, et al. AM J OBSTET GYNECOL 110: 547-555, June 15, 1971.

"Chromosome abnormalities in early spontaneous abortions," by D. T. Arakaki, et al. J MED GENET 7:118-124, June, 1970.

"Chromosome pathology in spontaneous abortions," by C. Zara. ARCH OSTET GINECOL 75:215-225, May-June, 1970.

"Chromosome studies in selected spontaneous abortions. 3. Early pregnancy loss," by D. H. Carr. OBSTET GYNECOL 37:570-574, May, 1971.

"Chromosome studies in selected spontaneous abortions. Polyploidy in man," by D. H. Carr. J MED GENET 8:164-174, June, 1971.

"Cytogenetic investigation of spontaneous abortions," by A. M. Kuliev. HUMANGENETIK 12:275-283, 1971.

"Development and retention durations of 716 zygotes, products of precocious spontaneous abortions," by J. Bouê, et al. C R ACAD SCI 272:2992-2995, June, 1971.

"Electrolytes, enzymes and hormones in women with spontaneous and habitual abortions," by B. Kiutukchiev, et al. AKUSH GINEKOL (Sofiia) 10:89-98, 1971.

"Etiology of repeated spontaneous abortions," by M. Gaudefroy, et al. J SCI MED LILLE 89:309-311, August-September, 1971.

"Genetic aspects of spontaneous abortions," by J. Cousin. J SCI MED LILLE 89:313-315, August-September, 1971.

"Human chromosome abnormalities. 2. Occurrence in spontaneous abortion and antenatal detection by amniocentesis," by L. J. Butler. MIDWIFE HEALTH VISIT 7:105-108, March, 1971.

"In vitro lymphoblastic transformation of blood lymphocytes applied to the study of repeated spontaneous abortions," by D. Alcalay, et al. GYNECOL OBSTET 70:59-61, January-February, 1971.

"On combined estro-progestogenic and antireactional treatment in threatened abortion," by M. Goisis, et al. MINERVA GINECOL 23: 547-552, June, 1971.

"On the presence of anti-fetal antibodies in women after spontaneous abortion," by G. Gabbrielli, et al. BOLL SOC ITAL BIOL SPER 45:601-602, May 15, 1969.

"Pregnancy in the 4th month; spontaneous abortion. Acute hemorrhagic pancreatitis. (Presentation of a clinical case)," by P. Dulea, et al.

MED INTERNA 23:1513-1516, December, 1971.

"Procedure to follow in the case of a nonpregnant women consulting because of several previous spontaneous abortions," by M. Gaudefroy. J SCI MED LILLE 89:323-324, August-September, 1971.

"Procedure to follow in the case of a woman having had repeated spontaneous abortions and beginning another pregnancy," by L. Corette. J SCI MED LILLE 89:325-332, August-September, 1971.

"Prognostic importance of determining excretion of chorionic gonadotropin in the diagnosis of spontaneous abortion," by A. T. Berko. AKUSH GINEKOL 47:37-41, June, 1971.

"Role of mycoplasma infection in the genesis of spontaneous abortion," by M. A. Bashmakova, et al. VOPR OKHR MATERIN DET 16:67-70, February, 1971.

"Semiquantitative immunological determinations of chorionic gonadotropins with the gravimun test in normal pregnancy and in threatened abortion," by J. Nieder, et al. ZENTRALBL GYNAEKOL 92:721-727, June 6, 1970.

"Significance in classification of spontaneous abortion for genetic consultation rooms," by P. Dráč, et al. CESK GYNEKOL 36:491-492, October, 1971.

"Skin-vegetative changes in the anterior abdominal wall in normal pregnancy and threatened abortion," by S. I. Fofanov. AKUSH GINEKOL 44:26-31, October, 1968.

"'Spontaneous' abortion and haemorrhage following attempted amniocentesis in a carrier of haemophilia A," by S. D. Cederbaum, et al. LANCET 2:429-430, August 21, 1971.

"Spontaneous and induced abortion," WHO CHRON 25:104-111, March, 1971.

"Spontaneous abortion and preventive hormone therapy (results in 110 cases)," by D. Antonopoulos, et al. ZENTRALBL GYNAEKOL 92:706-707, May 30, 1970.

"Spontaneous abortion due to luteal insufficiency. Histologic documentation," by P. Hietter, et al. J SCI MED LILLE 87:317-319, April, 1969.

"Spontaneous and septic abortions in the city of Aberdeen, 1958-1968," by G. P. Milne. J BIOSOC SCI 3:93-95, January, 1971.

"Spontaneous interruption of pregnancy during the early period," by V. I. Grishchenko. AKUSH GINEKOL 45:59-62, September, 1969.

"Threatened and spontaneous abortion. A retrospective study of the disgnosis on admission," by A. Johannsen. ACTA OBSTET GYNECOL SCAND 49:95-99, 1970.

"Treatment of pregnant women with spontaneous abortion of hormonal origin and isthmicocervical insufficiency," by M. P. Chertova, et al. AKUSH GINEKOL 46:48-51, November, 1970.

"Treatment of spontaneous abortion with high doses of sex hormones and the child's state," by V. Sulovic, et al. BULL FED SOC GYNECOL OBSTET LANG FR 20:Suppl:304-306, 1968.

"Vaginal cytology and urinary pregnanediol levels in threatened abortion, actual abortion and missed abortion," by A. Pannain. ARCH OSTET GINECOL 74:14-49, January-February, 1969.

STATISTICS

"Abortion mortality statistics," by R. L. Burt. OBSTET GYNECOL 38:950-951, December, 1971.

"Analysis of 2,746 abortions treated at their Managua General Hospital," by C. Guido, et al. INT SURG 56:125-127, August, 1971.

"Clinical and statistical considerations of recurrent abortion," by G. Pritsivelis, et al. MINERVA GINECOL 21:1067-1069, August 31, 1969.

"Diagnosis and management of internal abortion. Clinico-statistical study on 204 cases," by G. Zucconi, et al. RIV OSTET GINECOL 24:323-333, November, 1969.

"Imminent abortion, a statistical investigation of symptomatology and results of treatment," by N. B. Mossing, et al. UGESKR LAEGER 133:1206-1209, June 25, 1971.

"Official statistics of legal abortions in England," by K. Händel. MED KLIN 65:524-526, March 12, 1971.

"Statistical analysis of applicants and of the induced abortion workup. Grady Memorial Hospital, January-December, 1970," by L. D. Baker, et al. J MED ASSOC GA 60:392-396, December, 1971.

"Statistics on abortion in New York State from questionnaire," by G. Schaefer. CLIN OBSTET GYNECOL 14:258-265, March, 1971.

"Use of the statistical method of paired combinations in studying aspects of regulating family size," by A. I. Markov. SOV ZDRAVOOKHR 29:43-46, 1970.

STERILITY

"Abortion and sterility of neuro-endocrine origin," by J. Belaisch. ANN ENDOCRINOL 31:975-977, September-October, 1970.

"The control of fertility," by J. McEwan. PRACTITIONER 206:406-407, March, 1971.

"A demographic study on the relationships of nuptiality, child mortality, and attitude toward fertility to actual fertility in Hsueh-Chia township in Taiwan. I. Relationship of marriage cohort and marriage age to actual fertility," by H. Y. Wu. J FORMOSAN MED ASSOC 69: 243-255, May 28, 1970.

"Evaluation of fertility control of periodic abstinence," by W. M. Moore. PRACTITIONER 205:38-43, July, 1970.

"Fertility in balanced heterozygotes for a familial centric fusion translocation, t(DgDg)," by J. A. Wilson. J MED GENET 8:175-178, June, 1971.

"The teaching of fertility control and population problems in the medical schools of Brazil," by J. Yunes. REV SAUDE PUBLICA 4:79-84, June, 1970.

"Trends in pregnancy and fertility in a rural area of East Pakistan," by J. Stoeckel, et al. J BIOSOC SCI 2:329-335, October, 1970.

"Uterine malformations in relation to sterility and infertility," by G. Magli, et al. RASS INT CLIN TER 51:1259-1267, October 30, 1971.

"Uteroplasty in infertility caused by congenital malformations," by J. S. Contreras, et al. GINECOL OBSTET MEX 26:305-314, September, 1969.

"Women--the impact of advances in fertility control on their future. A presidential address," by G. S. Jones. FERTIL STERIL 22:347-350, June, 1971.

STERILIZATION

"Abortion and sterilization: an insight into obstetrician-gynecologists' attitudes and practices," by A. T. Fort. SOC BIOL 18:192-194, June, 1971.

"Impact on hospital practice of liberalizing abortions and female sterilizations," by A. D. Claman, et al. CAN MED ASSOC J 105:35-41, July 10, 1971.

"The Parliament requested overhaul in sterilization law," LAKARTID-NINGEN 67:5732, December 2, 1970.

"Sterilization. A case of extensive practice in a developing nation," by D. O. Cowgill, et al. MILBANK MEM FUND Q 49:363-378, July, 1971.

"Sterilization and family planning," by M. Elstein. PRACTITIONER 205:30-37, July, 1970.

"Sterilization on abortion," by D. Gudgeon. LANCET 1:1240, June 12, 1971.

"Surgeon, sterilization and abortion," by R. M. Soderstrom. NORTHWEST MED 70:167, March, 1971.

"Vaginal hysterectomy: a modality for therapeutic abortion and sterilization," by L. E. Laufe, et al. AM J OBSTET GYNECOL 110:

1096-1099, August 15, 1971.

"Vaginal tubal ligation at time of vacuum curettage for abortion," by
S. R. Sogolow. OBSTET GYNECOL 38:888-892, December, 1971.

"Voluntary male sterilization," MED J AUST 1:455-456, February 27,
1971.

SURGICAL TREATMENT AND MANAGEMENT
see also: Techniques of Abortion

"Aggressive management of incomplete or inevitable abortion. Report
of 1002 septic and aseptic patients," by J. L. Breen, et al. J MED
SOC NJ 67:711-715, November, 1970.

"Aggressive treatment of septic abortion," by L. G. Keith, et al. AM
FAM PHYSICIAN 3:98-103, June, 1971.

"Combination of a surgical and drug treatment in isthmo-cervical
insufficiency during pregnancy," by H. Hertel, et al. GEBURT-
SHILFE FRAUENHEILKD 29:9-15, January, 1969.

"Experience in the use of the NAPP-1 apparatus for fluothane anesthesia in minor gynecologic surgery," by V. A. Glotova, et al. NOV
MED PRIBOROSTR 2:41-45, 1970.

"Pregnancy continuing to term despite a surgical evacuation procedure in the early weeks," by R. Gaskell. MANCH MED GAZ 50:14-
16, 1971.

"Surgical treatment and prevention of isthmo-cervical insufficiency
causing prematurity, habitual abortion and premature delivery," by
R. Tokhin. AKUSH GINEKOL (Sofiia) 8:473-481, 1969.

"Surgical treatment of cervico-segmental insufficiency during pregnancy," by G. Taricco. MINERVA GINECOL 21:1121-1127, September 15, 1969.

"Surgical treatment of habitual abortion," by J. Bovec. MED PREGL
24:135-136, 1971.

"Termination of pregnancy from the surgical viewpoint," by E. F.

SURGICAL TREATMENT AND MANAGEMENT

Drews, et al. MED KLIN 66:1-8, January 1, 1971.

"Threatened abortion. Development and treatment," by M. Maretti, et al. MATERN INFANC 29:71-78, January-March, 1970.

"Transvaginal treatment of uterine perforation," by A. Tsuji. SANFU-JINKA JISSAI 20:519-528, May, 1971.

TECHNIQUES OF ABORTION
see also: Induced Abortion
Surgical Treatment and Management

"Amniocentesis and abortion: methods and risks," by F. Fuchs. BIRTH DEFECTS 7:18-19, April, 1971.

"Amniocentesis: medical and social implications," by R. Adams. REV MED SUISSE ROMANDE 91:389-400, June, 1971.

"The art of abortion. 1. Curettage of the pregnant uterus," by B. W. Newton. POSTGRAD MED 50:131-161, August, 1971.

"The art of abortion. 2. Induction of labor and other methods," by B. W W. Newton. POSTGRAD MED 50:213-220, September, 1971.

"Aspiration abortion without cervical dilation," by S. Goldsmith, et al. AM J OBSTET GYNECOL 110:580-582, June 15, 1971.

"Clinical experience with basal temperature rhythm," by J. P. Durkan. FERTIL STERIL 21:322-324, April, 1970.

"Clinical experiences with pregnancy interruption with a vacuum extractor," by C. Flämig, et al. ZENTRALBL GYNAEKOL 91:1567-1570, November 29, 1969.

"Combined use of the aspiration method and abortion forceps in induced abortion between the 13th and 18th week of pregnancy," by A. Atanasov, et al. AKUSH GINEKOL (Sofiia) 9:223-228, 1970.

"Critical study of single-time and double-tine methods of artificial pregnancy interruptions," by W. Weise, et al. ZENTRALBL GYNAEKOL 92:841-848, June 27, 1970.

"The duration of the positive pregnosticon-planotest reaction

224

following evacuation of the uterine cavity," by E. Reinold.
Z GEBURTSHILFE GYNAEKOL 174:75-79, 1971.

"Emergency room vacuum curettage for incomplete abortion," by B.
R. Marshall. J REPROD MED 6:177-178, April, 1971.

"Ketamine for dilatation and curettage," by S. Galloon. CAN
ANAESTH SOC J 18:600-613, November, 1971.

"Late abortion and difficulties of evacuation of the uterus," by H.
Serment, et al. BULL FED SOC GYNECOL OBSTET LANG FR
21:174-176, April-May, 1969.

"Management of incomplete abortion as an outpatient procedure," by
A. Allen, et al. CENT AFR J MED 17:91-96, May, 1971.

"Management of incomplete abortion with vacuum curettage," by D.
L. Hill. MINN MED 54:225-228, March, 1971.

"Methods of abortion," by W. T. Fullerton. J BIOSOC SCI 3:128-131,
January, 1971.

"My experience in uterine perforation," SANFUJINKA JISSAI 20:611-
612, May, 1971.

"My experience in uterine perforation--self-examination," SANFUJINKA
JISSAI 20:612-613, May, 1971.

"My method in prevention of uterine perforation," by F. Kikuchi.
SANFUJINKA JISSAI 20:604-606, May, 1971.

"My method in prevention of uterine perforation," by G. Ozawa.
SANFUJINKA JISSAI 20:607-608, May, 1971.

"My method in prevention of uterine perforation," by T. Shinorara.
SANFUJINKA JISSAI 20:609, May, 1971.

"My method in prevention of uterine perforation," by Y. Tamano.
SANFUJINKA JISSAI 20:608-609, May, 1971.

"My method in prevention of uterine perforation," by H. Yoshida.
SANFUJINKA JISSAI 20:606-607, May, 1971.

"Our experience with the Krause method in the Clinica y Maternidad Conchita," by L. B. de Anda. GINECOL OBSTET MEX 26:641-647, November, 1969.

"Paracervical block anaesthesia for evacuation of the uterus," by V. E. Aimakhu. WEST AFR MED J 20:277-279, August, 1971.

"Prognosis of threatened abortion. A comparative study with the use of vaginal cytology and urinary gonadotropin immunoassay," by A. F. Youssef, et al. AM J OBSTET GYNECOL 109:8-11, January, 1971.

"Results in 1,000 cases of therapeutic abortion managed by vacuum aspiration," by K. C. Loung, et al. BR MED J 4:477-479, November 20, 1971.

"Rupture of the bladder secondary to uterine vacuum curettage: a case report and review of the literature," by S. N. Rous, et al. J UROL 106:685-686, November, 1971.

"Simple technique of uterine evacuation," by R. P. Soonawala. LANCET 2:640-641, September 18, 1971.

"The single instrument abortion during the first 3 months of pregnancy and its quota of disorders with inflammatory complications," by W. Altmann. ZENTRALBL GYNAEKOL 92:984-993, August 1, 1970.

"Suction curettage for early abortion: experience with 645 cases," by B. N. Nathanson. CLIN OBSTET GYNECOL 14:99-106, March, 1971 1971; also in MOD TREAT 8:64-71, February, 1971.

"Suction evacuation of uterus for incomplete abortion," by S. Rashid, et al. J OBSTET GYNAECOL BR COMMONW 77:1047-1048, November, 1970.

"Technique of dilatation and curettage for abortion," by G. Schaefer. MOD TREAT 8:50-63, February, 1971.

"Vacuum aspiration, using pericervical block, for legal abortion as an outpatient procedure up to the 12th week of pregnancy," by B. M. Beric, et al. LANCET 2:619-621, September 18, 1971.

TECHNIQUES OF ABORTION

"Vacuum curettage in septic abortion," J REPROD MED 7:198, October, 1971.

"Vacuum extraction in febrile abortion," by G. Göbel. DTSCH GESUNDHEITSW 26:305-308, February 11, 1971.

"Vacuum termination of pregnancy," by S. C. Lewis. BR MED J 4: 365, November 6, 1971.

"Vaginal tubal ligation at time of vacuum curettage for abortion," by S. R. Sogolow. OBSTET GYNECOL 38:888-892, December, 1971.

THERAPEUTIC ABORTION
"Abortion. Is it a therapeutic procedure in psychiatry?" by C. V. Ford, et al. JAMA 218:1173-1178, November 22, 1971.

"Abortion: is it a therapeutic procedure in psychiatry?" by C. V. Ford, et al. J AMER MED ASS 218:1173-1178, November 22, 1971.

"Analysis of internal indications for termination of pregnancy," by V. Fialová, et al. CESK GYNEKOL 36:344-346, July, 1971.

"The British canidate for termination of pregnancy: a quantified survey of psychiatric referrals," by R. G. Priest. BR J PSYCHI-ATRY 118:579-580, May, 1971.

"Coagulation failure after vaginal termination of pregnancy," by S. V. Sood. BR MED J 4:724, December 18, 1971.

"Content of microelements in blood and placental tissue in normal pregnancy and abortion," by P. I. Fogel. PEDIATR AKUSH GINEKOL 2:33-37, 1971.

"Coordination of outpatient services for patients seeking elective abortion," by C. H. Siener, et al. CLIN OBSTET GYNECOL 14: 48-59, March, 1971.

"Decidual-cell necrosis after injection of hypertonic saline for therapeutic abortion," by B. Gustavil, et al. LANCET 2:826, October 9. 1971.

"The efficacy and acceptability of intravenously administered prostaglandin F as an abortifacient," by A. I. Csapo, et al. AM J OBSTET GYNECOL 111:1059-1063, December 15, 1971.

"Efficacy and tolerance of intravenous prostaglandins F 2 and E 2," by C. H. Hendricks, et al. AM J OBSTET GYNECOL 111:564-579, October 15, 1971.

"Extend the indications of medical abortion," by H. Zaidman. GYNE-COL OBSTET 70:243-244, March-April, 1971.

"Fetal indications for therapeutic abortion," by A. C. Barnes. ANNU REV MED 22:133-144, 1971.

"The fifth horseman. A specter of therapeutic abortion," by R. L. Burt. OBSTET GYNECOL 37:616-617, April, 1971.

"Genetics in therapeutic abortion," by A. C. Christakos. SOUTH MED J 64:Suppl:105-108, February, 1971.

"Guidelines for therapeutic abortion in Oregon: adopted September 26, 1971 by the Oregon Medical Association House of Delegates," NORTHWEST MED 70:854, December, 1971.

"Iatrogenic paracervical implantation of fetal tissue during therapeutic abortion. A case report," by L. R. Ayers, et al. OBSTET GYNE-COL 37:755-760, May, 1971.

"Indications for therapeutic abortion in Aberdeen, 1956-1967," by K. J. Dennis. J BIOSOC SCI 3:101-105, January, 1971.

"Induction of mid-trimester therapeutic abortion by intra-amniotic urea and intravenous oxytocin," by I. Craft, et al. LANCET 2: 1058-1060, November 13, 1971.

"Induction of therapeutic abortion by intra-amniotic injection of urea," by J. O. Greenhalf, et al. BR MED J 1:28-29, January 2, 1971.

"Induction of therapeutic abortion with urea," by J. O. Greenhalf. BR MED J 2:107, April 10, 1971.

"Induction of therapeutic abortion with urea," by M. Pugh, et al. BR MED J 1:345, February 6, 1971.

"Mechanism of selection and decision-making in therapeutic abortion," by C. Farmer. J BIOSOC SCI 3:121-127, January, 1971.

"Memorandum on The Medical Termination of Pregnancy Bill 1971; presented to Shrimati Indira Gandhi, Prime Minister of India, by Archbishop Angelo Fernandes," OR 39(183)4, September 30, 1971.

"Methoxyflurane in therapeutic abortion," by M. H. Lawrence. BR J CLIN PRACT 25:414-416, September, 1971.

"The organization and function of therapeutic abortion committees," by E. Wilson. CAN HOSP 48:38-40, December, 1971.

"Outpatient termination of pregnancy," by S. C. Lewis, et al. BR MED J 4:606-610, December 4, 1971.

"The oxytocic effect of acridine dyes and their use in terminating mid-trimester pregnancies," by B. V. Lewis, et al. J OBSTET GYNAE-COL BR COMMONW 78:838-842, September, 1971.

"The oxytocic effect of acridine dyes and their use in the termination of mid-trimester pregnancies," by V. Lewis, et al. J REPROD FERTIL 25:456-457, June, 1971.

"Parental consent not necessary to minor's therapeutic abortion: California," NEWSLETTER (SOC HOSP ATTORNEYS) 4:1, July, 1971.

"Personality factors and referral for therapeutic abortion," by P. C. Olley. J BIOSOC SCI 3:106-115, January, 1971.

"Psychiatric aspects of therapeutic abortion," by P. H. Linton. SOUTH MED J 64:Suppl:1:108-110, February, 1971.

"The psychiatrist and therapeutic abortion," by G. C. Sisler. CAN PSYCHIATR ASSOC J 16:275-277, June, 1971.

"Psychiatrist as consultant for therapeutic abortion," by R. L. Sadoff, et al. PENN MED 74:63-64, May, 1971.

"Pulmonary tuberculosis and pregnancy. Indications for therapeutic abortion in patients with pulmonary or extrapulmonary TBC," by C. Fossati. RASS INT CLIN TER 51:159-169, February 15, 1971.

"Radiographic study of extra-amniotically injected hypertonic saline in therapeutic abortion," by B. Gustavii, et al. ACTA OBSTET GYNECOL SCAND 50:315-320, 1971.

"Results in 1,000 cases of therapeutic abortion managed by vacuum aspiration," by K. C. Loung, et al. BR MED J 4:477-479, November 20, 1971.

"A review of therapeutic abortions at a southern university hospital," by G. L. Fields, et al. WOMAN PHYSICIAN 26:414-416, August, 1971.

"Some operative and postoperative hazards of legal termination of pregnancy," by S. V. Sood. BR MED J 4:270-273, October 30, 1971.

"Some thoughts on therapeutic abortion," by A. P. Chatowsky. RI MED J 54:462-466, September, 1971.

"Therapeutic abortion," CAN MED ASS J 105:638-639, September 18, 1971.

"Therapeutic abortion," by E. Borreman. CAN MED ASSOC J 104:421, March 6, 1971.

"Therapeutic abortion," by P. G. Coffey. LAVAL MED 42:611-612, June, 1971.

"Therapeutic abortion," by J. R. Dobson, et al. NZ MED J 74:274, October, 1971.

"Therapeutic abortion," by R. W. Elford. CAN MED ASSOC J 105: 638-639, September 18, 1971.

"Therapeutic abortion," by C. Heine. CAN MED ASSOC J 104:421, March 6, 1971.

"Therapeutic abortion," by A. C. Keast. S AFR MED J 45:888-891, August 14, 1971.

"Therapeutic abortion," by R. E. Reed. NC MED J 32:287-288, July, 1971.

"Therapeutic abortion," by S. J. Williams, et al. LANCET 2:1197, November 27, 1971.

"Therapeutic abortion and acculturation," by H. M. Donovan. NURS FORUM 10:378-381, 1971.

"Therapeutic abortion and cultural shock," by R. Zahourek. NURS FORUM 10:8-17, 1971.

"Therapeutic abortion and induction of labour by the intravaginal administration of prostaglandins E2 and F2," by S. M. Karim, et al. J OBSTET GYNAECOL BR COMMONW 78:294-300, April, 1971.

"Therapeutic abortion as a possible source of Rh immunization," by S. R. Hollán, et al. ACTA MED ACAD SCI HUNG 27:337-340, 1970.

"Therapeutic abortion at the obstetrical clinic of Clermont-Ferrand from 1958 to 1969. 24 cases," by G. Petit, et al. MED LEG DOMM CORPOR 3:418-422, October-December, 1970.

"Therapeutic abortion: attitudes of medical personnel leading to complications in patient care," by J. R. Wolff, et al. AM J OBSTET GYNECOL 110:730-733, July 1, 1971.

"Therapeutic abortion by intrauterine instillation of prostaglandins," by M. P. Embrey, et al. BR MED J 1:588-590, March 13, 1971.

"Therapeutic abortion by intrauterine instillation of prostaglandin E2," by G. Roberts, et al. J OBSTET GYNAECOL BR COMMONW 78:834-837, September, 1971.

"Therapeutic abortion. Current status of the question," by P. Piraux, et al. BULL FED SOC GYNECOL OBSTET LANG FR 20:454-456, November-December, 1968.

"Therapeutic abortion experience in North Carolina under the liberalized 1967 law," by W. J. May. NC MED J 32:186-187, May, 1971.

"Therapeutic abortion follow-up study," by A. J. Margolis, et al. AM J OBSTET GYNECOL 110:243-249, May 15, 1971.

"Therapeutic abortion follow-up study," by A. J. Margolis, et al.

TRANS PAC COAST OBSTET GYNECOL SOC 38:122-128, 1970.

"Therapeutic abortion: a follow-up study," by A. B. Sclare, et al. SCOTT MED J 16:438-442, October, 1971.

"Therapeutic abortion in California. Effects of septic abortion and maternal mortality," by G. K. Stewart, et al. OBSTET GYNECOL 37:510-514, April, 1971.

"Therapeutic abortion in a Canadian city," CAN MED ASSOC J 103: 1085 passim, November 1, 1970.

"Therapeutic abortion in a Canadian city," by J. G. Stapleton. CAN MED ASSOC J 104:70, January 9, 1971.

"Therapeutic abortion in north-east Scotland: introduction," by G. Horobin. J BIOSOC SCI 3:87-88, January, 1971.

"Therapeutic abortion: medical and social sequels," by A. B. Bames, et al. ANN INTERN MED 75:881-886, December, 1971.

"Therapeutic abortion. Nurses' involvement and moral grounds," by G. Mathew. NURS J INDIA 62:305-306, September, 1971.

"Therapeutic abortion: a prospective study. I," by H. Brody, et al. AM J OBSTET GYNECOL 109:347-353, February 1, 1971.

"Therapeutic abortion: the psychiatric nurse as therapist, liaison, and consultant," by R. Zahourek, et al. PERSPECT PSYCHIATR CARE 9:64-71, 1971.

"Therapeutic abortion: a psychiatric view," by J. M. Donahue. J INDIANA STATE MED ASSOC 64:833-834, August, 1971.

"Therapeutic abortion. A social work view," by F. Addelson. AM J OBSTET GYNECOL 111:984-992, December 1, 1971.

"Therapeutic abortion. A study of psychiatric applicants at North Carolina Memorial Hospital," by J. R. Partridge, et al. NC MED J 32:131-136, April, 1971.

"Therapeutic abortion. Who needs a psychiatrist?" by C. V. Ford, et al. OBSTET GYNECOL 38:206-213, August, 1971.

"Therapeutic abortions," by D. R. McCoy. MIDWIVES CHRON 84: 376-377, November, 1971.

"Therapeutic abortions at University Hospitals, 1951-1969, with emphasis on current trends," by D. W. Wetrich, et al. J IOWA MED SOC 60:691-696, October, 1970.

"Therapeutic abortions in California," by E. W. Jackson, et al. CALIF MED 115:28-33, July, 1971.

"Therapeutic abortions: National Association for Mental Health position statement," MENT HYG 55:130, January, 1971.

"Therapeutic abortions. A review of 567 cases," by P. H. Brenner, et al. CALIF MED 115:20-27, July, 1971.

"Therapeutic abortions topic of study and discussion at operating room nurses' conference," by I. Adams. HOSP ADMIN CAN 13: 38+, September, 1971.

"Therapeutic interruption of pregnancy in the 3d trimester," by L. C. Ayala, et al. GINECOL OBSTET MEX 27:661-681, June, 1970.

"Vaginal hysterectomy: a modality for therapeutic abortion and sterilization," by L. E. Laufe, et al. AM J OBSTET GYNECOL 110:1096-1099, August 15, 1971.

THREATENED ABORTION

"Amnioscopy in patients with bad obstetric history and high risk pregnancies," by K. H. Ng. MED J MALAYA 26:59-61, September, 1971.

"Clinical experience in midwifery. Threatened abortion," by K. Zenki. JAP J MIDWIFE 25:47-49, January, 1971.

"Colpocytodiagnosis of threatened abortion," by O. I. Lopatchenko. VOPR OKHR MATERIN DET 15:27-30, December, 1970.

"Content of chorionic gonadotropins in urine of women with threatened abortion," by A. T. Berko. PEDIATR AKUSH GINEKOL 1:37-40, January-February, 1971.

"Content of silicon, aluminum, titanium in blood in normal pregnancy and threatened abortion," by L. I. Priakhina. PEDIATR AKUSH GINEKOL 1:35-37, January-February, 1971.

"Content of vitamin E in blood and estriol excretion in women with threatened abortion," by L. Ia. Davidov, et al. PEDIATR AKUSH GINEKOL 1:33-35, January-February, 1971.

"Definition and etiology of threatened abortion," by A. Mestrallet. LYON MED 18:Suppl:17-19, 1971.

"Determination of C-reactive protein in metrorrhagic blood with special reference to the diagnosis of threatened abortion," by C. Zanoner. FRIULI MED 24:413-421, July-August, 1969.

"Effect of therapy in threatened abortion," by F. S. Baranovskaia, et al. PEDIATR AKUSH GINEKOL 1:41-44, January-February, 1971.

"Hormonal studies and clinical observations in patients with threatening abortion or premature birth, respectively treated with depot-17-alpha-hydroxyprogesterone-caproate," by F. Tóth, et al. Z GEBURTSHILFE GYNAEKOL 175:168-175, October, 1971.

"Inhibition of prostaglandin release and the control of threatened abortion," by A. Tothill, et al. LANCET 2:381, August 14, 1971.

"Long-term results of treatment with a delayed-action progestational hormone in threatened abortion," by P. Scillieri. MINERVA GINECOL 22:413-416, April 15, 1970.

"On the use of isoxysuprine in threatened abortion," by A. Julitta, et al. MINERVA GINECOL 21:867-868, July 15, 1969.

"Possibility of prognosis of threatened abortion," by G. P. Mandruzzato, et al. MINERVA GINECOL 22:476-477, May 15, 1970.

"Progesterone depot in threatened abortion," by A. P. Camilleri, et al. OBSTET GYNECOL 38:893-895, December, 1971.

"The prognosis of threatened abortion," by A. Johannsen. ACTA OBSTET GYNECOL SCAND 49:89-93, 1970.

"Prognosis of threatened abortion," by J. M. Thoulon. LYON MED 18:Suppl:21-25, 1971.

"Prognosis of threatened abortion. A comparative study with the use of vaginal cytology and urinary gonadotropin immunoassay," by A. F. Youssef, et al. AM J OBSTET GYNECOL 109:8-11, January, 1971.

"Results of gestanon therapy in women with threatened and habitual abortion," by Ts. Despodova. AKUSH GINEKOL (Sofiia) 9:208-213, 1970.

"Role of progesterone in the 1st trimester of pregnancy and in the treatment of threatened abortion," by L. P. Bengtsson. REV FR GYNECOL OBSTET 63:73-81, March, 1968.

"Study of fetal erythrocytes in metrorrhagias caused by threatened abortion," by F. Pietropaolo, et al. QUAD CLIN OSTET GINE-COL 25:39-44, January, 1970.

"Study of vaginal smears by luminescent microscopy in normal pregnancy and in threatened abortion," by O. S. Badiva. PEDIATR AKUSH GINEKOL 1:44-46, January-February, 1969.

"Threatened abortion. Development and treatment," by M. Maretti, et al. MATERN INFANC 29:71-78, January-March, 1970.

"Threatened abortions and their prognosis in the light of cytohormonal and enzymatic studies," by A. Dzioba, et al. WIAD LEK 24:649-652, April 1, 1971.

"Threatened and spontaneous abortion. A retrospective study of the diagnosis on admission," by A. Johannsen. ACTA OBSTET GYNECOL SCAND 49:95-99, 1970.

"Treatment of threatened abortion," by P. Magnin. LYON MED 18: Suppl:27-31, 1971.

"Treatment of threatened abortion and premature labor with Duvadilan," by H. Neumann, et al. ZENTRALBL GYNAEKOL 92:1100-1108, August 22, 1970.

"Ultrasonic diagnosis: abortions and threatened abortions," by S. Levi. GYNECOL OBSTET 70:333-342, May-June, 1971.

TOXOPLASMAS

"Abortion in women with latent toxoplasma infections," by P. Janssen, et al. KLIN WOCHENSCHR 48:25-30, January 1, 1970.

"Epizootics of toxoplasmosis causing ovine abortion," by W. A. Watson, et al. VET REC 88:120-124, January 30, 1971.

"A field trial of the fluorescence antibody test for toxoplasmosis in the diagnosis of ovine abortion," by J. F. Archer, et al. VET REC 88:206-208, February 20, 1971.

"Further field studies on the fluorescent antibody test in the diagnosis of ovine abortion due to toxoplasmosis," by J. F. Archer, et al. VET REC 88:178-180, February 13, 1971.

"Ovine abortion due to experimental toxoplasmosis," by W. A. Watson, et al. VET REC 88:42-45, January 9, 1971.

"Pregnancy interruption during toxoplasmosis," by P. Hengst. DTSCH GESUNDHEITSW 26:1611-1614, August 19, 1971.

"Repeated abortion and toxoplasmosis," by A. D'Alberton, et al. ANN OSTET GINECOL 91:415-419, June, 1969.

"The role of toxoplasmosis in abortion," by A. C. Kimball, et al. AM J OBSTET GYNECOL 111:219-226, September 15, 1971.

"Role of toxoplasmosis in the pathogenesis of abortions of unclear etiology," by J. Kicinski, et al. POL TYG LEK 26:1319-1322, August 23, 1971.

"Trial of a killed vaccine in the prevention of ovine abortion due to toxoplasmosis," by J. K. Beverley, et al. BR VET J 127:529-535, November, 1971.

TRANSCYCLINE

"Use of transcycline in fever states following induced abortion," by J. A. Cacault. BULL FED SOC GYNECOL OBSTET LANG FR 21:116-124, April-May, 1969.

TRANSPLACENTAL HEMORRHAGE
see also: Hemorrhage

"Abruptio placentae," by B. McDonnell. MIDWIFE HEALTH VISIT
7:177-181, May, 1971.

"Abruptio placenta with renal failure," by S. Johnson. MIDWIVES
CHRON 85:344-345, October, 1971.

"The nurse and placenta praevia and abruptio. Her function in protecting both mother and child," by G. Rosenheim, et al. BEDSIDE
NURSE 3:31-32, December, 1970.

"Transplacental hemorrhage during voluntary interruption of pregnancy," by K. M. Lakoff, et al. J REPROD MED 6:260-261, June,
1971.

VETERINARY ABORTIONS
see: Research and Abortions

WOMEN'S LIBERATION
see also: Laws and Legislation
Sociology, Behavior and Abortion

"Abortion committee 1965: woman's right to abortion as considerate
and early as possible," by G. Bergstrom, et al. LAKARTIDNIN-
GEN 68:4137-4150, September 8, 1971.

"Abortion: 'a woman's right to decide'," by P. Worthington. DAILY
TELEGRAPH 11, September 1, 1971.

"Birth control--the views of women," by J. A. Hurst. MED J AUST 2:
835-838, October 31, 1970.

"Doctor, I want an abortion," PATIENT CARE 5:28-33, April 15,
1971.

"French women admit having abortions," CAN HOSP 48:1 , May 15,
1971.

"Response to the appeal of 343 women for abortion," by N. Jouravleff.
PRESSE MED 79:2246-2248, November 20, 1971.

"What every woman should know about abortion," by J. E. Brody. READ DIGEST 98:119-122, February, 1971.

"What every woman should know about abortion," by G. M. Landau. PARENTS 46:42-43+, January, 1971.

YOUTH

"Abortion and the unemancipated minor," by M. Lipman. CALIF NURSE 67:8, September, 1971.

"Abortion in Japan; cond from Family Life, December, 1970," by P. Popenoe. C DGST 35:27-29, September, 1971.

"Abschaffung des 218 StGB?" by E. W. Böckenförde. STIMM ZEIT 188:147-167, September, 1971.

"Adolescent attitudes toward abortion: effects on contraceptive practice," by I. W. Gabrielson, et al. AMER J PUBLIC HEALTH 61:730-738, April, 1971.

"18-year-old may consent to abortion: Washington (D.C.) Hospital Center," NEWSLETTER (SOC HOSP ATTORNEYS) 4:5, March, 1971.

"Parent and child: minor's right to consent to an abortion," SANTA CLARA LAW 11:469, Spring, 1971.

"Parental consent not necessary to minor's therapeutic abortion: California," NEWSLETTER (SOC HOSP ATTORNEYS) 4:1, July, 1971.

AUTHOR INDEX

Abernathy, J. R. 37
Abrahams, C. 20
Abroms, G. M. 39
Adadevoh, B. K. 67
Adams, R. 19
Adams, I. 89
Addelson, F. 88
Adler, P. 26
Aehnelt, E. 61
Agliozzo, M. A. 40
Agüero, O. 93
Ahmed, Z. 8
Aimakhu, V. E. 64
Aitken-Swan, J. 81
Akpokodjc, J. U. 62
Alcalay, D. 47
Allen, A. 55
Alpern, H. D. 29
Alsobrook, H. B., Jr. 32, 56
Altemeier, W. A. 50
Altmann, W. 80, 93
Anderson, G. G. 70
Andreev, D. 57
Andrews, E. J. 81
Angeli, G. 74
Anglin, C. S. 33
Antonopoulos, D. 81
Arakaki, D. T. 26
Archer, J. F. 41, 43
Arehart, J. L. 76
Aresin, N. 58
Arnstein, H. S. 36

Arnold, C. B. 90
Aronov, B. Kh. 46
Artal, R. 30
Arthure, H. G. 17, 21, 58
Ascari, W. Q. 7
Atanasov, A. 28
Atanasov, I. 50
Auer, A. 96
Aurele, J. 75
Avčin, M. 38
Ayers, L. R. 46

Badivo. P. S. 83
Baird, D. 10
Baker, L. D. 82
Ball, D. 10
Bames, A. B. 88
Baranovskaia, F. S. 35, 89
Barcai, A. 40
Barnes, A. C. 41
Barnharnsupawat, L. 46
Barron, S. L. 75
Barry, A. P. 17, 52
Bashmakova, M. A. 76
Batko, B. 79
Beasley, J. D. 39, 93
Beauman, S. 13
Beauvais, P. 18
Beazley, J. M. 85
Becker, W. 50
Belaisch, J. 8
Bell, L. N. 18

239

Dzioba, A. 79, 89

Eames, J. R. 43
Edlow, J. B. 59
Edmiston, S. 75
Edmunds, L. 44
Ehrlich, P. R. 7
Eisenberg, H. 55, 95
Elford, R. W. 86
Eliakis, E. 46
Elstein, M. 82
Embrey, M. P. 49, 64, 70, 87
Empereur-Buisson, R. 74
Endres, R. J. 11
Engel, R. 42
Eser, A. 53, 78
Esteve, H. 6
Evans, J. C. 11
Evans, R. 94

Fairchild, E. 79
Farmer, C. 56
Fenlon, J. W. 65
Fialová, V. 19
Fields, G. L. 75
Filshie, G. M. 92
Finnis, J. M. 6
Fischl, I. 95
Fishbein, M. 81
Fitzgerald, J. 19, 86
Flämig, C. 27
Fofanov, S. I. 80
Fogel, P. I. 29
Fomina, I. P. 92
Ford, C. E. 43
Ford, C. V. 5, 11, 88
Fort, A. T. 8
Fossati, C. 72
Fossati, S. 22
Fotheringham, J. B. 55
Fox, R. W. 13
Franciosi, R. A. 59
Franke, H. 21

Freda, V. J. 28
Freedman, R. 41
Freilich, H. 60
Friesen, R. F. 68
Frigoletto, F. D. 36
Fuchs, F. 19
Fujikura, T. 25
Fullerton, W. T. 57
Furier, I. K. 62

Gabbrielli, G. 62
Gabrielson, I. W. 18
Gallon, S. 51
Galvin, S. 5
Gandhi, H. S. 21
Garcia, D. Q. 48
Garcia, A. G. 56
Faskell, G. 68
Gaudefroy, M. 37, 69, 95
Gaumont, R. 79
Gendel, E. S. 35
Georgiev, B. 24
Gerber, R. J. 13, 15
Gerchow, J. 53
Giaquinto, M. 92
Gilbert, L. 54
Gillen, M. 96
Gillespie, A. 92, 93
Gillet, J. Y. 37
Gillon, R. 54
Gillott, J. 82
Giroud, P. 38
Gitter, M. 77
Glatova, V. A. 38
Glenister, T. 66
Gluckman, L. K. 10
Göbel, G. 93
Godsick, W. H. 57
Goetz, O. 77
Goisis, M. 44, 62
Golob, E. 26
Gold, E. M. 12
Gold, S. 71

Moore, W. M. 38
Morgan, B. I. 51
Morsa, J. 80
Mosena, P. W. 47
Mosier, W. 90
Mossing, N. B. 46
Motulsky, A. G. 72
Muller, C. 80
Murooka, H. 44
Murray, R. R. 11
Murray, S. 75
Muziorelli, A. 27
Myers, L. 5, 8, 46

McCance, C. 13
McCormick, R. A. 95
McCoy, D. R. 88
McDermott, J. F., Jr. 14
McDonald, A. D. 10, 78
McDonnell, B. 17
McEwan, J. 30
McKernan, M. F. 73
McKie, B. D. 71
McLaren, H. C. 11
McLaughlin, M. C. 15
McLellan, J. 44
McWhirter, W. A. 65

Nabriski, S. A. 39
Nahmias, A. J. 65
Nathanson, B. N. 32, 83
Neitz, W.A. 36
Neme, B. 79
Neumann, H. 90, 91
Newman, M. J. D. 96
Newman, S. J. 21
Newmann, K. 66
Newton, B. W. 20
Newton, P. 28
Ng, K. H. 19
Nicolini, G. 47
Nieder, J. 78
Nishimura, H. 74

Nixon, R. 69
Notter, A. 36
Nowlan, A. 53
Nussbaum, P. E. 73

O'Boyle, P. 11, 24, 47, 91
O'Brien, M. 58
Ohrberg, K. 72
Ooi, O. S. 32
Olds, S. 95
Olley, P. C. 65
Orlandi, C. 47
Ornstedt, S. 40
Osofsky, J. D. 72
O'Sullivan, J. V. 35
Ottosson, J. O. 52
Overstreet, E. W. 47, 55
Ozawa, G. 59

Pakter, J. 10, 84
Palagi, R. 62
Palenzona, C. 28
Palliez, R. 93, 94
Palmgren, B. 26
Palmade, J. 25
Pannain, A. 94
Papp, Z. 31
Partridge, J. R. 88
Pearson, J. F. 66
Penev, I. 56, 70
Penfield, A. J. 15
Pehrson, S. L. 83
Perez, J. L. deS. 75
Petit, G. 87
Petzoldt, K. 85
Pfiefer, F. M. 12
Philadelphy, I. 28
Piechowiak, Z. 20
Pietropaolo, F. 83
Pigeaud, H. 85
Piguit, L. 34
Pike, L. A. 42
Pion, R. J. 20